Logical Models of Legal Argumentation

Edited by

Henry Prakken

Computer/Law Institute, Faculty of Law
Free University of Amsterdam, The Netherlands

and

Giovanni Sartor

The Queen's University of Belfast, Northern Ireland

Reprinted from *Artificial Intelligence and Law*
Volume 4, Nos. 3–4, 1996

Kluwer Academic Publishers

Dordrecht / Boston / London

A C.I.P. catalogue record for this book is available from the Library of Congress.

ISBN 0-7923-4413-8

Published by Kluwer Academic Publishers,
P.O. Box 17, 3300 AA Dordrecht, The Netherlands.

Kluwer Academic Publishers incorporates
the publishing programmes of
D. Reidel, Martinus Nijhoff, Dr W. Junk and MTP Press.

Sold and distributed in the U.S.A. and Canada
by Kluwer Academic Publishers,
101 Philip Drive, Norwell, MA 02061, U.S.A.

In all other countries, sold and distributed
by Kluwer Academic Publishers Group,
P.O. Box 322, 3300 AH Dordrecht, The Netherlands.

Printed on acid-free paper

Printed in the Netherlands

Table of Contents

Artificial Intelligence and Law **4:** 157–161, 1996.

Editors' Introduction

Historical remarks

Only a few years ago the very title of this special issue would appear to many readers as expressing an oxymoron if not a blatant contradiction. Both in legal theory and AI & law logic and (dialectical) argumentation have often been conceived as opposite and incompatible approaches to legal reasoning. In legal theory, legal logicians tended to focus on a deductive reconstruction of a judges' justification of a decision, without taking into account the dialectical process which had led to the selection of the chosen justification. Others instead emphasized the adversarial and discretionary nature of legal reasoning, involving reasonable evaluation of alternative choices: it has therefore condemned the attempts to force legal reasoning into the structure of logical deduction (cf. the well-known studies of (Toulmin, 1958) and (Perelman, 1969)).

Also in the AI & law domain logic and dialectic-based approaches for a long time followed separate tracks. Logic found its favourite application domain in legislation: the basic idea was to represent legislation as a set of consistent statements (rules), from which legal conclusions could be deductively derived (cf. (Sergot et al., 1986)). Dialectics found instead its favourite application domain in case-based reasoning: the basic idea was to model legal reasoning via the adversarial citation of pro and contra cases (cf. e.g. (Ashley, 1990)).

However, in the last years the separation between logic and dialectic seems to be coming to an end. In legal philosophy a number of elaborate and mature proposals are being advanced, e.g. by (Alexy, 1989) and (Peczenik, 1989), who offer a unifying framework for legal reasoning which merges logical and dialectical approaches to law. Also within AI & law the two developments converge. CBR researchers have acknowledged the use of rules, and of theory formation, in legal argumentation (cf. e.g. (Rissland & Skalak, 1991; Branting, 1994)), while logically inclined researchers have developed logical models of defeasible legal argumentation (e.g. the various studies of Loui, Gordon, Hage, Prakken and Sartor).

The theme of this volume

This special issue contains contributions from the latter development. There is a growing body of research in this area, in which two main topics can be distinguished: studies on inference, and studies on procedure. The first line of research intends to answer the question what are the defeasible conclusions obtainable from a given pool of premises, while the latter focuses on how the pool of premises is (and may be) formed in the dialectical interaction of the parties.

This special issue mainly considers the first area, in which AI & law research has already obtained significant results, both in the development of theoretical analyses and in the establishment of computable formalisms. We believe that the significance of these results extends beyond the boundaries of the AI & law community. For legal philosophy a new form of legal logic is emerging, whose features (its ability of dealing with conflicting sets of premises, the possibility of deriving defeasible conclusions, the adherence to the intuitive structure of legal reasoning) make it attractive for the theoretical analysis of legal reasoning. And for general AI research on logics of nonmonotonic reasoning it is perhaps significant that in one of the few domains in which such logics have been applied to real examples, in particular argument-based and dialectical approaches have been successful.

The papers of this volume

The collection presented in this special issue does not cover all the research being accomplished but offers, we believe, a representative selection. Let us first introduce the single contributions and then shortly comment on the different approaches they express and on their connection with the main trends of current research.

Jaap Hage's *A Theory of Legal Reasoning and a Logic to Match* develops an ambitious comprehensive account of law, considering both its knowledge structures and reasoning methods. Hage distinguishes two levels of legal knowledge: the primary level includes principles and goals, while the secondary level includes rules. Principles and goals express reasons pro or con a conclusion. Without the secondary level these reasons would in each case have to be weighed to obtain a conclusion, but according to Hage rules are meant to summarise the outcome of the weighing process in advance for certain classes of cases. However, Hage argues in detail that in the end also rule application boils down to weighing reasons in concrete cases: reasons can be given for or against the application or validity of a rule, for or against an exception to a rule, and for or against analogous or 'a contrario' application when a rule's conditions are not completely met. The result of Hage's analysis is a rich model of legal reasoning, which is finally given a logical formalisation with an extension-based semantics in the spirit of default logic.

In *A Dialectical Model of Assessing Conflicting Arguments in Legal Reasoning* Henry Prakken and Giovanni Sartor define a dialogue game for assessing conflicting arguments. A (defeasible) proof that an argument is justified takes the form of a debate between opposing parties; an argument is justified if the proponent can make the opponent run out of moves in every way of attack. The individual arguments are expressed in a logic-programming language with both weak and strong negation, and conflicts between arguments are decided with the help of priorities on the rules which themselves are defeasibly derived as conclusions within the system. Thus also debates on the choice between conflicting arguments can be modelled. The dialogue game can be given a semantic justification in terms of a unifying framework for nonmonotonic reasoning which has arisen from research in the semantics of logic programming.

In this framework the differences between many nonmonotonic logics (such as logic programming, circumscription, default logic and autoepistemic logic) are reduced to different ways of producing extensions of given theories with the help of assumptions. In the present volume the framework is outlined by two of its developers, Kowalski and Toni, in *Abstract Argumentation.* They also outline a dialectical proof theory, which, unlike Prakken & Sartor's dialogue game, is for 'credulous' instead of 'sceptical' reasoners. The main contribution of Kowalski & Toni's present paper is a methodology for representing defeasible rules in logical languages that have a nonprovability operator (like logic programming's negation as failure). They claim that their methodology does not require the development of new or extended nonmonotonic logics, as is done by Hage and Prakken & Sartor, but can be applied within existing systems.

While the three papers just introduced present completely formalised logical systems, Freeman and Farley use logic implicitly, in *A Model of Argumentation and its Application to Legal Reasoning*. Their semiformally described dialectical model allows arguments to be constructed from rules (or 'warrants') with reasoning steps of multiple types, including deductive rule application but also weak steps, such as abduction or a contrario reasoning. Freeman and Farley also specify how an argument can be attacked. Both the form and the force of an attack depend on the types of the reasoning steps in the attacked argument, but the force of an attack also depends on the epistemic nature of a warrant (e.g. 'evidential' or 'definitional'.) The process of argumentation is modelled as a dialogue game, in which the central control mechanism is the notion of burden of proof, acting as move filter, turntaking mechanism and termination criterion.

The contribution of Alexander Peczenik, *Jumps and Logic in the Law. What can One Expect from Logical Models of Legal Argumentation*, evaluates the other papers in this issue from the point of view of legal philosophy. Peczenick first considers some aspects of legal reasoning that have escaped traditional logical analysis, such as the application of principles and general goals (which have a *prima-facie* character and have to be weighed and balanced), and weak inference steps, such as analogy and abduction. For all those aspects Peczenik argues that models of formal argumentation, like those of the present issue, offer valuable insights; thus they extend the scope of logical methods in legal argumentation. Nevertheless he argues that these systems, 'foundationalist' as they are, still fail to grasp the notion of coherence, which concept offers a wider account of legal rationality. While being aware that formalisation of coherence is extremely difficult, Peczenik provides an in depth analysis of this concept, illustrating its role in epistemology and in legal thinking.

A comparison of the papers

All the papers in this special issue focus on the defeasible aspect of legal reasoning, where one body of information can give rise to conflicting reasonable conclusions, and where new information can overturn an earlier reached conclusion. But there are also differences. While Freeman & Farley and Prakken & Sartor take their starting point in the notion of an argument, in Hage this notion is left implicit in the notion of an extension of a given theory; also Kowalski & Toni start with an extension-based account, but later they enrich it with an explicit notion of an argument. Furthermore, although all the papers address both examples and technical issues, in Hage and especially Freeman & Farley the emphasis is more on a typology of reasoning phenomena, while Kowalski & Toni and Prakken & Sartor focus more on the technical properties of their systems. And while most of the papers only focus on reasoning with rules, Hage also analyses the role of principles and goals.

The papers reflect that there are several grounds for attacking arguments. To start with, they can be attacked on the strength of their premises. All papers except Freeman & Farley observe that the criteria for comparing conflicting premises are themselves a matter of legal debate. Prakken & Sartor and Hage also analyze debates on the applicability and (Hage) validity of rules. That not only the strength of premises but also the form of an inference step can make arguments susceptible to attack is recognised by Freeman & Farley, who define how, for instance, abductive and a contrario arguments can be attacked. Also Hage analyses these reasoning forms. In Prakken & Sartor and Kowalski & Toni, on the other hand, only the use of logic programming's negation as failure gives a structural ground for attack. While Prakken & Sartor regard such attacks as logically different from attacks on a conclusion, Kowalski & Toni claim that the latter can be reduced to the former.

Finally, three papers, Prakken & Sartor, Freeman & Farley and Kowalski & Toni, state their theories in the for lawyers familiar form of a dialogue game between a proponent and an opponent of a claim.

Significance for AI & law

As we hope to show with this collection, research on formal models of legal argumentation, in spite of its novelty, can already exhibit a number of significant results. In particular, it illustrates that logic can be put to use in ways that do not suffer from the problems faced by attempts to model law as a deductive system. These problems have been discussed by e.g. (Ashley, 1992, pp. 169–7) (cf. also (Gardner, 1987; Berman & Hafner, 1987)), who, among other things, observes that deductive models have problems with syntactic and semantic ambiguity; in this paper Hage shows how disputes on interpretation can be formalised. Ashley also points at the problems caused by conflicts among legal rules; clearly, this is well addressed by systems for defeasible argumentation (and several other nonmonotonic logics). Finally, Ashley observes that legal rules often leave exceptions and other conditions for their application unstated; the systems presented in this issue show that these features can be preserved in logical formalisations of the rules.

Moreover, formal models of dialectical argumentation open many new prospects for future development in legal inquiry. Here we just mention two very promising directions for further research.

Firstly, these models offer a framework for the integration of rule-based and case-based reasoning. Some work on this has been done by (Loui et al., 1993) and (Loui & Norman, 1995), but in the present volume the papers mainly focus on reasoning with rules. Hage also discusses how HYPO-style case-based reasoning could be modelled in his reason-based logic, but much work remains to be done.

Secondly, a broader account of legal reasoning may be obtained by integrating research on legal inference and research on the procedural context of legal argumentation. Freeman & Farley, Prakken & Sartor and Kowalski & Toni make some steps in this direction, by employing the dialectical form, but their perspective is still restricted, since their dialogue games evaluate arguments only on structural and content-based grounds; they do not formalise the discourse rules for entering the premises into the debate, nor do they discuss under which conditions protocols for dialectical argumentation are fair and effective. Perhaps a future issue of this journal will answer (Gordon, 1995)'s call to study these questions.

HENRY PRAKKEN
GIOVANNI SARTOR

References

Alexy, R. 1989. *A Theory of Legal Argumentation. The Theory of Rational Discourse as Theory of Legal Justification*. Oxford: Clarendon.
Ashley, K. D. 1990. *Modeling Legal Argument: Reasoning with Cases and Hypotheticals*. Cambridge (Massachusetts): MIT.
Ashley, K. D. 1992. Case-based reasoning and its implications for legal expert systems. *Artificial Intelligence and Law* 1: 113–208.
Berman, D. H. & Hafner, C. D. 1987. Indeterminacy: A challenge to logic-based models of legal reasoning. In *Yearbook of Law, Computers and Technology* 3: 1–35. London: Butterworths.
Branting, L. K. 1994. A Computational Model of Ratio Decidendi. *Artificial Intelligence and Law* 2: 1–31.
Gardner, A.v.d.L. 1987. *An Artificial Intelligence Approach to Legal Reasoning*. Cambridge (Massachusetts): MIT.
Gordon, T. F. 1995. *The Pleadings Game. An Artificial Intelligence Model of Procedural Justice*. Dordrecht: Kluwer.
Loui, R. P., Norman, J., Olson, J. & Merrill, A. 1993. A Design for Reasoning with Policies, Precedents and Rationales. In *Proceedings of the Fourth International Conference on Artificial Intelligence and Law* 202–211. Amsterdam: ACM.
Loui R. P., & Norman, J. 1995. Rationales and Argument Moves. *Artificial Intelligence and Law* 3: 158–189.
Peczenik, A. 1989. *On Law and Reason*. Dordrecht: Kluwer.
Perelman, Ch. & Olbrechts-Tyteca, L. 1969. *The new rhetoric. A treatise on argumentation*. Notre Dame: University of Notre Dame press.
Rissland, E. L. & D. B. Skalak, D. B. 1991. CABARET: statutory interpretation in a hybrid architecture. *International Journal of Man-Machine Studies* 34 (1991), 839–887.
Sergot, M. J., Sadri, F., Kowalski, R. A., Kriwaczek, F., Hammond, P. & Cory, H. T. 1986. The British Nationality Act as a Logic Program. *Communications of the ACM* 29: 370–386.
Toulmin, S. E. 1958. *The Uses of Argument*. Cambridge: Cambridge University Press.

Artificial Intelligence and Law **4:** 163–197, 1996.

A Model of Argumentation and Its Application to Legal Reasoning

KATHLEEN FREEMAN and ARTHUR M. FARLEY
Computer and Information Science, University of Oregon, Eugene, OR 97403, U.S.A.

Abstract. We present a computational model of dialectical argumentation that could serve as a basis for legal reasoning. The legal domain is an instance of a domain in which knowledge is incomplete, uncertain, and inconsistent. Argumentation is well suited for reasoning in such weak theory domains. We model argument both as information structure, i.e., argument units connecting claims with supporting data, and as dialectical process, i.e., an alternating series of moves by opposing sides. Our model includes burden of proof as a key element, indicating what level of support must be achieved by one side to win the argument. Burden of proof acts as move filter, turntaking mechanism, and termination criterion, eventually determining the winner of an argument. Our model has been implemented in a computer program. We demonstrate the model by considering program output for two examples previously discussed in the artificial intelligence and legal reasoning literature.

Key words: argumentation, legal reasoning, burden of proof

Introduction

As the artificial intelligence (AI) and legal reasoning communities both realize, most legal decisions are reached against a background of incomplete, uncertain, and inconsistent knowledge (i.e., weak theory domains; Porter, et al., 1990). The best known AI methods for reasoning in such weak theory domains either rely on an absence of outright contradictions (e.g., probabilistic reasoning; Pearl, 1987) or are unable to support motivated decision making in the face of inconsistent information (e.g., default reasoning; Ginsberg, 1987). Both theoretical solutions place the problem of deciding what to believe outside their respective domains of discourse. Correct propagation of probabilities or computation of consistent extensions are their primary concerns. Choosing the proposition with highest probability or randomly choosing one of a set of consistent extensions are proposed as possible, simplistic decision procedures.

The legal domain, however, is concerned with justified decision making under conditions of incompleteness, inconsistency, and uncertainty. An adequate theory of legal reasoning must provide a sound basis for choosing what to believe, e.g., someone's guilt or liability. The practice of legal reasoning suggests a method for reasoning in weak theory domains that permits conclusions to be drawn relative to available evidence and perceived risks. Argumentation, with its emphasis on generating and comparing both supporting and refuting claims under situations of uncertainty and inconsistency, is well suited to serve as a framework for reasoning in weak theory domains (Pollock 1992, 1994). In addition, burden of proof introduces a mechanism for determining the outcome of an argument in the face of inevitable uncertainty.

As an example, consider the following "Bermuda" problem, based upon a classic example in (Toulmin, 1958):

> Usually anyone born in Bermuda can be assumed to be a British subject, unless both parents are aliens. People with British passports are generally British subjects. Statistics show that the majority of people who are English speaking and have a Bermudan identification number were born in Bermuda. Any person with a Bermudan identification number is eligible to obtain Bermudan working papers. We have just been introduced to Harry, who speaks English, has a passport that is not a British passport, and shows us his Bermudan working papers. We must decide whether or not Harry is a British subject.

The knowledge in this problem is inconsistent, with some evidence that supports a positive conclusion and other evidence that points to a negative conclusion. It also is incomplete, since knowledge that could help support one conclusion or the other, such as whether or not Harry was born in Bermuda or whether his parents were aliens, is not available. Finally, the knowledge is uncertain, containing hedges such as "usually" and "most". In light of these issues, how can we reach a reasonable decision?

One possibility is to resolve all of the problems prior to making a decision, i.e., supply missing knowledge, transform uncertain into certain knowledge, and disallow inconsistent information. Unfortunately, this solution is not often realistic, due to constraints on information gathering capabilities, time, and the state of real world knowledge. Another possibility is simply to forego the decision making process. But this is clearly unsatisfactory, as well. A lawsuit or criminal proceeding cannot fail to proceed because of inconsistent knowledge. There may be enough information to at least speculate about support for one or other of the claims. What is known may even be enough, if not to establish a claim conclusively, to support it adequately in a particular context. For example, someone choosing team members for a pick-up soccer game based on whether or not a person is a British subject would need much less convincing support for the claim than would someone attempting to establish it in a court of law, say for inheritance purposes.

We begin by exploring means for supporting the claim "Harry is a British subject" under these difficult conditions. The claim could be established by default, if it could be shown that Harry was born in Bermuda. There is some evidence for this, as Harry speaks English, but there is no input information about whether or not Harry has a Bermudan identification number. We do know that Harry has his working papers; thus, it is reasonable to speculate that he was able to obtain them because he has an identification number. We can follow this speculative chain of inferences to conclude tentatively that Harry is a British subject.

Reasoning in this way, while not deductive, is not irrational either; it has been termed plausible. *Plausible inference* (Polya, 1968; Rescher, 1976) is appropriate for reasoning under conditions of incomplete knowledge, particularly in situations such as the one above, where, if we rely on deductive inference alone, there is no way to build a case for the claim. However, plausible inference is certainly not a panacea. The support it gives a claim is at best tentative, i.e., refutable, defeasible. For example, if it could be shown that Harry obtained his working papers some other way, then there would be no reason to speculate that he has an identification number; the support for "identification number", and then "born in Bermuda" and "British subject" would collapse. Even when the support cannot be immediately refuted, its tentative nature remains, and should be reflected in our certainty about its conclusion.

In light of the uncertainty in support for claims based on plausible inference and because of the possibility of inconsistency in the knowledge base, an intelligent reasoner should not stop at this point. One could explicitly look for information that would tend to undercut the existing arguments supporting the claim. One could try to refute the case just made by showing Harry's parents were aliens or by looking for evidence that he was not born in Bermuda, for example. A suspicious adversary could look for evidence that Harry doesn't speak English or that he doesn't have his working papers. Furthermore, there might be information that seems to support the negation of the claim, i.e., "Harry is not a British subject". If found, such information would make the original claim that "Harry is a British subject" controversial, and, therefore, even more tentative. In the current example, there is anomalous data: the fact that Harry is said not to have a British passport. This can be used to weakly support the claim that Harry is not a British subject.

The Bermuda example is meant to highlight several key points about reasoning and decision making in real world, weak theory domains. Aspects of reasoning under these conditions, such as the use of plausible inference and the representation of uncertainty, are helpful to a point, but cannot completely resolve problems and may themselves add uncertainty to the knowledge. Support for claims may be tentative and, therefore, refutable. There may be simultaneous support for conflicting claims. Yet reasoning with inconsistent knowledge is useful because it may be all that is available, and we may be able to support a claim sufficiently for making a decision in a particular context. Even if the outcome remains inconclusive, claims are evaluated with respect to both their own support and support for alternative claims.

Our research addresses the use of argumentation as a basis for reasoning and decision making in weak theory domains. Argumentation has long been studied as an important reasoning method in many areas. It has been a topic of research in philosophy, (e.g., Rescher, 1977; Toulmin, 1958), rhetoric (e.g., Horner,1988), education (e.g., Kuhn, 1991), and, of course, legal reasoning (e.g., Gardner, 1987; Ashley, 1990). For example, Rescher (1977) writes, "... disputation and debate may be taken as a paradigmatic model for reasoning in pursuit of truth ... There is nothing new about this approach"; and "The aim of the inquiry is to arrive at defensible results ... [using] a heuristic method of inquiry ... [that] pits one thesis against its rivals, with the aim of refining its formulation, uncovering its basis of rational support, and assessing its relative weight ... Dialectic ... [is] a method for sifting the evidence so as to set it out systematically, in a rationally organized structure that exhibits the fabric of supporting reasons." Kuhn (1991) offers, "The major early philosophers – Plato, Socrates, Aristotle – were all centrally concerned with thinking, and all regarded the construction of arguments as the heart of thinking ..."

In this paper, we present a computational model of dialectical argument, computational in the sense that it has been formalized and implemented as a computer program. Later, we present traces of our program's behavior on several examples taken from the legal domain. Our model comprises argument both as supporting explanation and as dialectical process. As an explanation structure, argument consists of argument units connecting claims with supporting data. As dialectical process, an argument consists of an alternating series of moves made by opposing sides for and against a given claim. Inspired by legal reasoning, our model of argument incorporates the notion of burden of proof, roughly defined as what level of support must be achieved by one party to an argument to win the argument. Burden of proof acts as a move filter, turntaking mechanism, and termination criterion during the process of argumentation. We will provide operational definitions for several burden of proof levels that, while not directly corresponding to legal definitions, are motivated by those used in legal settings. Argumentation moves, coupled with burden of proof requirements, will provide us with means to make decisions that are skeptical, credulous, or located appropriately between these two extremes.

In the following sections, after we outline our model of argumentation, we briefly describe important elements of our program, written in Common Lisp, that implements the model. We then demonstrate the model by considering output from the program for two examples previously discussed in the AI and legal reasoning literature. These examples will illustrate the effects that different burdens of proof can have on argument process and outcome. We conclude with a discussion of related research and directions for future work.

Modeling Argument

Our model of argumentation is based on the following, complementary definitions of argument: (a) "the grounds ... on which the merits of an assertion are to depend" (Toulmin, 1958), and (b) "a method for conducting controversial discussions, with one contender defending a thesis in the face of object[ions] and counterarguments made by an adversary" (Rescher, 1977). There are two, distinct senses of argument posed by these definitions. The first defines argument as a supporting explanation, i.e., an entity; the second concentrates on argument as a dialectical process in which two or more agents engage. Thus, the representation of arguments as structured entities and the generation of arguments as dialectical processes are both crucial to our theory.

We make several simplifying assumptions about the type of arguments we hope to model. Of the five aspects of argumentation discussed in classical rhetoric (invention, arrangement, style, memory, and presentation/delivery), we concentrate on invention, i.e., the process of developing defensible support for an assertion. Of the three types of proof in classical rhetoric (logos, ethos, pathos), we deal solely with logos, i.e., logical reasoning (both formal and informal logic). Argumentation as studied here does not include negotiation, i.e., a claim which an arguer is attempting to establish or defeat may not be altered or changed. Persuasion per se is not a goal of the more logical aspects of argumentation, so the use of rhetorical devices intended only to persuade are not included in the model. Support for a claim will depend only on derivation of support for the claim and not on issues like the fairness of a ruling or costs that would be entailed by a particular decision. Finally, arguments will have two sides only, "pro" and "con" with respect to a claim. These restrictions are intended to focus the work on the more formal aspects of argument.

ARGUMENT STRUCTURE

For argument as supporting explanation, we define argument structures that organize relevant, plausible, available support for a claim, and also for its negation. We represent an argument in an extended version of the form given by Toulmin (1958). For Toulmin, an argument comprises *data* (evidence, grounds) said to support a *claim* (conclusion). The authority for taking the step from data to claim is called a *warrant.* The warrant may have backing, or justification. The data and the warrant may not be enough to establish the claim conclusively, i.e., the resultant claim may be *qualified.* The claim may be subject to *rebuttals*, special circumstances where the warrant would not hold. We refer to this basic structure, presented in Figure 1 in graphical form, as a "Toulmin argument unit", or tau.

Modifications to this structure are needed for several reasons: to formalize Toulmin's ideas; to provide a macro structure for arguments, e.g., extended chains of support for claims, multiple arguments for claims; and to explicate various sources of uncertainty, i.e., arguable points in the domain knowledge. In our representation, an argument consists of a set of claims. In addition to the claim as described above, the data and warrant parts of a tau are also seen as claims and are also qualified, with backing and rebuttal. (Since all the major elements of a tau are claims, we will refer to these simply as data, warrant, and conclusion, where needed to avoid ambiguity.) In our earlier example, "Harry was born in Bermuda" and "A person born in Bermuda will usually be a British subject" would be viewed as claims in their own right, as well as support for "Harry is a British subject". The proposition field of a claim comprises one or more clauses. If the claim contains multiple

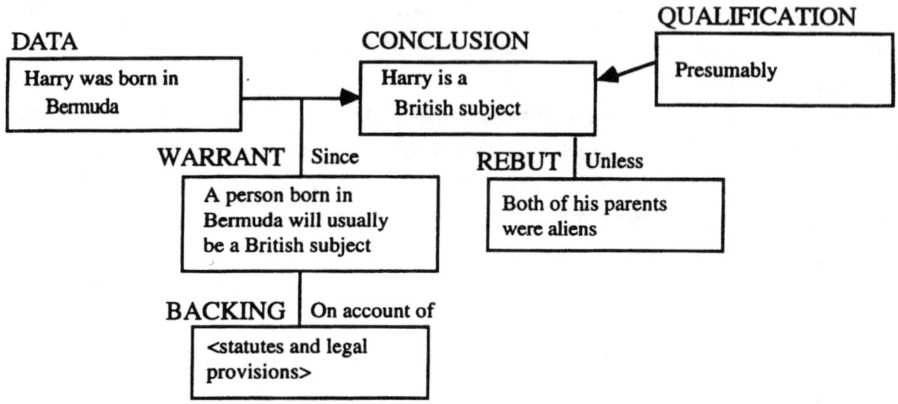

Figure 1. Basic Toulmin form for representing argument fragments.

clauses, they are assumed to be conjunctive. Figure 2 presents our expanded tau structure in a graphical form.

All claims must be supported, i.e., have backing. We allow two types of backing: *atomic*, as information from outside the immediate realm of the argument (e.g., "given", "observed", "hearsay", etc.) and *tau*, where a conclusion is supported by data through application of a warrant. A claim may have multiple backings. In the above example, the claim "Harry is a British subject" is supported by a tau. The claims "Harry was born in Bermuda" and "A person born in Bermuda will usually be a British subject" also need backing. A warrant will often have atomic backing, being given as input representing some law, for example. In fact, all warrants in the current model have atomic backing. Support for the datum "Harry was born in Bermuda" might also be atomic, or this claim could be the conclusion of another tau.

All claims have qualifications, which capture the level of support realized as a result of arguments made based upon uncertain knowledge and plausible reasoning. We use the following qualifications: *valid(!), strong(!-), credible (+) weak, (+-), and unknown (?).* The first four are ranked in decreasing order of support, while the last indicates a lack of (known) support. A valid qualification represents a high degree of certainty. Such a qualification may be the result of trusted observations of the environment and application of deductive reasoning steps. A strong qualification represents a default level of support; such support represents general regularities in the environment that have relatively rare exceptions. Credible is meant to represent lesser support for data or warrants that are more likely than not. A weak qualification reflects the tentative support realized as a result of plausible inference. A more precise, formal definition of the meaning of the qualification levels is given through their use and interaction in argument formation and resolution within our model, as will be presented below.

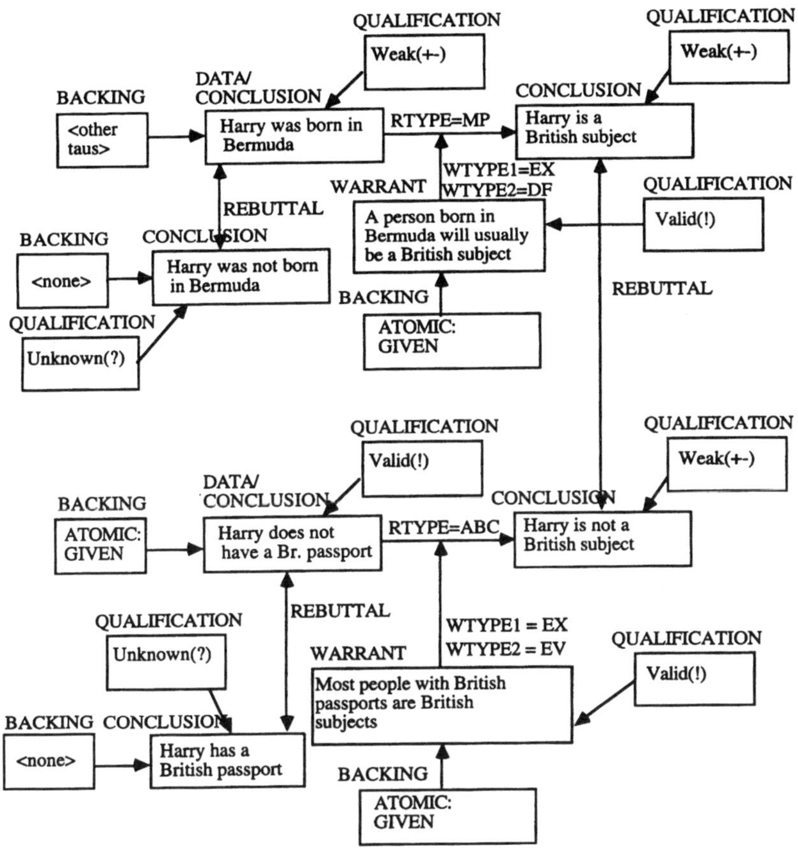

Figure 2. Expanded Toulmin argument unit (tau) structure.

Each claim has an associated rebuttal. In our representation, a rebuttal is a rival claim, currently defined as the negation of the claim, and the arguments that support the rival conjecture. For example, the rebuttal for the claim "Harry is a British subject" is "Harry is not a British subject", plus its backing (and vice versa). Exceptional circumstances are represented by warrants that support the negation of a claim, for example, "A person born in Bermuda to alien parents will usually not be a British subject".

Since warrants represent a relationship between two claims, i.e., data and conclusion, they have a slightly different structure from other claims. Our warrant structure represents the data and conclusion by two fields, *antecedent* and *consequent*, respectively. As noted earlier, all warrants have atomic backing in our current implementation of the model. In addition, a warrant does not have a direct rebuttal field, but does have two, associated type fields. The *wtype1* field classifies the relationship between the antecedent and consequent as *explanatory (ex)* or *sign (si)*. An example of an explanatory relationship is a causal link, because knowl-

(w1 ((british passport)) → ex ev ((british subject)) (!) (GIVEN))
(w2 ((bermuda born)) → ex df ((british subject)) (!) (GIVEN))
(w3 ((english speaking)(bermuda id#)) → si ev ((bermuda born)) (!) (GIVEN))
(w4 ((bermuda id#)) → ex df ((working papers)) (!) (GIVEN))
(w5 ((bermuda born)(alien parents)) → ex df ((not (british subject))) (!) (GIVEN))
(w6 ((special skills)) → ex df ((working papers)) (!) (GIVEN))
(w7 ((special skills)(quota met)) → ex df ((not (working papers))) (!) (GIVEN))
(w8 ((pays Bermuda taxes)) → ex ev ((british subject)) (!) (GIVEN))
(w9 ((lives in Bermuda)) → si ev ((british subject)) (!) (GIVEN))

Figure 3. Warrants for the Bermuda Problem.

edge of the antecedent "explains" knowledge of the consequent, e.g., antecedent "fire" causes (explains) its consequent "smoke". Other explanatory relationships, in addition to cause/effect, include definition, classification, diagnosis/symptom, enable/effect, and action/consequent (see, e.g., Porter, 1990). A sign relationship represents a correlational link between antecedent and consequent, for example, "Summer weekends are generally rainy." These capture noticed, but not necessarily explained, regularities in the world. Distinguishing between explanatory and sign warrants is important for reasoners using both deductive and plausible reasoning.

The *wtype2* field of a warrant represents the strength with which its consequent can be supported by the given antecedent. Representing information as to the strength of the connection between warrant fields is appropriate for reasoning with incomplete or uncertain knowledge. Current types are *sufficient (s), default (df)*, and *evidential (ev)*. The sufficient type is meant to represent certain relationships, e.g., definitions. The default and evidential types represent two levels of uncertain knowledge, with default indicating relationships that are usually the case (e.g., "birds fly"), and evidential referring to less certain links (e.g., "persons who live in Bermuda are often British subjects"). Warrants are expected to be written in the direction that reflects the strongest type. As an example, for a causal relation such as that between fire and smoke, since fire causes (is default grounds for concluding) smoke, "smoke" can therefore be said to be evidential grounds for concluding "fire". In the warrant that represents this relation, "fire" should be the antecedent and "smoke" the consequent, since that is the direction of the stronger relationship.

In Figure 3, we present a set of warrants that represents the general background knowledge for an expanded Bermuda problem. We add to our original problem, warrants regarding special skills and working papers as they relate to being a British subject. We use a propositional form for the warrants, where the implications indicate their type (wtype1) and strength (wtype2) by labels following the arrow. For example, in warrant w1, the antecedent proposition is "british passport" and the consequent is "british subject". The wtype1 field is "explanatory" and the wtype2 field is "evidential". The qualification is "valid" (!) and backing is atomic, as "given".

(d1 (english speaking) (!?) (GIVEN))
(d2 (british passport) (?!) (GIVEN))
(d3 (special skills) (!?) (GIVEN))
(d4 (quota met) (!?) (GIVEN))
(d5 (pays Bermuda taxes) (!?) (GIVEN))
(d6 (lives in Bermuda) (!?) (GIVEN))
(d7 (working papers) (!?) (GIVEN))

Figure 4. Harry's situation in the Bermuda Problem.

In Figure 4, we present a set of input claims that represents our knowledge regarding Harry as given in the Bermuda problem. Each claim is given in positive form, followed by two qualifications and a backing. All input claims have the atomic backing: "given". The first and second qualifications indicate levels of support for the positive and negative form of the claim, respectively. Thus, not having a British passport is indicated by support for the negative side of the claim "british passport". Here, all input data are considered accepted or certain; questionable input data could be represented by lesser qualifications, as will be considered in a later example. In the present example, for data-claim d1, the proposition is "english speaking"; the qualification for "english speaking" is "valid"(!); the qualification for "not english speaking" is "unknown"(?); and the backing for "english speaking" is atomic: "given".

To generate tau backing for a claim, a warrant is applied to data to support a conclusion. For example, the warrant w2 "A person born in Bermuda is usually a British subject" may be applied to the data element "born in Bermuda" to draw the conclusion "British subject". While the antecedent and consequent indicate the normal direction of a warrant's application, warrants can be used in other ways, as well. For example, the above warrant could be applied to the data element "British subject" to support the conclusion "born in Bermuda".

An important aspect of our model of argumentation is the use of warrants in differing "directions". Given a warrant with antecedent p and consequent q, we define several *reasoning steps* in Table I. The latter two reasoning steps, ABD and ABC, being forms of abductive reasoning, are considered to be fallacies in deductive reasoning (i.e., asserting the consequent and denying the antecedent, respectively). However, they are often appropriate for reasoning when knowledge is incomplete and uncertain. Polya (1968) discusses the role of similar reasoning steps as "patterns of plausible inference". He calls them "examining a ground" (MP, ABC) and "examining a consequent" (MT, ABD). Diagnostic reasoning is typically a form of abductive reasoning, where one is trying to infer causes of an observed symptom by reasoning backward over causal warrants. Although plausible reasoning types and less than valid warrants are available in our model, a user may choose to restrict their use at argument startup time; for example,

Table I. Reasoning steps.

Warrant	Data	Conclusion	Reasoning step
$p \rightarrow q$	p	q	modus ponens (MP)
$p \rightarrow q$	not q	not p	modus tollens (MT)
$p \rightarrow q$	q	p	direct abduction (ABD)
$p \rightarrow q$	not p	not q	contrapositive abduction (ABC)

sometimes only a valid argument (i.e., valid data and deductive reasoning steps with sufficient warrants) will serve.

The MT and ABC reasoning steps interact with conjunctive clauses in a warrant to generate disjunctions. For example, a warrant of the form "(X and Y) → (W and Z)" can be used with modus tollens reasoning to support the claim "not X" as follows: "(not W or not Z) → (not X or not Y)". Since our model assumes only conjunctive propositions as parts of warrants, the disjunction must be eliminated. The disjunction in the antecedent is handled by creating two warrants: "not W → (not X or not Y)" and "not Z → (not X or not Y)". The disjunction in the consequent field presents a more difficult problem. We address it by interpreting the "or" in the consequent as an exclusive or, so the two warrants become "(not W and Y) → not X" and "(not Z and Y) → not X" in support of claim "not X". Two others are created supporting "not Y", as well. As such, the current argument theory incorporates a limited form of disjunctive reasoning, but does not take on the issues of representing, reasoning, and arguing with full disjunction.

When deductive and plausible reasoning steps are present in the same system, as they are in our model, care must be taken to avoid inappropriate reasoning combinations, as Pearl (1987), among others, has discussed. For example, if the reasoner knows that "rain causes wet grass" and "sprinkler on causes wet grass", an unrestricted combination of modus ponens and abductive reasoning would allow the reasoner to derive the conclusion "sprinkler on" from the data "rain". This is unacceptable, though reasoning from data "wet grass" to "sprinkler on" (i.e., abductively) is reasonable in isolation.

To permit generation of acceptable conclusions while blocking generation of unacceptable ones, the reasoning steps interact with warrant type fields. Modus ponens/abduction combinations are not permitted for two explanatory warrants, unless both warrants are "evidential". The justification for this is that the data field of the explanatory warrant being used with modus ponens reasoning already explains its conclusion, and, therefore, abductive reasoning, which essentially is speculation about a plausible explanation, or cause, for a claim, is irrelevant in this context. In the above example, as "rain" explains how the grass came to be wet there is no reason to speculate "sprinkler on" as another explanation for the wet grass. When both warrants have a wtype2 field of "evidential", then the reasoning combination is permitted.

Table II. Link qualifications.

Warrant type	Reasoning step	link qualification
$\rightarrow$ s	MP, MT	valid
$\rightarrow$ s	ABD, ABC	weak
$\rightarrow$ df	MP	strong
$\rightarrow$ df	MT, ABD, ABC	weak
$\rightarrow$ ev	MP	credible
$\rightarrow$ ev	MT, ABD, ABC	weak

For example, if "high humidity" or "grey skies" were evidential data for conclusion "rain" (i.e., "high humidity $\rightarrow$ rain"; "grey skies $\rightarrow$ rain"), it seems reasonable to conclude "grey skies" starting from data "high humidity". This is because "high humidity" gives only a partial cause for conclusion (using modus ponens reasoning) "rain", i.e., there is still room to speculate as to additional (partial) causes, e.g., "grey skies". Similarly, when at least one warrant has a wtype1 field of "sign", the reasoning combination is permitted. Since sign warrants indicate a correlation rather than causal relation, speculating about causes remains appropriate in this situation.

The qualification associated with a claim is that associated with its strongest supporting argument. The qualifications on input data are given as atomic backing at input time; such a qualification will change if better support for the claim is derived from a tau backing. The qualification on any conclusion of a tau backing is the least of the qualifications associated with the tau: the qualification(s) on the data support, the qualification on the warrant, and the qualification derived from the warrant type and reasoning step applied. We call this latter qualification the "link qualification", as defined in Table II.

Deductive reasoning steps give strengths reflecting warrant types, while plausible, abductive steps provide only "weak" link qualification.

The weakest link approach to propagating support over warrants for claims and its appropriateness for plausible reasoning has been thoroughly discussed elsewhere (Rescher, 1976; Pollock, 1991). Rescher (1976) appeals to tradition: "[Plausible reasoning] bases its approach on the traditional modal principle that the conclusion of a piece of reasoning takes its status from that of the 'weakest' premis[e] *(pars deterior).*" Pollock (1991) argues that human reasoning must make use of a "weakest link principle for defeasible arguments", as other methods for propagating uncertainty seem too complex for everyday reasoning.

Argument Process

In the previous section, we described a representation for arguments as supporting explanations. The representation, based on a standard Toulmin format, includes non-deductive reasoning types, qualified claims, explanatory and correlational war-

Table III. Argument moves

Moves	Given	Show	Defeated
Support C	C	$X \rightarrow C \wedge X$	
		$C \rightarrow X \wedge X$	
		$\sim C \rightarrow X \wedge \sim X$	
		$X \rightarrow \sim C \wedge \sim X$	
Refute C			
undercut C			
invalid	$X \rightarrow C$	$\sim X$	
antecedent	$\wedge X$		
specific	$X \rightarrow C$	$X \wedge C \rightarrow \sim C$	*
exception	$\wedge X$	$\wedge Y$	
inapplicable	$X \rightarrow \sim C$	$Y \rightarrow \sim C$	*
evidence	$\wedge \sim X$	$\wedge$	
unneeded	$C \rightarrow X$	$Y \rightarrow X$	*
explanation	$\wedge X$	$\wedge$	
rebut C			
reductio ad	C	$C \rightarrow Z$	
absurdum		$\wedge \sim Z$	
rival	C	$X \rightarrow \sim C$	
support		$\wedge X$	
missing	C	$X \rightarrow C$	
support		$\wedge \sim X$	
rival	C	$\sim C \rightarrow X$	
implication		$\wedge X$	

rants, and sufficient, default, and evidential warrants. These features are appropriate for representing and reasoning about knowledge that is incomplete or uncertain. They explicate uncertainty in the support for a claim, i.e., arguable points. However, having only a structural model does not capture the procedural character of argumentation.

In this section, based upon the representation just outlined, we expand our model of argumentation to include argument as dialectical process, where arguments supporting alternative claims are refuted and defended in turn. Argument as dialectical process includes the tasks of supporting and refuting claims, and choosing actions relevant to these tasks. In successful refutation, supporting arguments for a claim are shown to be invalid or controversial. Dialectical arguments result in the intertwining, over time, of argument structures generated by Side-1 in support of an input claim and by Side-2 in support of its negation. A qualification on a claim is either a *Side-1 check* or a *Side-2 check*. A *check condition* for a side is such that, if the other side cannot refute that side's arguments, it wins the argument (as in a chess game).

We define the primary tasks of dialectical argumentation to be (a) supporting a claim; and (b) refuting a claim or its supporting arguments. Tasks are implemented by argument moves. Table III catalogs the set of argument moves we consider here.

Dialectical argument begins with Side-1 attempting to find support for the input claim. Finding support for a claim results in the generation of argument structures. Given a claim, search for support proceeds in a goal-directed fashion by looking for backing for the claim. If a claim is already in the data base with atomic backing, then the task is done. If a claim already has tau backing, the backing is checked to ensure that it does not loop (i.e., no claim is being used to support itself in the argument) or contradict (i.e., no negation of a claim is being used to support the claim) claims further up the argument tree. Otherwise, when the claim has no atomic backing or reusable tau backing, then possible tau backings for the claim are generated by searching for warrants that are relevant to the claim, i.e., contain the claim in their antecedent or consequent fields. Loops and contradictions are pruned throughout this process.

If a new tau backing is created, argument generation continues recursively by searching for backing for claims from the supporting proposition field of the relevant warrant. The argument generation process is completed when all (sub)claims are supported. At this point, the argument information structures are updated. A new tau structure is generated for each warrant that supports a (sub)claim, with qualification and backing fields of all claims updated to reflect the new support. If no initial support can be found through the above process, the argument ends with a loss for Side-1. If Side-1 is able to find support for the claim, control passes to Side-2, which tries to refute the argument for the claim(s) established by Side-1.

For example, given the expanded Bermuda example and the input claim "Harry is a British subject", Side-1 to the argument could generate support for the claim based on "Harry was born in Bermuda". This support is in turn supported by the data that Harry speaks English and has his Bermudan id#. "Working papers" is used to support the claim "bermuda id#", via abductive reasoning. The qualification on the conclusion "Harry is a British subject" will be weak, due to the reliance on a plausible reasoning step.

We distinguish two types of refutation: *undercutting* and *rebutting* (similar to Pollock, 1987). Undercutting is accomplished by finding weaknesses in purported support for a claim. With respect to the structure of a tau, undercutting questions the sufficiency of the data support and the link fields (i.e., warrant type and reasoning type). The model includes four undercutting moves, as presented in Table III. Questioning the data that supports a conclusion amounts to attempting to refute the antecedent of the tau, moving the argument a step back (the "invalid antecedent" move). Following up on a less than certain warrant and/or reasoning type in the support for a claim leads to argument moves that: (a) search for exceptions to default rules (the "specific exception" move); (b) attempt to show that weak evidence is irrelevant in the face of other, strong evidence (the "inapplicable evidence" move); (c) try to find alternative explanations for data, defeating claims that had been hypothesized as explanations for the same data using abductive reasoning (the "unneeded explanation" move).

If an undercutting move is successful, it results in a change to the qualification of a claim and possibly the withdrawal of an argument. In the latter case, such moves are said to be defeating moves, as indicated by the * entries in Table III. These moves are in response to an argument for which an exception is found (i.e., a more specific counter argument is found), or to a weak argument made by the other side, i.e., those based on plausible, not deductive reasoning steps. In the example Bermuda problem, the claim "bermuda id#" was hypothesized as an explanation for data "working papers". When the problem contains additional knowledge, e.g., "special skills" and "special skills $\rightarrow$ df working papers", "working papers" can be shown to be otherwise explainable (the "unneeded explanation" move), and should be withdrawn as support for "bermuda id#". The qualification of the claim "bermuda id#" would change from "+-?" to "??" as a result of this undercutting argument that defeats its prior support.

For a non-defeating undercut, the new qualification would reflect the resultant controversy. For example, if there were evidence that "not bermuda id#" (the "invalid antecedent" move), then the qualifications on the claims "bermuda id#", "bermuda born" and "british subject" would all change (e.g., from"+-?" to "+-+-"). Similar to non-defeating undercutting moves, directly rebutting arguments find alternative arguments for the negation for a claim and serve (only) to make the original conclusion controversial. Whether this is a sufficient outcome for a given side of an argument will depend on the burden of proof. For example, in the Bermuda problem, the argument for the claim "Harry is not a British subject", supported by the "Harry does not have a British passport" data uses the "missing support" move to rebut the argument in support of the original claim.

When a side is in control of the argument, it must select which argument move to apply. Ordering heuristics, guidelines for selecting argument moves, determine the course of the actual argument. They are used to order both the moves that implement a dialectical argumentation task and the warrants that implement a particular move. The ordering heuristics are meant to reflect two goals: to generate the strongest arguments possible for the active side and to generate coherent arguments that are responsive to those put forward by the other side. Argument moves are currently ordered according to the following criteria: (a) moves that are defeating are preferred over moves that can only make a claim controversial; (b) moves that attack a supporting argument closer to the overall claim are preferred; (c) specific moves are preferred over general ones; and (d) undercutting moves are preferred over rebutting moves.

For example, to refute the argument "(english speaking)(bermuda id#) $\rightarrow$ ev/mp (bermuda born) $\rightarrow$ df/mp (british subject)", the move "find exception to (bermuda born) $\rightarrow$ (british subject)" is preferred over the "invalid antecedent" (i.e., question data "bermuda born") move, since an exception can defeat a tau, while the invalid antecedent move can only make a tau controversial. The "invalid antecedent

– bermuda born" move is preferred over "invalid antecedent – english speaking", since "bermuda born" is closer to the top claim in the argument structure. "Invalid antecedent – english speaking" would be preferred to "rebut british subject", because the undercutting move responds to a particular argument put forward by the other side.

An argument move may be realized by more than one relevant warrant. In our present implementation, the selection of warrants is ordered according to the following criteria: (a) strong reasoning types (modus ponens and modus tollens) are preferred over plausible reasoning types; (b) strong warrant types are preferred over weaker warrant types; and (c) warrants where the data support part already has consistent support or where nothing is known about its support are preferred over warrants where the data support is controversial, or negated. For example, to support claim "bermuda born", the warrant "(english speaking)(bermuda id#) → ex/ev(bermuda born)" would be rated above "(bermuda born) → ex/ev(polo player)", using modus ponens rather than abductive reasoning. But "(parents living in bermuda during year of birth) → ex/df(bermuda born)" would be preferred to the first warrant, because the default warrant type is stronger than the evidential warrant type. Finally, "(attended school in bermuda) → ex/ev(bermuda born)", where nothing is yet known about "attended school in bermuda", would be ranked above "(early memories of bermuda) → ex/ev(bermuda born)" where the current qualification for "early memories of bermuda" is "?+", i.e., in cases where "not (early memories of bermuda)" is already supported, the best outcome would be only a controversial qualification.

The ordering heuristics anticipate moves that the other side may use in trying to refute a claim. Strong reasoning steps are more difficult to defeat; those closer to the root claim leave fewer opportunities for alternative support; defeating arguments eliminate controversial elements; weaker reasoning types allow more opportunities for defeating refutations. Controversial or negated data can be used to support a claim weakly at best.

This completes an overview of the basic elements of our model of dialectical argumentation. Given a set of warrants, some input data, a claim, and a burden of proof, our system proceeds to generate a dialectical argument, both structure and process. Control switches from side to side as check conditions are realized. Deciding which moves are sufficient to generate a check condition for a particular side, when an argument process is complete, and who wins, all depend upon a given burden of proof.

Burden of Proof

Now we turn our attention to the definition of burden of proof and discuss its impact on argument generation and conclusion. When knowledge is incomplete, uncertain, and inconsistent, a reasoner cannot count on deriving claims that are deductively valid. Since claims cannot be proved conclusively, a new definition of "proof" is needed that makes sense for weak theory domains. Inspired by the legal domain, we include a burden of proof mechanism in our argument model. Different burdens of proof are mandated at different stages of the legal process and for different types of legal action. For example, the arguments required to indict someone need not be as convincing as those needed to convict; the arguments needed to convict in one type of trial need not be as strong as those needed to convict in another type of trial. The higher the cost of being wrong, the more strict are the requirements that are imposed. By including burden of proof in the model, we are able to "prove" claims in weak theory domains and allow the notion of "proof" to vary appropriately in response to argument context. In addition, we will see that burden of proof acts as a heuristic to control inference during the argument generation process.

There are two aspects to the notion of burden of proof in our model: (i) which side in the argument bears the burden; (ii) what level of proof is required. As we consider only two sides to an argument (for and against the input claim), we assume that Side-1 always bears the burden of proof for the input claim, which might be stated as the negation of a proposition.

A *defendable argument* is one that cannot be defeated with the given warrants and input data. This has been called a *plausible argument* elsewhere (Sartor, 1993). We define the following levels of support for satisfying the burden of proof:

- *scintilla of evidence (se)*
  find at least one defendable argument
- *preponderance of the evidence (pe)*
  find at least one defendable argument
  outweigh the other side's rebutting arguments
- *dialectical validity (dv)*
  find at least one credible, defendable argument
  defeat all of the other side's rebutting arguments
- *beyond a reasonable doubt (brd)*
  find at least one strong, defendable argument
  defeat all of the other side's rebutting arguments
- *beyond a doubt (bd)*
  find at least one valid, defendable argument
  defeat all of the other side's rebutting arguments

In the case of preponderance of evidence, *outweigh* means having a stronger qualification for the input claim than for its rebuttal or a greater number of arguments for the claim with the same qualification as for its rebuttal.

As mentioned earlier, we borrow the names of several legal burdens of proof in our model, as this element of the model has been inspired by legal tradition. Our corresponding concepts for the burdens of proof clearly differ from those in the law, but do reflect an increasing stringency of requirements. Legal notions of burden of proof extend to substantive and procedural policies related to actual trials that do not apply in our restricted model of argumentation. One area for further research would be to develop our current notions to be more in line with legal concepts in a system designed to assist lawyers in trial procedure and argument formation.

Burden of proof plays several roles in the process of argumentation: (i) as a basis for deciding relevance of particular argument moves; (ii) as a basis for deciding sufficiency of a side's move (whether a check condition has been realized); (iii) as a basis for declaring an argument over; and (iv) as a basis for determining the outcome (decision) of an argument. For example, if we have imposed a burden of proof of dialectical validity and Side-2 has presented an argument rebutting Side-1's claim, Side-1 cannot merely find another argument supporting the input claim; Side-1 must defeat the rebuttal or concede the argument. However, if the burden of proof were only preponderance of the evidence, then another argument in favor of the claim by Side-1 could be sufficient to outweigh Side-2's rebuttal. For a burden of proof of beyond a reasonable doubt, Side-1 must find an initial argument based upon valid application of a sufficient or default warrant; otherwise, it must concede defeat without Side-2 even needing to make a move, as strong support must be found for the input claim under this burden of proof.

We illustrate the impacts of burden of proof upon argument process and outcome when we consider two examples of legal argumentation below. First, we consider important elements of our computer implementation of the model of argumentation.

DART: IMPLEMENTING THE ARGUMENTATION MODEL

DART (*D*ialectical *Ar*gumen*t*ation) is a computer program written in Common Lisp that implements our model of dialectical argumentation. Given a warrants set, an input data base, a claim to prove, and a proof level, DART generates a dialectical argument as a side effect of its attempt to prove the input claim. The argument generated is represented using the modified Toulmin representation described earlier.

The main components of DART are the Find_Support, Followup_Support, and Refute modules, as shown in Figure 5. The goal of Find_Support is to establish support for a given claim (or claims). If there is no current support for the claim, Find_Support attempts to generate support. This is accomplished through use of a basic matching step; the warrants base is searched for warrants that could provide support for the claim. The matcher examines warrants in terms of all reasoning step possibilities, i.e., support for claim C could be supplied by warrant "X → C" using modus ponens, "not C → X" using modus tollens, "C → X" using abduction, and "X → not C" using the abduction-contrapositive reasoning step.

Potentially supportive warrants are checked for allowable reasoning steps and warrant types. They are also checked to ensure that support from the warrant would not conflict with or repeat support already generated further up the argument chain. Say a side in the argument wishes to find support for a claim "C", and the warrants base contains a warrant "X → ex/evC", a potentially supportive warrant. If "C" is itself being used to support or help support the claim "not X", then "X → C"

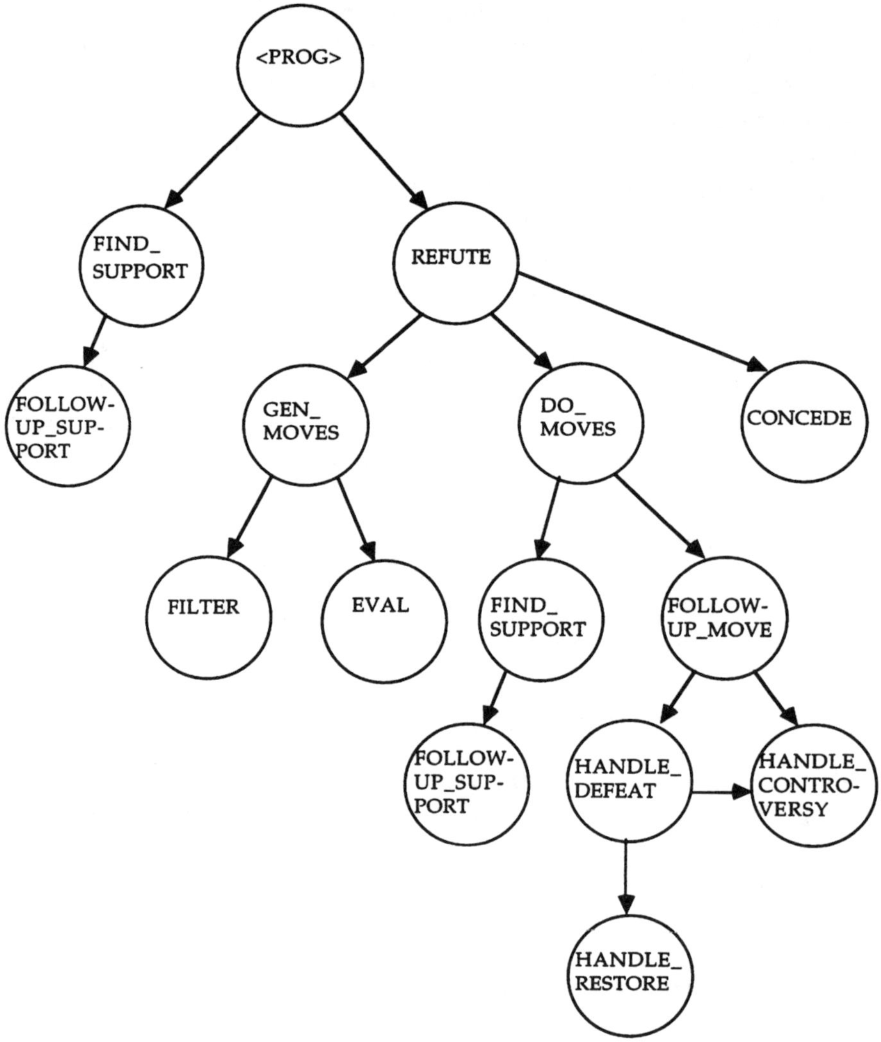

Figure 5. Control structure among the major procedures of DART.

cannot be used, as it would cause the argument to be internally inconsistent (i.e., "X $\rightarrow$ C $\rightarrow \ldots \rightarrow$ not X"). If a possible warrant passes all of the constraint checks, it is added to a set of usable warrants.

If the set of usable warrants is empty when the matcher finishes checking the warrants base, Find_Support has failed to find support for the claim, and returns nil. Otherwise, each warrant is evaluated according to the ordering heuristics and a sorted list of usable warrants is returned. The data support part of the next warrant (e.g., "X", when "X $\rightarrow$ C" is being used to support "C") then becomes the new claim, and Find_Support calls itself recursively.

When the proposition part of the input claim to Find_Support is supported in the data base, Find_Support calls Followup_Support to generate an argument structure in the format of the modified Toulmin representation. The support for the current claim is propagated along a warrant to become data support for another claim, and so on along the argument chain. A tau structure is generated to record the link between each data support and conclusion combination. The qualification and backing fields of each claim in the argument are updated to reflect the new support. For example, when Find_Support is called for claim "C", and the warrants base contains warrants of the forms "X → C" and "Y → X", and the data base contains a claim node showing that "Y" has atomic backing, then the argument structure generated by Find_Support would include three claims ("X", "Y", and "C") and two taus (one that is backing for "X" based on data support "Y", and one that is backing for "C" based on data support "X").

At the beginning of the argument generation process, Find_Support is called by Side-1 to generate support for the argument's top level (input) claim. If this initial call to Find_Support is successful, the qualification on the top level claim of the argument becomes a Side-1 check, and control of the argument is given to Side-2. Side-2's task is then to refute the current argument established by the other side. If Side-2 succeeds, i.e., establishes a Side-2 check qualification, control is given to Side-1 to attempt to refute the refutation. Turn-taking continues in this manner until one side concedes the argument.

After Side-1 finds an argument in support of the claim, Side-2 calls Refute to argue against the current argument. The most recent additions to the argument, the elements just generated by the other side, are used by the Refute matcher in an attempt to generate a coherent response. The matcher considers the new claims and their tau backings in light of a table of relevant argument moves, i.e., for each new tau that contributes to the support of the claim that the current side wishes to refute, DART generates argument moves that will, if successful, refute the tau. Some moves attempt to exploit weak points in the tau, e.g., weak warrant and reasoning types. A move that is always generated is to question the data support field of a given tau, since if the data support can be shown to be controversial, the conclusion it purports to support will also be controversial. A rebuttal move for the top claim is also always generated.

The possible argument moves are filtered with respect to the burden of proof level, as well as input reasoning and warrant type constraints. For example, when the burden of proof level is "scintilla of evidence", and the current side is Side-2, the only moves that would survive this filtering process would be the defeating moves. This is because to win the overall argument, Side-2 must actually force the withdrawal of (defeat) Side-1's argument; moves that can only make the claim controversial are therefore ignored.

A successful refutation will either defeat a tau or cause it to become controversial. When a tau is defeated, it is removed from the current argument structure, as are any taus that depended on the defeated tau for support. If the defeated tau was

(w1 ((burglar)) → ex s ((felon)) (!? GIVEN))
(w2 ((fleeing suspect) (felon)) → ex df ((deadly force is reasonable)) (!? GIVEN))
(w3 ((not (apprehension possible))) → ex df ((deadly force is reasonable)) (!? GIVEN))
(w4 ((two officers present)) → ex df ((apprehension possible)) (!? GIVEN))

(d1 (burglar) (!? GIVEN))
(d2 (fleeing suspect) (!? GIVEN))
(d3 (not (armed suspect)) (!? GIVEN))
(d4 (private residence) (!? GIVEN))
(d5 (unoccupied residence) (!? GIVEN))
(d6 (< ten dollars taken) (!? GIVEN))
(d7 (two officers present) (!? GIVEN))
(claim (deadly force is reasonable) (?? NIL))

Figure 6. Background knowledge for the deadly force case.

itself a defeater tau, then the taus that were removed at that time are restored to the current argument. When a tau is shown to be controversial, its claim becomes controversial. This will in turn cause each tau supported by that claim to become controversial, and so on to the root of the argument. Thus, at the end of a successful refute move, taus will have been added, removed, and/or restored, and new claim qualifications propagated to the top argument claim. Followup_Move is called to give the results of the move as program output. At this point, the Refute module tests the qualification of the top claim to see if it is now a "check" for the current side, in accordance with requirements from burden of proof specified. If it is, control of the argument is turned over to the other side. If it is not a check qualification, the current side executes the next move or concedes the argument, if there are no more moves.

Legal Reasoning Examples

As noted above, the primary source of inspiration for including burden of proof in our model of argumentation comes from the legal domain, which has long relied on this notion as means for making decisions in uncertain, often inconsistent, contexts. As such, we demonstrate our model of argument and burden of proof by considering two examples that have previously appeared in the AI and legal reasoning literature.

In the first example, adapted from (Marshall, 1989), we show how the argument model deals straightforwardly with inconsistent information. We consider the initial knowledge regarding the case, as presented in Figure 5. According to the warrants given, a burglar is a felon, by definition. When pursuing a fleeing felon or when apprehension is not possible, the use of deadly force is reasonable. When two officers are present, (non-violent) apprehension is usually possible. According to the facts of the given situation, an unarmed burglar is fleeing from an unoccupied, private residence, from which less than ten dollars has been stolen. There are at least two officers available to stop the burglar. The input claim is that deadly force is reasonable.

Side-1 is able to make a strong argument for the input claim (deadly force is reasonable) based on MP applications of warrants w1 and w2 based upon input data d1 and d2. Side-2 can respond with an argument using an MP application of w4 followed by a plausible, ABC application of warrant w3, which leads only to weak support for the counterclaim. As long as the burden of proof standard is less than or equal to the preponderance of the evidence, Side-1 can clearly win because its arguments are stronger.

Below, we give DART output for the argument process outlined above. Let us assume that the burden of proof borne by Side-1 is dialectical validity. The argument starts with Side-1 attempting to generate support for the input claim (deadly force is reasonable). As the claim is not already supported, the warrant base is searched for warrants that can be used to provide tau support for the claim. A set of usable warrants is generated, and warrants are checked for compliance with constraints, including allowable reasoning types and warrant types. In addition, the data support part of the warrant may not repeat or contradict any claims that are already part of the argument chain being developed. The set of available warrants is then heuristically ordered according to the criteria described earlier. Here, warrants W2 and W3 are both applicable and are equally ranked; W2 is checked first because it precedes W3 in the knowledge base.

```
Side 1 is looking for support for (DEADLY FORCE IS REASONABLE)
Burden of proof on side 1 is dialectical validity.

  Looking for support for claim (DEADLY FORCE IS REASONABLE)
  Check warrant(s) (W2 W3) for support for (DEADLY FORCE IS REASONABLE).

  Trying W2 with ((AND (FLEEING SUSPECT) (FELON)))
  to support (DEADLY FORCE IS REASONABLE).

  Looking for support for claim (FLEEING SUSPECT)
    Support found in data base for (FLEEING SUSPECT)

  Looking for support for claim (FELON)
  Check warrant(s) (W1) for support for (FELON).

    Trying W1 with ((AND (BURGLAR)))
    to support (FELON).

    Looking for support for claim (BURGLAR)
    Support found in data base for (BURGLAR)

  Support found for warrant W1
Support found for warrant W2
```

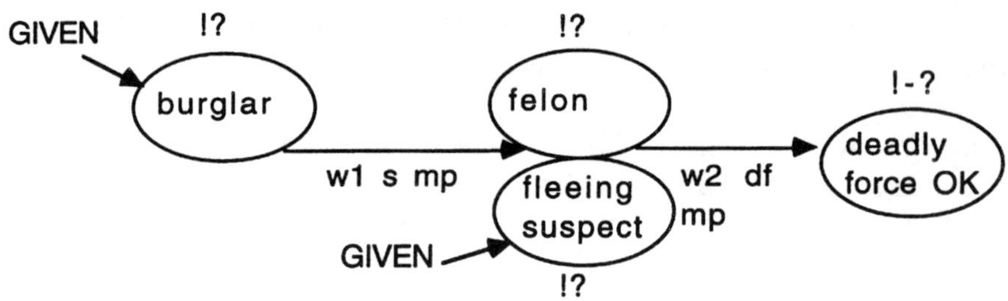

Figure 7. Structure of initial Side-1 argument.

Side-1 has found support for the claim, and generates the following argument structure:

Claim ((DEADLY FORCE IS REASONABLE)) is supported by ((FELON) (FLEEING SUSPECT))
Warrant id: W2 - Wtype1: EX - Wtype2: DF - Rtype: MP
New tau id: #:255
Claimnode qualification is: (!- ?)

Claim ((FELON)) is supported by ((BURGLAR))
Warrant id: W1 - Wtype1: EX - Wtype2: S - Rtype: MP
New tau id: #:254
Claimnode qualification is: (! ?)

Claim (BURGLAR) is already supported.
Backing is GIVEN
Claimnode qualification is: (! ?)

Claim (FLEEING SUSPECT) is already supported.
Backing is GIVEN
Claimnode qualification is: (! ?)

This argument can be graphically represented, as shown in Figure 7. In summary, there is support for the use of deadly force, because there is support for the claim that the suspect was fleeing a felony crime. The support for the (felon) subclaim comes from warrant W1, which definitively classifies a burglar as a felon. Support for subclaims (burglar) and (fleeing suspect) are found in the input data base. As the warrants are of types sufficient and default, and the reasoning step used for both warrants is modus ponens, the qualification on the top claim is strong, i.e. (!-?); no support has been found for the counterclaim.

Since Side-1 has succeeded in generating an argument in support of the input claim, control of the argument is given to Side-2; it must attempt to refute Side-1's support for the claim. First, argument moves that can be used to refute Side-1's argument are collected, including moves generated but not used by Side-2 in previous turns. Since this is Side-2's first turn, there are no old moves. Next, new moves are generated, based on Side-1's last argument in support of the top claim. Moves are generated tau by tau, and seek to expose weak reasoning types, warrant types, and data support, as discussed above.

Possible NEW argument moves are:
Find exception for rule
(AND (FELON) (FLEEING SUSPECT)) → (AND (DEADLY FORCE IS REASONABLE))
Refuted tau would be #:2̂55

Question data: find support or bolster (OR (NOT FELON) (NOT FLEEING SUSPECT))
Refuted tau would be #:2̂55

Question data: find support or bolster (AND (NOT BURGLAR))
Refuted tau would be #:2̂54

Find support for (AND (NOT DEADLY FORCE IS REASONABLE))
Refuted tau would be TOP

In this example, a move to attempt to find an exception to the default warrant is generated. (Recall from Table 3 that an exception move uses a more specific warrant.) Since that is the only possible weak spot in the current argument, the only other moves available to Side-2 are to check for inconsistent knowledge, i.e., support for claims that would contradict the data claims used in the current argument. Support for, say, (not (fleeing suspect)) would cause the claim (fleeing suspect), and, as a result, Side-1's entire argument to become controversial. The generated moves have already been checked for compliance with input reasoning type and warrant type constraints; next, moves are filtered that are not strong enough to achieve the qualification needed to refute with respect to the input burden of proof level. For dialectical validity, Side-2 needs only to show that support for the top claim is controversial; all of the generated moves are retained. Next, the set of moves is heuristically ordered, according to the criteria given earlier. The result of the sorting is to put the exception move first, which could result in the defeat of the current argument, followed by undercutting, question data ("invalid antecedent") moves, followed by a rebut the top claim move.

New argument moves, in sorted order, are:

Find exception for rule
(AND (FELON) (FLEEING SUSPECT)) → (AND (DEADLY FORCE IS REASONABLE))
Refuted tau would be #:2̂55

Question data: find support or bolster (OR (NOT FELON) (NOT FLEEING SUSPECT))
Refuted tau would be #:2̂55

Question data: find support or bolster (AND (NOT BURGLAR))
Refuted tau would be #:2̂54

Find support for (AND (NOT DEADLY FORCE IS REASONABLE))
Refuted tau would be TOP

Side-2 now attempts each move in turn, until a move results in Side-2 successfully responding to Side-1's argument, or until there are no more moves. The first three moves fail to find support, but the fourth is successful, as follows:

Next move for side 2 is:

Find support for (AND (NOT DEADLY FORCE IS REASONABLE))

Looking for support for claim (NOT DEADLY FORCE IS REASONABLE)
Check warrant(s) (W3) for support for (NOT DEADLY FORCE IS REASONABLE).

Trying W3 with ((AND (APPREHENSION POSSIBLE)))
to support (NOT DEADLY FORCE IS REASONABLE).

Looking for support for claim (APPREHENSION POSSIBLE)
Check warrant(s) (W4) for support for (APPREHENSION POSSIBLE).

Trying W4 with ((AND (TWO OFFICERS PRESENT)))
to support (APPREHENSION POSSIBLE).

Looking for support for claim (TWO OFFICERS PRESENT)
Support found in data base for (TWO OFFICERS PRESENT)
Support found for warrant W4
Support found for warrant W3

This results in the following counterargument being generated:

Claim ((NOT DEADLY FORCE IS REASONABLE)) is supported by
((APPREHENSION POSSIBLE))
Warrant id: W3 - Wtype1: EX - Wtype2: DF - Rtype: ABC
New tau id: #:258
Claimnode qualification is: (!- +-)

Claim ((APPREHENSION POSSIBLE)) is supported by
((TWO OFFICERS PRESENT))
Warrant id: W4 - Wtype1: EX - Wtype2: DF - Rtype: MP
New tau id: #:257
Claimnode qualification is: (!- ?)

Claim (TWO OFFICERS PRESENT) is already supported.
Backing is GIVEN
Claimnode qualification is: (! ?)

Tau #:258: ((AND (APPREHENSION POSSIBLE)) →
(NOT DEADLY FORCE IS REASONABLE))
makes top claim: (DEADLY FORCE IS REASONABLE) controversial - FS.

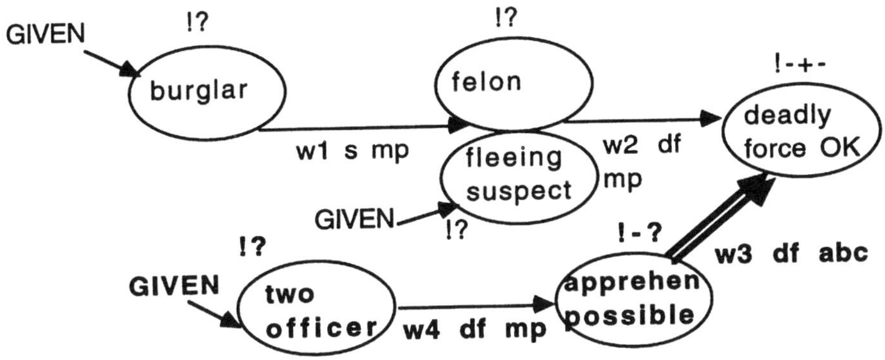

Figure 8. Side-2 rebuttal to the initial argument.

Qualification for claim (DEADLY FORCE IS REASONABLE) is (!- +-)

Graphically represented, the overall argument is as presented below in Figure 8. Side-2 has succeeded in rebutting Side-1's argument, by making a case for the negation of the input claim. Side-2's argument relies in part on the plausible, ABC application of warrant w3, so the support for the rebutting claim is only weak.

For a burden of proof of dialectical validity, this is sufficient for a Side-2 check. Control of the argument is returned to Side-1, which must attempt to defend its claim against this refutation. Side-1 must defeat the argument presented by Side-2, so only a subset of argument steps otherwise available are relevant at this point. Once again, a set of argument moves is generated, filtered, and sorted, with the following result:

When the burden of proof is dialectical validity, usable NEW argument moves, in sorted order, are as follows:

Find strong support for (AND (DEADLY FORCE IS REASONABLE))
to show that weak evidence (AND (APPREHENSION POSSIBLE))
  for claim (AND (NOT DEADLY FORCE IS REASONABLE)) is irrelevant.
Refuted tau would be #:$\hat{2}58$

Find exception for rule
  (AND (TWO OFFICERS PRESENT)) → (AND (APPREHENSION POSSIBLE))
Refuted tau would be #:$\hat{2}57$

Since Side-2's argument uses a default warrant, Side-1 generates an exception move. Since it uses a plausible inference type, Side-1 generates the move to attempt to show that the weak inference is faulty. In addition, "question data" moves are generated for all data used in Side-2's argument, along with a move to look for additional support for the top claim. All of the moves except for the two defeating moves are filtered. This is because the question data and rebuttal moves can at best show that the top claim is controversial; for dialectical validity, Side-1 must provide non-controversial support for its top claim. Thus, the non-defeating moves are rejected as too weak for the current situation. Side-1 attempts the remaining moves in order:

```
Next move for side 1 is:
Find strong support for (AND (DEADLY FORCE IS REASONABLE))
to show that weak evidence (AND (APPREHENSION POSSIBLE))
for claim (AND (NOT DEADLY FORCE IS REASONABLE)) is irrelevant.

Looking for support for claim (DEADLY FORCE IS REASONABLE)
Check warrant(s) (W3) for support for (DEADLY FORCE IS REASONABLE).

  Trying W3 with ((AND (NOT APPREHENSION POSSIBLE)))
  to support (DEADLY FORCE IS REASONABLE).

    Looking for support for claim (NOT APPREHENSION POSSIBLE)
    Check warrant(s) (W4) for support for (NOT APPREHENSION POSSIBLE).

    Trying W4 with ((AND (NOT TWO OFFICERS PRESENT)))
    to support (NOT APPREHENSION POSSIBLE).

    Looking for support for claim (NOT TWO OFFICERS PRESENT)
    No warrant support found.
  No support found.
No support found.
move failed

Next move for side 1 is:
Find exception for rule (AND (TWO OFFICERS PRESENT)) →
    (AND (APPREHENSION POSSIBLE))
  Looking for support for claim (NOT APPREHENSION POSSIBLE)
  No warrant support found.
move failed

Side 1 has no more arg moves.
Side 2 wins.

Claim (DEADLY FORCE IS REASONABLE) was NOT established.
Burden of proof on side 1 was: dialectical validity
```

Side-1 fails either to make a dialectically valid case for the reasonableness of deadly force, because it appears that non-violent apprehension is possible with two officers present and it cannot show an exception to the rule that non-violent apprehension is possible with two officers. Side-2's case, though weak, is defendable; thus, Side-1 loses the argument that (deadly force is reasonable) at the dialectical validity proof level.

If the proof level were preponderance of the evidence, Side-1 would win the argument, as it has the stronger argument. For that proof level, the argument would proceed initially as shown above; Side-1 makes its initial case for the input claim. Then, during Side-2's turn, the set of argument moves would be generated and ordered, also as described above. But at this proof level, all the moves fail, including the rebuttal move that succeeded above. This is because DART would filter the move that succeeded for dialectical validity, since, at best, it could offer only weak support. This would not be enough for Side-2 to prevail for proof level preponderance of the evidence, because Side-1 already has established strong support for its claim. Side-2 would concede the argument during its first turn; (deadly force is reasonable) is supported for proof level preponderance of the evidence.

For proof level scintilla of evidence, Side-1, of course, would again prevail. But the argument process would be even more streamlined. Once again, Side-1 would generate its support for the input claim. However, this time Side-2 must actually defeat Side-1's support to win the argument. When its turn comes, the only move even attempted is the one defeating move, to find an exception to the default warrant used by Side-1. That move fails, and Side-2 must concede the argument.

Warrant w2 is meant to reflect the import of a Tennessee law intending to discourage felons from fleeing the scene of a crime. The law gave police free reign to use deadly weapons as a means of stopping them. The U.S. Supreme Court, in Tennessee v. Garner, felt the rule was open to abuse and contrary to the intent of federal statutes that required some indication of threat of danger to property, the public, or the police prior to allowing the use of deadly force. Suppose we change w2 to w2' to reflect this new perspective and add w5 as one of several possible supporting warrants, as follows:

```
(w2' ((dangerous suspect)(fleeing suspect)(felon)
  → ex df ((deadly force is reasonable)) (!? GIVEN))
(w5 ((armed suspect) → ex ev ((dangerous suspect))(!? GIVEN))
```

In this case, Side-1 cannot even generate an argument in favor of the input claim (deadly force reasonable), thus, it can win no argument at any proof level. If the claim is changed to the counterclaim that deadly force is not reasonable, Side-1 has two weak arguments. One is based on ABC application of w3, as seen earlier, and the other is based on ABC applications of w5 followed w2', i.e., (not (armed)) leads to (not (dangerous)), which supports (not (deadly force is reasonable)). Note that support for the negation of only one proposition of a conjunctive condition is sufficient for ABC application of the warrant. Thus, the counterclaim can win arguments up to proof level of preponderance of the evidence. The revised warrants base is highly controversial; neither side can generate a credible argument in its favor. This suggests the opportunity for introduction of new warrants providing stronger arguments in support of either side. The use of dynamic sets of warrants,

(w1 ((loose bricks)) $\rightarrow$ ex df ((maintenance deficiency)) (!? GIVEN))
(w2 ((maintenance deficiency)) $\rightarrow$ ex df ((landlord responsible)) (!? GIVEN))
(w3 ((landlord responsible)) $\rightarrow$ ex s ((not (tenant responsible))) (!? GIVEN))
(w4 ((loose bricks)(near road)) $\rightarrow$ ex df ((danger)) (!? GIVEN))
(w5 ((danger)) $\rightarrow$ ex df ((tenant responsible)) (!? GIVEN))
(w6 ((loose bricks)(near road)(seldom used)) $\rightarrow$ ex df ((not (danger))) (!? GIVEN))

(d1 (loose bricks) (!? GIVEN))
(d2 (near road) (!? GIVEN))
(d3 (seldom used) (!? GIVEN))
(claim (landlord responsible) (?? NIL))

Figure 9. Background knowledge for maintenance argument.

where new warrants can be introduced during the process (as is often done during legal arguments), is an element of argumentation yet to be addressed by our model.

The next problem, which has been used to demonstrate application of default and rule-based reasoning in a legal context, is from (Prakken, 1991). The knowledge from the problem is represented by the following warrants and data, as Figure 9.

That is, loose bricks in a rental unit are usually a maintenance deficiency, and taking care of maintenance deficiencies is usually the responsibility of the landlord, not the tenant. However, if the loose bricks are near a road, they constitute a danger; the tenant, not the landlord, is usually responsible for any danger. However, loose bricks near a road that is seldom used are usually not considered a danger. In this case, there were loose bricks near a road, and the road was seldom used. Is the landlord responsible?

Side-1 must try to find strong support for the input claim (landlord responsible). It is able to do this through MP application of warrants w1 and w2 based on input data d1. Below is a trace of DART as it searches for this support.

```
Side 1 is looking for support for (LANDLORD RESPONSIBLE)
Burden of proof on side 1 is dialectical validity.

Looking for support for claim (LANDLORD RESPONSIBLE)
Check warrant(s) (W2 W3) for support for (LANDLORD RESPONSIBLE).

  Trying W2 with ((AND (MAINTENANCE DEFICIENCY)))
  to support (LANDLORD RESPONSIBLE).

  Looking for support for claim (MAINTENANCE DEFICIENCY)
  Check warrant(s) (W1) for support for (MAINTENANCE DEFICIENCY).

    Trying W1 with ((AND (LOOSE BRICKS)))
    to support (MAINTENANCE DEFICIENCY).

    Looking for support for claim (LOOSE BRICKS)
```

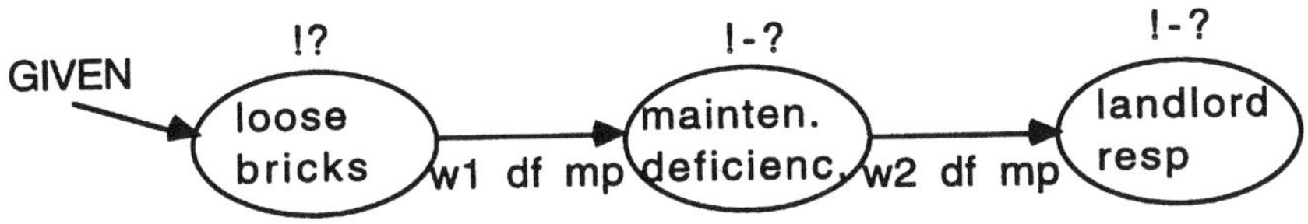

Figure 10. Initial maintenance argument by Side-1.

Support found in data base for (LOOSE BRICKS)
Support found for warrant W1
Support found for warrant W2

Having found the necessary argument chain providing strong support for the claim, Side-1 builds the following structure of interrelated taus, as shown in Figure 10:

Claim ((LANDLORD RESPONSIBLE)) is supported by ((MAINTENANCE DEFICIENCY))
Warrant id: W2 - Wtype1: EX - Wtype2: DF - Rtype: MP
New tau id: #:$\hat{1}$99
Claimnode qualification is: (!- ?)

Claim ((MAINTENANCE DEFICIENCY)) is supported by ((LOOSE BRICKS))
Warrant id: W1 - Wtype1: EX - Wtype2: DF - Rtype: MP
New tau id: #:$\hat{1}$98
Claimnode qualification is: (!- ?)

Claim (LOOSE BRICKS) is already supported.
Backing is GIVEN
Claimnode qualification is: (! ?)

Side-2 must try to refute this initial argument supporting the input claim. It considers a number of moves, in the following order, as a trace of DART indicates:

When the burden of proof is dialectical validity,
New argument moves, in sorted order, are:

Find exception for rule (AND (MAINTENANCE DEFICIENCY))
→ (AND (LANDLORD RESPONSIBLE))
Refuted tau would be #:$\hat{1}$99

Find exception for rule (AND (LOOSE BRICKS))
→ (AND (MAINTENANCE DEFICIENCY))
Refuted tau would be #:$\hat{1}$98

Question data: find support or bolster (AND (NOT MAINTENANCE DEFICIENCY))
Refuted tau would be #:$\hat{1}$99

Question data: find support or bolster (AND (NOT LOOSE BRICKS))

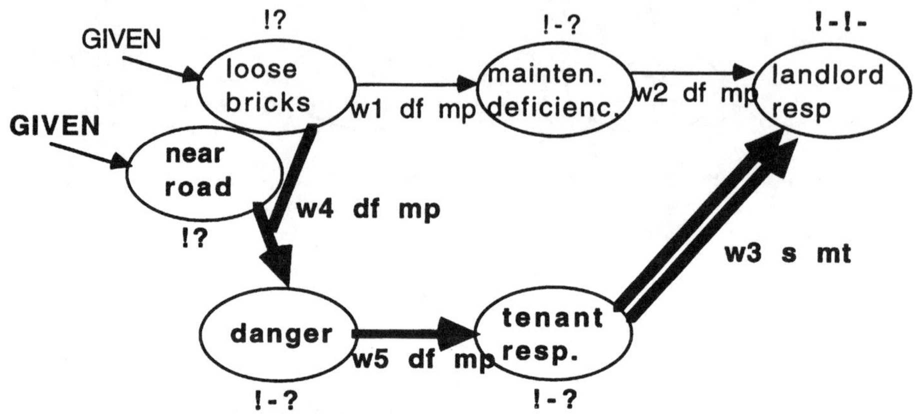

Figure 11. The argument after Side-2's rebuttal.

Refuted tau would be #:1̂98

Find support for (AND (NOT LANDLORD RESPONSIBLE))
Refuted tau would be TOP

That is, Side-2 will attempt to dispute Side-1's case by establishing exceptions to the default rules, and by checking each of the claims put forward by Side-1. The last move above succeeds. Side-2 can refute the argument by finding an argument for the negation of the input claim. This argument shows that loose bricks near a road constitute a danger for which the landlord is not responsible, using warrants w4 and w5 and an MT application of the sufficient warrant W3. The resultant argument structure now can be pictured as shown in Figure 11.

Although several moves are now available to Side-1, including questioning whether the tenant is really near the road, or whether the bricks are really loose, or making another case for landlord responsibility, the only moves that will be of any use with the dialectical validity burden of proof are the defeating moves, as follows:

When the burden of proof is dialectical validity,
New argument moves, in sorted order, are:

Find exception for rule (AND (DANGER)) → (AND (TENANT RESPONSIBLE))
Refuted tau would be #:2̂03

Find exception for rule (AND (NEAR ROAD) (LOOSE BRICKS)) → (AND (DANGER))
Refuted tau would be #:2̂02

The second option above succeeds. Side-1 can show that the data d3 in the current situation matches the conditions of warrant w6, an exception to the w2 default rule about danger. As such, warrant w6 can be used to show that loose

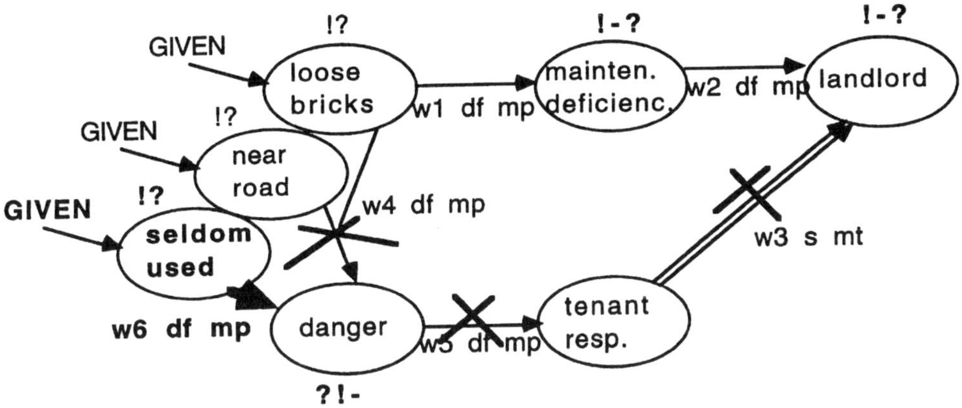

Figure 12. Argument structure after Side-1's successful response.

bricks near a road that is seldom used do not constitute a danger after all. Side-2's argument for there being danger is thereby defeated, causing it to be withdrawn and reinstating the original argument that the landlord is responsible. The argument is defeated as an exception (i.e., more specific rule) has been found that contradicts the earlier conclusion. Side-2 can generate no more counterarguments; Side-1, having defended a strong argument for the landlord's responsibility, will win this argument for any proof level up to and including beyond a reasonable doubt. Figure 12 shows the ultimate argument structure.

If the burden of proof on Side-1 had been only scintilla of evidence, Side-2 would not have put forward even its single refutation. The argument move, even if successful, would not have been strong enough to defeat Side-1's argument outright; this would have been needed for Side-2 to win the argument at this proof level. Side-2 would have tried its two defeating, find exception moves, but as we have seen, they both fail. On the other hand, if the burden of proof on Side-1 were beyond a doubt, Side-1 would have to concede the argument immediately, as there are no sufficient warrants available to support the input claim with valid qualification.

If we next consider the counterclaim, i.e., (not (landlord responsible)), as the input claim, Side-1 could generate a supporting argument based on warrants w4, w5, and w3 as above, with input data d1 and d2. But, as we have already seen, an argument based on warrant w4 can be defeated using warrant w6. Side-1 has no other argument for (not landlord responsible) and must concede. Thus, the claim (not landlord responsible) cannot be established with even a scintilla of evidence. Lastly, suppose we consider that the input evidence about the road being seldom used is only hearsay and at best can be given a qualification of credible. This would change the input to include (d1 (seldom used) (+ ? HEARSAY)). The undercutting argument by Side-1 using warrant w6 would no longer be considered a defeating argument; due to the uncertain input data, it would be of lower qualification than the argument it is attacking. Side-1 has no way of defeating outright Side-2's counterargument. Thus, in this case, both the claim and the counterclaim could only win arguments for proof level scintilla of evidence.

Related Research

The AI and law community has seen growing interest in research addressing issues of the formalization of argumentation. The notion of interargument defeat has been addressed by several recent efforts. More specific arguments viewed as exceptions, and thus defeaters, was pursued by Poole (Poole, 1985) and adopted by others (Prakken, 1991; Loui et al., 1993). Since we allow unsound, weak reasoning steps to be applied, we introduce other opportunities for defeat between arguments. Any counterargument based solely on MP reasoning steps, regardless of qualification on the links, is seen as sufficient to defeat a plausible, weak argument step supporting a particular claim. A weak argument is fragile, but may prove to be a crucial factor when left unanswered, as in our first, deadly force example above.

In other related research, the work of Sartor (Sartor, 1993) comes closest to capturing our various notions of proof level. He defines a *plausible argument* to be one with no defeating counterargument. This would be an argument sufficient to win a scintilla of evidence argument for a particular claim. He then describes a *justifying argument* as a plausible argument for a claim and no plausible argument for its counterclaim or negation. This is what we require of a dialectically valid argument; Prakken introduces related concepts, as well (Prakken, 1991). Neither explore the application of burden of proof at different proof levels as an important element of control for generating coherent, dialectical arguments. They both assume that all arguments are generated and then these relationships are used to prune the sets of contrasting, competing arguments.

Reason-Based Logic (RBL) has been proposed as an extension of first-order predicate logic to handle situations of conflicting reasons supporting a conclusion (Hage, et.al., 1994; Hage, 1995). Properties of rules, such as "applies" or "valid", and relationships between rules, such as "outweighs" or "replaces", are represented and reasoned about explicitly. This allows conflicting proofs or reasons to be mediated and a decision reached in RBL. In a related, logical framework, Sartor and Prakken (1995) attempt to formalize the the notion of conflicting and justified arguments. In addition, they also make explicit reasoning about priorities among rules based upon principles of rule superiority, e.g., lex superior, lex specialis, lex posterior, an ability that is especially important in the legal domain.

In terms of dialectic process, Gordon's (Gordon, 1993) work on formalizing the process of pleadings, i.e., deciding what issues must be decided before the court in a given case, directly addresses steps in a dialog between sides of an issue. He introduces several types of actions that can be taken – concede, deny, defend, and declare – and several types of statements that can be made – claim, argument, rebuttal, and denial. He then provides rules whereby the actions are allowed in terms of the active statements of the pleading process. He demonstrates his system, also implemented, on a number of interesting examples. As the system is aimed at identifying issues and not deciding a main claim, burden of proof is not a factor in the process. This work complements that presented here and could be combined with our work to create a more explicit control model in conjunction with the argument representation presented here.

Conclusion

Our computational model of argument comprises both senses of argument: argument as supporting explanation and argument as dialectical process. It incorporates features appropriate for reasoning in weak theory domains, including plausible inference and uncertainty representation. We demonstrate that burden of proof is a useful aspect of a computational model of argumentation when applied as a basis for practical decisionmaking. We demonstrate the impacts of different burden of proof levels in two examples of legal argument contexts discussed in previous literature. Our model has been implemented and tested on a number of classic reasoning problems across a variety of weak theory domains, including those discussed here from the legal arena. The model as implemented exhibits reasonable behavior when applied to these examples drawn from formal argumentation and artificial intelligence research (Freeman, 1993).

We hope that our model can serve as a framework for further exploration concerning models of argumentation as a means for practical and legal reasoning. We are investigating several extensions to our model, including adding of a new warrant type case that will incorporate elements of case-based reasoning. Such warrants would have facts of prior cases as antecedents, with conclusions representing case outcomes. A particular case may give rise to multiple warrants, representing various, differing interpretations of the reasoning, precedent, or outcome of a case (Ashley, 1990). In particular, focusing on a subset of facts from a case as the relevant antecedents of a derived warrant represents one issue to be addressed. To reflect adequately the way cases are used in arguments, partial matching and matching by analogy on the structure of fact sets involved in particular cases would also have to be allowed, as explored in the GREBE system (Branting, 1991). How this capability would interact with warrant qualifications and burden of proof to generate typical argument strategies involving the use of cases (Rissland, 1985; Skalak and Rissland, 1991) suggests further, interesting research questions.

As in the second example above, where the federal law takes precedence over a state statute, giving differing weights or priorities to warrants (beyond that of strength of qualification) is another direction for exploration. This factor has been used by a number of recent researchers, who put explicit, hierarchical preferences on warrants (Loui et al, 1993; Prakken, 1993; Sartor, 1993) and reason directly about these priorities. Combining these new modeling capabilities with a generalized definition of burden of proof in a dialectical, process model of argumentation would advance progress toward an adequate computational model of legal argumentation. The formal, computational study of argument is still in its infancy. Introducing the many nuances of this field of discourse into operational models of argument structure and argument process, including the sophisticated techniques of legal argumentation, will require continued, significant effort.

Acknowledgements

We wish to thank the anonymous reviewers of an earlier draft of this paper, whose comments assisted us in improving its presentation substantially.

References

Ashley, K. D. (1990) *Modeling Legal Argument: Reasoning with Cases and Hypotheticals*. Cambridge, MA: MIT Press, 93–102.

Barth, E. M. and Krabbe, E.C.W. (1982) *From Axiom to Dialog: A Philosophical Study of Logics and Argumentation*. Berlin, NY: Walter de Gruyter.

Branting, K. L. (1991) Reasoning with portions of precedents. *Proceedings of the Third International Conference on Artificial Intelligence and Law* (ICAIL–91), 145–154.

Freeley, A. (1990) *Argumentation and Debate: Critical Thinking for Reasoned Decision Making* (7th ed.). Belmont, CA: Wadsworth Publishing Company.

Freeman, K. (1993) *Toward Formalizing Dialectical Argumentation*. PhD Thesis, Department of Computer and Information Science, University of Oregon.

Ginsberg, M. L. ed. (1987) *Readings in Nonmonotonic Reasoning*, Los Altos, CA, Morgan Kaufmann.

Gardner, A. (1987) *An Artificial Intelligence Approach to Legal Reasoning*. MIT Press : Cambridge, MA, 1987.

Gordon, T. F. (1993) The pleadings game: formalizing procedural justice. *Proceedings of the Fourth International Conference on Artificial Intelligence and Law* (ICAIL–93), 10–19.

Hage, J. C. Leenes, R. and Lodder, A. (1994) Hard cases: a precedural approach. *Artificial Intelligence and Law*, 2, 113–167.

Hage, J. C. (1995) Teleological reasoning in reason-based logic, *Proceedings of the Fifth International Conference on Artificial Intelligence and Law* (ICAIL–95), 11–20.

Horner, W. (1988) *Rhetoric in the classical tradition*. St. Martins Press: New York, NY.

Kuhn, D. (1991) *The skills of Argument*. Cambridge University Press: Cambridge. UK.

Loui, R. P., Norman, J., Olson, J. and Merrill, A. (1993) A design for reasoning with policies, precedents, and rationales. *Proceedings of the Fourth International Conference on Artificial Intelligence and Law* (ICAIL–93), 202–211.

Marshall, C. (1989) Representing the structure of legal argument. *Proceedings of the Second International Conference on Artificial Intelligence and Law* (ICAIL–89), 121–127.

Pearl, J. (1987). Embracing causality in formal reasoning. *Proceedings of AAA1–87*, 369–373.

Pearl, J. (1988) *Probabilistic Reasoning in Intelligent Systems: Networks of Plausible Inference*. Morgan Kaufmann: San Mateo, CA.

Pollock, J. (1987). Defeasible reasoning. *Cognitive Science* 11, 481–518.

Pollock, J. (1991). A theory of defeasible reasoning. *International Journal of Intelligent Systems* 6, 33–54.

Pollock, J. (1992). How to reason defeasibly. *Artificial Intelligence* 57, 1–42.

Pollock, J. (1994). Justification and defeat. *Artificial Intelligence* 67, 377–407.

Poole, D. L. (1985), On the comparison of theories: Preferring the most specific explanation, *Proceedings IJCAI–85*, 144–147.

Polya, G. (1968). *Mathematics and plausible reasoning* (2nd ed.) (v. II). Princeton, NJ: Princeton University Press.

Porter, B., Bareiss, R., and Holte, R. (1990). Concept learning and heuristic classification in weak theory domains. *Artificial Intelligence* 45, 229–263.

Prakken, H. (1991) A tool in modelling disagreement in law: preferring the most specific argument. *Proceedings of the Third International Conference on Artificial Intelligence and Law* (ICAIL–91), 165–174.

Prakken, H. (1993) A logical framework for modelling legal argument. *Proceedings of the Fourth International Conference on Artificial Intelligence and Law* (ICAIL–93), 1–9.

Prakken, H. and Sartor, G. (1995) On the relation between legal language and legal argument: assumptions, applicability, and dynamic priorities. *Proceedings of the Fifth International Conf. on Artificial Intelligence and Law* (ICAIL–95), 1–11.

Rescher, N. (1976). *Plausible Reasoning.* Assen/Amsterdam, The Netherlands: Van Gorcum.

Rescher, N. (1977). *Dialectics: A controversy-oriented approach to the theory of knowledge.* Albany, NY: State University of New York Press.

Rissland, E. L. (1985) Argument moves and hypotheticals. In C. Walter (ed.) *Computing Power and Legal Reasoning*, St. Paul, MN: West Publishing.

Sartor, G. (1993) A simple computational model for nonmonotonic and adversarial legal reasoning. *Proceedings of the Fourth International Conference on Artificial Intelligence and Law* (ICAIL–93), 192–201.

Skalak, D. B. and Rissland, E. L. (1991), Argument moves in a rule-guided domain. *Proceedings of the Third International Conference on Artificial Intelligence and Law* (ICAIL–91), 1–11.

Toulmin, S. (1958). *The uses of argument.* Cambridge, UK: Cambridge University Press, 1958.

Artificial Intelligence and Law **4:** 199–273, 1996.

A Theory of Legal Reasoning and a Logic to Match*

JAAP HAGE
University of Limburg, Department of Metajuridica, E-mail: jaap.hage@metajur.unimaas.nl

Abstract. This paper describes a model of legal reasoning and a logic for reasoning with rules, principles and goals that is especially suited to this model of legal reasoning. The paper consists of three parts. The first part describes a model of legal reasoning based on a two-layered view of the law. The first layer consists of principles and goals that express fundamental ideas of a legal system. The second layer contains legal rules which in a sense summarise the outcome of the interaction of the principles and goals for a number of case types. Both principles, goals and rules can be used in legal arguments, but their logical roles are different. One characteristic of the model of legal reasoning described in the first part of the paper is that it takes these logical differences into account. Another characteristic is that it pays serious attention to the phenomena of reasoning about the validity and acceptance of rules, respectively principles and goals, and about the application of legal rules, and the implications of these arguments for the use of rules, principles and goals in deriving legal conclusions for concrete cases.

The second part of the paper first describes a logic (Reason-Based Logic) that is especially suited to deal with legal arguments as described in terms of the previously discussed model. The facilities of the logic are illustrated by means of examples that correspond to the several aspects of the model.

The third part of the paper deals with a number of logico-philosophical reflections on Reason-Based Logic. The occasion is also used to compare these presuppositions with theories of defeasible reasoning based on the comparison of arguments.

Key words: legal reasoning, reasoning with principles and rules, non-monotonic logic

1. Introduction for Non-Logicians: Why Bother about Non-Monotonic Logics?

Many persons with an interest in the field of AI and Law, especially those with a legal background, sometimes wonder what is the use of all the research in complicated logics and in particular so-called non-monotonic ones.** In the first place, one might argue, because the essence of legal reasoning has to do with

---

* The ideas developed in this paper are based on the draft of my book 'Reasoning with rules' which will be published by Kluwer Academic Publishers in the Law and Philosophy Series. The book offers not only more elaborate and sometimes different treatments of the topics of this paper, but also pays more attention to the philosophical background of this work.

** A logic is monotonic if the sentences that can be derived from a superset of a theory are a superset of the sentences that can be derived from the theory. So if $\Rightarrow$ stands for derivability, the monotonicity of a logic means that if $T \Rightarrow S$, then $T, P \Rightarrow S$. A logic that is not monotonic is non-monotonic.

Informally, the non-monotonicity of a logic means that the addition of new information to a theory can make sentences underivable which used to be derivable on the basis of the smaller theory. A legal example would be that new information about an exception makes a rule inapplicable and the conclusion of this rule underivable.

making the right decisions, that is with matters of evaluation, rather than logic. And in the second place because the logic that seems to be used is rather simple. We have a rule with a number of conditions, and if these conditions are satisfied, the rule conclusion is drawn, and otherwise not. There may be discussions about whether the rule conditions are satisfied, but that is the evaluative issue that is at stake, not the logical one. And to the extent that the evaluative discussion makes use of logic, it is the same simple logic of rule application again. In other words, all the logic that is needed is the logic that accounts for the application of rules. Technically this means that no other logic is necessary than that which accounts for the validity of Modus Ponens arguments.

This is a simple argument against the usefulness of logics, and although many will see that it is too simple, many will also have the feeling that for *most* of their legal work they hardly use any complex reasoning, let alone logic. One of the purposes of this paper is to show that ordinary legal reasoning is much more complex than it might seem at first sight. By means of examples which are not too unrealistic, I will try to illustrate that legal reasoning involves more than simple rule application, and that a logic that takes this complexity into account will be non-monotonic. In other words, I will try to show that the intuitions of many lawyers about what they are logically doing are wrong, and that – often unknowingly – lawyers argue in ways that are logically rather complex.

However, even if it is granted that legal reasoning is more complex than just applying applicable rules, it has not yet been shown that AI and Law needs non-monotonic logics. In particular not, because non-monotonic logics tend to be computationally inefficient, and are therefore not so suitable as the basis of legal inference mechanisms.

This objection overlooks that logics need not fulfil a role in the inference mechanism of (legal) knowledge systems, but that they can also be an intermediary between on the one hand a jurisprudential account of legal reasoning, and on the other hand the specification of an inference engine for legal knowledge systems. Jurisprudence is a domain theory which is too much interwoven with characteristics of legal systems to provide the specifications for an inference engine. A logic that gives a satisfactory account of the reasoning involved in legal decision making, abstracts from the legal background that will dominate the jurisprudential theory. Still it does not commit to a particular inference mechanism for knowledge systems. A logic rather provides a list of desiderata, demands that we would like to make on an inference mechanism, but which may have to be compromised against demands of implementation.*

This paper is meant for non-logicians who are prepared to take logic seriously. It is, however, not meant as an introduction to non-monotonic reasoning for lawyers. Such an introduction can be found in [Prakken 1993]. This paper rather wants to show how particular characteristics of legal reasoning ask for complex, even

* By the way, this is also a reason why a logical account of legal reasoning should not be compromised by the aim to end up with something which is computational tractable.

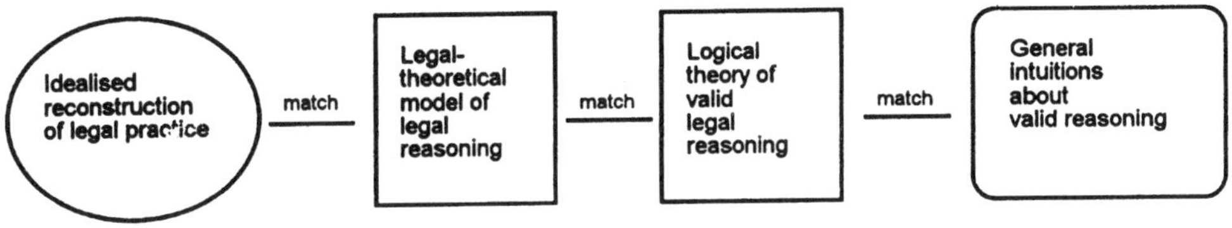

Figure 1. Matches between legal practice, legal theory, legal logic and logical intuitions.

non-monotonic logics, and how a logic which takes these characteristics seriously may look like. Moreover, it hopes to demonstrate by means of extensive examples, how a particular non-monotonic logic, Reason-Based Logic, can be used to model these relatively complex forms of legal reasoning.

2. Introduction for Logicians

The recent proliferation of logical systems has made it impossible to assume that there is something like THE LOGIC, a universal theory about valid reasoning, which holds true for all fields in which arguments play a role. It is rather the case that we must choose a logic that is most adequate for the kind of reasoning task that we are dealing with. In the field of Artificial Intelligence and Law, a number of logics has been proposed (e.g. [Gordon 1994], [Prakken and Sartor 1995], [Hage 1995] to mention some of the most recent versions). To make a reasoned choice between these logics, or to prefer a combination of them or still some other logic, we need a standard to measure these logics against.

Because these logics are meant to deal with legal reasoning, the proper standard is whether they give an adequate account of valid legal reasoning. The problem in this connection is, however, that we lack an independent account of valid legal reasoning. On the one hand we need a theory of valid legal reasoning to measure logics against, while on the other hand we need a logical theory to distinguish between valid and invalid legal reasoning. The 'solution' to this dilemma is to develop simultaneously a theory of valid legal reasoning and a matching logic for legal reasoning. The jurisprudential part of this dual theory must be acceptable as an idealised reconstruction of legal practice, while the logical part must match our intuitive understanding of valid reasoning. In the end, we need three matches: the account of valid legal reasoning must match legal practice, while the legal-logical theory must match both general logical intuitions and the legal-theoretical account of legal reasoning. Cf. Figure 1.

These three matches are reflected in the three main parts of which this paper consists. Part A (Sections 3 to 18) of the paper contains a jurisprudential account of the legal reasoning which is involved in 'solving' particular cases. This account is based on a two-layered model of the law. The first layer consists of principles and goals that express fundamental ideas of a legal system. The second layer contains legal rules which in a sense summarise the outcome of the interaction of the principles and goals for a number of case types. Both principles, goals and rules can be used in legal arguments, but their logical roles are different. One characteristic of the proposed model of legal reasoning is that the model takes these logical differences into account. Another characteristic is that it pays serious attention to the phenomena of reasoning about the validity and acceptance of rules, respectively principles and goals, and about the application of legal rules, and the implications of these arguments for the use of rules, principles and goals in deriving legal conclusions for concrete cases.

Part B (Sections 19 to 35) of the paper describes Reason-Based Logic (further: RBL), a non-monotonic logic that mirrors a number of aspects of legal reasoning that are part of the previously described model. By means of examples that illustrate the several parts of the model of legal reasoning, it is shown how RBL matches this model.

To show that RBL is not merely a formal description of the model, but a logic on its own right, part C (Sections 36 to 39) of the paper contains some logico-philosophical reflections on RBL, pictures RBL against the background of a general theory of valid reasoning, and finally compares RBL to logics based on the comparison of arguments.

A. The Two Layers of the Law

3. Two Kinds of Legal Reasoning

At first sight it seems that at least two different kinds of reasoning occur within the law.* The first kind of reasoning is illustrated by the application of a legal rule whose conditions are satisfied. The result of this application is that the rule conclusion is drawn by means of an argument which is very similar to a Modus Ponens argument. In fact, several authors have described the application of a rule as a case of deduction [e.g. MacCormick 1978, and Alexy 1978]. The following is an example of this type of legal reasoning:

Rule:	*Thieves are punishable.*
Fact:	*John is a thief.*
Conclusion:	*John is punishable.*

The second kind of reasoning is maybe best exemplified when a particular case is to be classified (or not) by an evaluative term, where there is no antecedent legal basis in the form of rules or case law for making this classification. For instance, what amounts to *creating danger* in the case of making genetic modifications to some bacterium? Arguments in such a case will consist of adducing reasons that plead for and against the dangerous nature of the modifications, where none of these reasons

* I do not claim that the two kinds of reasoning described here are exhaustive as a categorisation of kinds of legal reasoning. Another obvious distinction is the one between rule-based reasoning and case-based reasoning.

will be decisive by itself and the final decision depends on the 'weighing' of all available reasons. This type of reasoning cannot without distortion be modelled as a Modus Ponens argument, nor as any other kind of deductive argument.*

These two kinds of reasoning are reminiscent of Dworkin's distinction between legal rules and legal principles. According to Dworkin [1978, pp. 22f.], rules apply in an all-or-nothing fashion. If the conditions of a valid legal rule are satisfied, the conclusion of this rule must follow. A principle, on the contrary, 'states a reason that argues in one direction, but does not necessitate a particular decision' (p. 26). As a consequence of this first difference, Dworkin mentions a second difference, namely that other than rules, principles have a dimension of weight or importance. According to Dworkin 'When principles intersect ... one who must resolve the conflict has to take into account the relative weight of each.' Rules, on the contrary, cannot be weighed: 'If two rules conflict, one of them cannot be a valid rule' (p. 27).

To facilitate the discussion of these two types of reasoning, I will call them *rule-based reasoning* and *principle-based reasoning*, where the latter includes reasoning on the basis of goals (cf. Section 8).

4. Principle-Based Reasoning

A discussion of principle-based reasoning can very well start with the notion of a reason. A reason is an elementary or compound fact which is significant for the presence of some other fact, or for believing that some other fact is present. For instance, the compound fact that John took away Mary's car and that Mary did not allow John to take her car away, is a reason why John is a thief. The compound fact that somebody saw John climbing out of a window of Mary's house at three at night and that the following morning Mary found her antique clock missing in a (for her) unexplainable way, is a reason to believe that John is a thief (of the clock). The former fact makes John into a thief; it is a *constitutive* reason. The latter fact is evidence for John's being a thief; it is an *epistemic* reason. In both cases the reason forms a basis for an argument to the conclusion that John is a thief, although the significance of the reason for the conclusion is somewhat different.

One important characteristic of reasons is that they are amenable to 'weighing'. There can both be reasons for and against a particular conclusion, and if this is the case, the judgement on the conclusion depends on all the available reasons.** Let us consider another example. John sells the clock he has stolen from Mary to Gerald. The fact that John was not the owner of the clock is a reason why the sale does not make Gerald the owner of the clock. However, the fact that Gerald could

* With distortion it is possible to model any finite argument as a Modus Ponens argument. Suppose we have an argument consisting of the set of premises S and the conclusion C. This argument can be modelled as a Modus Ponens argument by adding the 'hidden' premise that the conjunction of the elements of S materially implies C. Seemingly valid arguments can be made invalid by adding 'hidden' elements to the antecedent of an implication.

** The need for weighing reasons is also stressed by, amongst others, Raz [1975 and 1979] and Peczenik [1989].

not know that John had stolen the clock and that he paid a reasonable price for it is a reason why Gerald should become the owner. These reasons why Gerald has not, respectively has become the owner of the clock have to be weighed in order to determine the final legal consequence.

Another important characteristic of reasons is that they are – as Hare [1963] called the phenomenon – *universalisable*. If a fact of a type T is significant for a conclusion of the type C, then all facts of the type T are significant for conclusions of the type C. This presupposes, of course, that facts of the type T are significant *because* they belong to type T and the conclusion belongs to type C. So, if the fact that he is a thief is a reason why John is punishable, the fact that somebody is a thief is in general a reason why this person is punishable. The latter formulation can be considered as the expression of a *principle*: Thieves are punishable.

If any fact of the type R is a reason for a conclusion of the type C, this can be universalised into the formulation of the principle 'If there is a case of R, then there is a case of C'. Notice, however, that the formulation expresses no more than a principle. It does not state that all cases of R are cases of C. In fact it does not *state* anything. The formulation of the principle only *denotes* a connection between types of facts, that is the connection that facts of the type R are a reason for facts of the type C.

5. Directions of Fit

The distinction between stating and denoting which I made in connection with formulations of principles, can be clarified by another distinction, namely the distinction popularised by Searle [1983] between directions of fit. The distinction between directions of fit is explained by Searle by borrowing an example of Anscombe's [Anscombe 1957]. I will use the same example. Suppose I make a shopping list which I use in the supermarket to put items in my trolley. A detective follows me and makes a list of everything that I put in my trolley. After I am finished, the list of the detective will be identical to my shopping list. However, the lists had different functions. If I use the list correctly, I place exactly those items in my trolley that are indicated on the list. My behaviour is to be adapted to what is on my list. In the case of the detective it is just the other way round; the list should reflect my shopping behaviour. If we consider my behaviour as (part of) the world, we can say that my shopping list has the world to word direction of fit, because my behaviour must fit the words on the list. The detective's list, on the contrary, has the word to world direction of fit, because his list must fit the world (my behaviour).

In this example, the world to word direction of fit is illustrated by means of a directive. The shopping list directs my behaviour and in that way makes the world fit the words. The word to world direction of fit is illustrated by means of a description. The list of the detective describes what is put in my trolley. However, directives are not the only case of world to word fit. Baptising is another example of a case in which the world (having a particular name) fits words (those used for baptising).

My interest in the world to word fit focuses on still a different case, namely that of *constitutive* principles (or rules). Suppose that we adopt a particular standard for determining which behaviour counts as coward. This standard runs that a soldier who flees at the approach of the enemy is coward. Notice that the standard is not a descriptive sentence which is true or false depending on the facts of the world. On the contrary, the adoption of this standard *makes* that certain facts occur in the world. Without the standard, there is only a soldier who flees at the approach of the enemy. Assuming the standard, there is also a coward. Adoption of the standard makes that certain facts also count as other facts. The fleeing of the soldier becomes to count as an act of cowardice. This is a clear case of the world to word direction of fit: thanks to the standard the world counts an additional fact (a case of cowardice) which would not be present without the standard.*

Do not misunderstand this. Physically the world would be the same with or without the standard. The difference created by the adoption of the standard is in the layer of facts built on top of the purely physical ones. In this connection Hare writes about 'supervenience' [Hare 1952, p. 80f]: Some facts supervene on other ones; they are present to the extent that these other facts are also present. A logical example is that the truth of the sentence p & q is supervenient on the truth of the sentences p and q.

The same thing can also be approached from a slightly different angle: The standard (a kind of principle) that soldiers who flee at the approach of the enemy are coward makes the fact that a particular soldier fled at the approach of the enemy into a reason why this soldier is coward. The principle makes a particular fact into a reason, which is a kind of constitution.

Given the distinction between directions of fit, we can also make another distinction. On the one hand we have descriptive sentences which are statements, which have the word to world direction of fit, and which are consequently true or false. On the other hand we have (amongst others) principles, which have the world to word direction of fit, and therefore do not state but rather express a connection between types of facts.

Although the distinction between directions of fit does not dictate a different logic for on the one hand reasoning with statements, and on the other hand reasoning with principles, rules and goals, it provides at least the beginning of an explanation of the differences in logical behaviour between these two categories. We will see that the distinction plays an important role in the model of legal reasoning that will be developed and in the logic that corresponds to this model.**

---

* Notice the clear connection with the phenomenon of institutional facts as discussed in several papers in [MacCormick and Weinberger 1986]. Cf. also [Searle 1995].

** Another approach to the same fundamental distinction can be found in [Toulmin 1958], where warrants are strictly distinguished from data and from their backings.

6. The Narrow View of Principles

The phenomenon that reasons (insofar as they are based on principles) have to be weighed against each other is a consequence of the narrow view of principles. Consider the following example: Gerald bought an antique clock from John, who stole the clock. Gerald does not become the owner of the clock, because his predecessor, John, was not the owner either. This reason is based on the principle that nobody can transfer a right that he has not got himself, the so-called nemo plus-principle.

Suppose moreover that Gerald thought that John was the owner of the clock, and that he paid a reasonable price for the clock. These facts form a reason why Gerald should become the owner of the clock, but they are not taken into consideration by the nemo plus-principle. This principle only has an eye for one particular aspect of the case, namely that John was not the owner of the clock. All other aspects, whether they are legally relevant for the outcome or not, are not taken into consideration by this principle.

That is what I mean by the narrow view of principles. Principles only have attention for the aspect of a case that corresponds to the condition part of the principle, and leave everything else out of consideration. Although the latter also counts for rules, rules aim – as I will argue in Section 9 – to take all legally relevant aspects of a case into account. A typical legal principle, such as the nemo plus-principle, does not even attempt to avoid narrow-mindedness.

The narrow view of principles is compensated for by the possibility that a reason generated by a principle is outweighed by one or more reasons that plead in a different direction. In our example, the fact that John was not the owner of the clock as a reason against Gerald becoming the new owner, may be outweighed by the reason that Gerald acted in good faith and paid a reasonable price for the clock. In other words, the narrow view of principles is counteracted by the possibility of colliding principles (and goals) which underlie reasons that plead in a different direction. By basing the final conclusion on the interaction of all available reasons, the narrow view of principles does not become a major disadvantage.

7. Reasoning with Principles

One principle of Penal Law might be that if somebody committed a crime, he ought to be punished. Since this is only a principle, it does not imply anything more than that having committed a crime is a reason for being punished. In particular it does not imply that everybody who committed a crime ought to be punished.

Suppose that John committed a crime. On the basis of the principle that if somebody committed a crime, he ought to be punished, this fact becomes a reason why John ought to be punished. If there are no reasons why John ought not to be punished, or if these reasons are outweighed by the reason that John committed a crime, this reason leads to the conclusion that John ought to be punished.

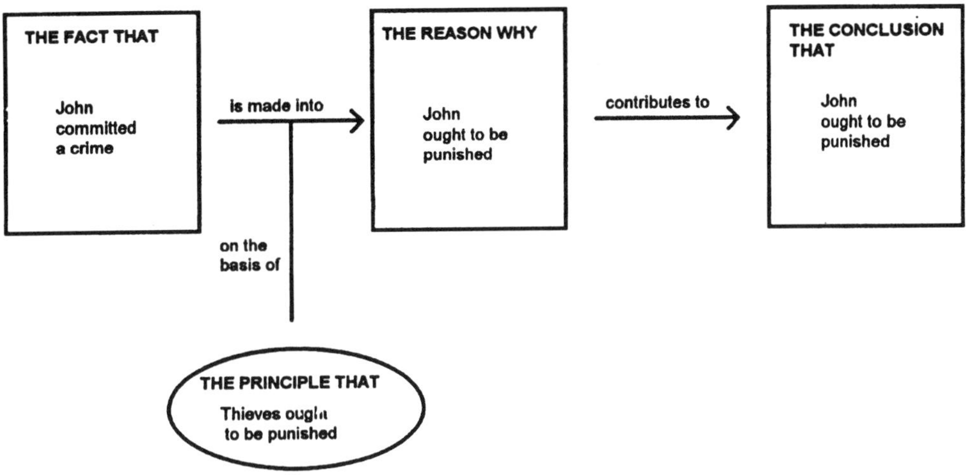

Figure 2. Reasoning with principles.

It turns out that the argument to the conclusion that John ought to be punished consists of two steps. The first step leads from the fact that John committed a crime to the intermediate conclusion that this fact is a reason why John ought to be punished. The second step leads from this reason, possibly in combination with other reasons, to the conclusion that John ought to be punished. Notice that both steps are cases of constitution, and are on the *ontological* level. The principle *makes* a fact into a reason, and this reason *makes* it the case that (or – if there are also other reasons – contributes to) the final conclusion that John ought to be punished. The argument is the mental (verbal) reproduction of this constitution. Cf. Figure 2, which on purpose makes use of the structure proposed by Toulmin.

8. Goals

Not only principles, but also goals can underlie reasons. In this connection, goals are to be taken in a very broad sense, which includes governmental policies, values, interests, and – in some sense of the word – rights [cf. Alexy 1985]. In contrast to principles, which can underlie all kinds of reasons such as reasons for classification, reasons to believe, reasons in the sense of causes, and reasons for acting, goals can only underlie deontic reasons, that is reasons for acting, reasons why something ought to be done (is forbidden / permitted), or reasons why something ought (not) to be the case, or may (not) be the case.*

Suppose that we have the goal to protect juveniles from harmful environments. Suppose, moreover, that John is a juvenile thief, and that punishing him (imprisonment) would bring John into a harmful environment. The goal to protect juveniles

* The limitation that goals can only underlie deontic reasons is not as serious as it might seem, because of the phenomenon of *deontic collapse*. Cf. [Hage 1995 and Reasoning].

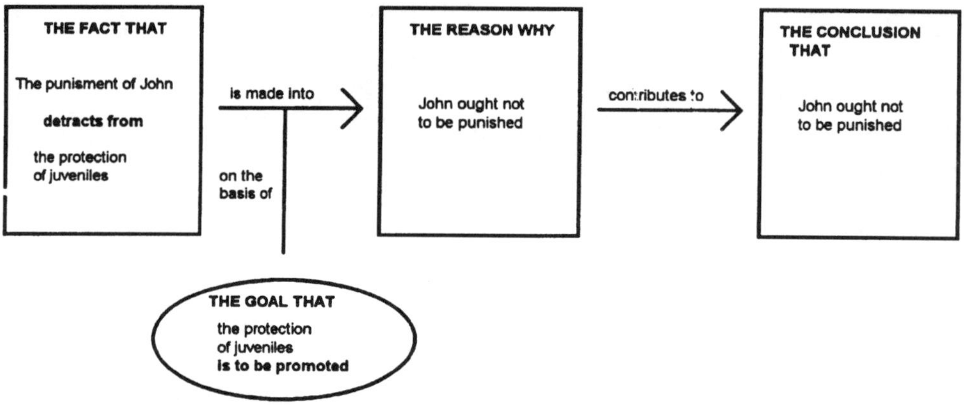

Figure 3. A goal-based argument.

from harmful environments makes the fact that punishing John detracts from this goal into a reason against punishing John. Cf. Figure 3.

This example can be generalised to the following informal rules:

- The goal to promote state S makes the fact that some action A contributes to S into a reason why A ought to be performed, or into a reason to perform A.
- The goal to promote state S makes the fact that some action A detracts from S into a reason why A ought not to be performed, or into a reason against performing A.
- The goal to promote state S makes the fact that some state T contributes to S into a reason why T ought to be the case.
- The goal to promote state S makes the fact that some state T detracts from S into a reason why T ought not to be the case.

Goals suffer from the same narrowness of view that also characterises principles. Take for instance the goal to protect parties in good faith. The fact that if Gerald becomes the owner of the antique clock which he bought, this contributes to the protection of parties in good faith, is made into a reason for the conclusion that Gerald ought to become the owner of the clock. The goal only has an eye for one aspect of this case. The fact that John, who sold the clock to Gerald, was not the owner of the clock is not taken into account. That is why the reason based on the goal to protect parties in good faith has still to be weighed against the reason based on the nemo plus-principle.

9. Rules

Both (legal) principles and goals reflect that some aspects of a case pull the legal solution of this case in a certain direction. Since both will usually be unwritten, so that their precise contents can be subject to dispute, and since both give only rise to reasons which need to be weighed against other reasons with uncertain outcome, legal reasoning solely on the basis of goals and principles suffers from legal insecurity. The use of legal rules is one way to minimise this evil. In the first place because rules are often written down so that, except for the uncertainty of interpretation, the contents of the rules are known. In the second place because rules determine the outcome of the cases to which they are applied. It is this second characteristic which requires some more attention.

Consider again the example of Gerald who, in good faith, bought an antique clock from John who had stolen the clock. There is both a reason why Gerald ought to become the owner of the clock, based on the goal to protect parties who acted in good faith, and a reason why Gerald does not become the owner, based on the nemo plus-principle. Suppose that the weighing of these reasons leads to the conclusion that Gerald becomes the owner.* To prevent that a next time in a comparable case these same reasons have to be weighed again, with the risk that the outcome will be different, a rule can be adopted to the effect that if somebody in good faith obtained a right from somebody who did not have the capacity to transfer this right, this party in good faith still obtains this right. Given this rule, the next time it is not necessary to identify and weigh the original reasons anymore. Instead it is possible to apply the rule and let the rule determine the legal consequences of the case

A *stereotypical* rule differs fundamentally from a *stereotypical* principle. A principle identifies a particular *aspect* that may be part of many divergent types of cases and attaches to the presence of this aspect in a case the tendency to solve the case in a particular way. Because the case may have other relevant aspects, there may also be tendencies to solve the case in a different way. A rule identifies a particular *type of case* and indicates the consequences of this type of case. Types of cases are characterised by sets of characteristics which will be mentioned in the rule conditions. Each of these characteristics may represent an aspect of the case that is made relevant by a legal principle. The rule has the pretension to take all relevant aspects of the case into account and to indicate the outcome of the case *based on all relevant aspects*. Because of this pretension, there is no need to weigh the outcome of the rule against other possible outcomes, because the reasons for these alternatives are (at least in theory) taken into account in the rule, and need not to be taken into account again.

In our example, the outcome of the rule needs not to be reconsidered in the light of the reason based on the nemo plus-principle why Gerald does not become the owner. This principle has been taken into account in making the rule and needs not to be considered anymore if the rule is applied.

In the terminology of Raz [1975], the facts that make a rule apply in a particular case are an *exclusionary reason* for the rule conclusion. This means that they are both a reason for the conclusion of the rule, and a reason not to apply competing

* There appears to be a problem with weighing the reasons, because they seemingly do not conflict. One reason is a reason why Gerald *ought* to be come the owner, while the other reason is a reason why Gerald *actually* has become the owner. Because of the phenomenon of *deontic collapse* [Hage Reasoning], this problem disappears.

goals and principles.* If these competing goals and principles are not applied, they do not generate reasons, and as a consequence the reason based on the rule needs not to be weighed against other reasons anymore. The rule applies in an all-or-nothing fashion.

However, although a principle or goal that is replaced by a rule does not generate a reason anymore that can compete with the reason generated by the rule, this does not mean that they have no role in legal reasoning anymore. Just because a rule replaces particular goals and principles, these goals and principles are relevant for the *interpretation* of the rule [Soeteman 1991]. The exclusion of goals and principles by applicable rules only means that these principles and goals loose their *independent* function in solving the cases in which their application is excluded.

The same phenomenon can also be described in terms of *replacing reasons*. The reason based on the rule comes instead of, replaces, the original reasons based on the principle and the goal. These latter reasons, which have been replaced, do not occur anymore [cf. Hage 1995].

Despite the distinction between stereotypical rules and principles, many principles (including goals) and rules will not be stereotypical and take an intermediate position on a scale the extremes of which are formed by the stereotypical principle and the stereotypical rule. Take for instance the moral principle not to hurt other people except in cases of self-defence. This principle is the result of taking the exception of self-defence into account in reformulating the one-sided principle that one ought not hurt other people. Originally there would be two reasons for and against hurting some other person. One reason is that the hurting was necessary to defend oneself; the other that it was a human being who suffered the hurting. If the self-defence reason outweighs the reason that a human being is hurt, and the result is universalised, the outcome is the principle not to hurt except in case of self-defence.

Because there are so many more issues involved in the question whether one may hurt another person (agreement, for instance), it would be overdone to call the more complex principle a rule. Still, this principle has in common with a rule that it replaces the original principles (not to hurt human beings, and self-defence is allowed) and that the application of these latter is excluded by the application of the complex principle. There can be principles and goals which are the result of combining other principles and/or goals and which replace these latter principles and goals.

There can also be rules which do not replace *all* principles and goals which might be relevant for the type of case with which the rule deals. For instance, the rule formulated above that if a party in good faith obtained a right from a person who did not have the capacity to transfer the right, this party still obtained the right,

* My use of the notion of an exclusionary reason is similar but not identical to Raz's use. According to Raz, an exclusionary reason is a second order reason not to act for some reasons, while in my view an exclusionary reason is a reason not to apply a rule, goal or principle, with the effect that some reasons do not even arise. For the present purposes this difference has only theoretical significance.

does not take the factor into account whether the original owner was to be blamed for loosing the power over his property. It may be argued that an owner who lost his good through theft deserves a better protection against parties in good faith than the owner who lend out his property, thereby causing the appearance that somebody else had the capacity to transfer the ownership. A factor that was not taken into account in formulating a rule is arguably not replaced as a reason by the application of this rule. A rule need not exclude the application of all possibly relevant goals and principles. There may be principles and goals that remain applicable in addition to an applicable rule [cf. Raz 1979, p. 22]. Such a rule is less of a rule than the stereotypical one.

There seems to be no clear boundary between, on the one hand, complex goals and principles which are the result of combining other principles and goals, and, on the other hand, less than perfect rules, which do not take into account all factors that are relevant for the type of case they deal with. One extreme is the stereotypical principle, which deals only with one aspect of a case, and which does not exclude any other principle or goal. The other extreme is the prototypical rule which takes into account all factors that may be relevant for the type of case governed by this rule, and which excludes the application of all principles and goals that deal with factors which occur in cases of this type. Most principles and rules will be somewhere in between these extremes. In fact, because it is practically impossible to determine in advance all aspects which may be relevant for all cases which belong to a particular type, stereotypical rules probably do not even exist.

10. Reasoning with Rules

Still there remains an important difference between on the one hand rules, and on the other hand principles and goals, and this difference is that most rules are the product of some kind of decision making, while principles and goals generally are not [Raz 1975, p. 71]. This difference is especially clear in the contrast between rules which are the product of legislation and unwritten principles and goals, but is also present if rules are abstracted from case law. Where rules are the product of decision making, there are additional reasons to apply them if their conditions are satisfied, based on authority, economy of deliberation and – in the case of legal rules – on legal security.

Because rules generate exclusionary reasons, reasoning with rules is somewhat different from reasoning with principles. If a rule is applied to a case, there is a reason for the conclusion of the rule for this case. This reason replaces all other reasons which might be relevant for the case, and the application of the goals and principles which might underlie these reasons would be excluded. The reason generated by the rule is the only available one, and the rule governs the case on its own. The rule applies in an all-or-nothing fashion, just like Dworkin described the application of rules.

Because ideally a rule takes all relevant factors in a case into account, for all possible cases there should only be one rule that deals with that case. In other words, it should not be possible that rules conflict. This unrealistic ideal is to a certain extent upheld by the presence of conflict rules that dictate which rule is applicable in case of a rule conflict. The application of the other rule is then excluded. Notice that in the case of principles and goals, conflict rules are superfluous. Collisions are so to speak built into goals and reasons, because goals and principles only have an eye for one or a limited number of the relevant aspects of a case. These collisions are dealt with by weighing the colliding reasons, not by excluding some of them.

Because sometimes a rule does not take all relevant aspects of a case into account, it may be the case that the rule is not applied, even though it is applicable. The reasons which were 'overlooked' by the rule may become reasons not to apply the rule to this particular case. Moreover, there may also be reasons to apply a rule to a case although the conditions of the rule are not (all) fulfilled in this case. Most of these aspects of reasoning with rules are dealt with more elaborately in the Sections 14 and 15.

11. The Two Step-Model of Reasoning with Principles and Rules

Principles contribute to the conclusions of arguments in that they generate reasons for their conclusions. A model of reasoning with principles should incorporate a step that determines whether the reasons generated by a principle are decisive. That is why an adequate model of reasoning with principles contains a step that deals with the interaction of the reasons generated by the principles.

Therefore there are two steps involved in the model of reasoning with principles that is presented here. The first step consists of applying all relevant and valid principles, in order to gather all reasons which plead for or against a conclusion. The second step consists of a 'weighing' process, in which it is established which conclusion follows from the collected reasons.

The first step can again be subdivided in three steps. For each possible principle which deals with the conclusion of the argument, it must first be established whether it is valid. Second, it must be decided whether the principle's conditions are satisfied by the case to which the principle is to be applied. And third, it is to be determined whether the principle, given the (non)satisfaction of its conditions, is to be applied to the case at hand.

The reasons which were found by applying principles are divided in a set of reasons which plead for the conclusion and a set of reasons which plead against the conclusion. The weighing of reasons can be dealt with in a rational manner if one of these sets can be argued to outweigh the other set. If this is not possible, there is no rational solution to the weighing problem.

The main elements of the two step-model are depicted in Figure 4. In the following sections, I discuss all of the steps involved in the model.

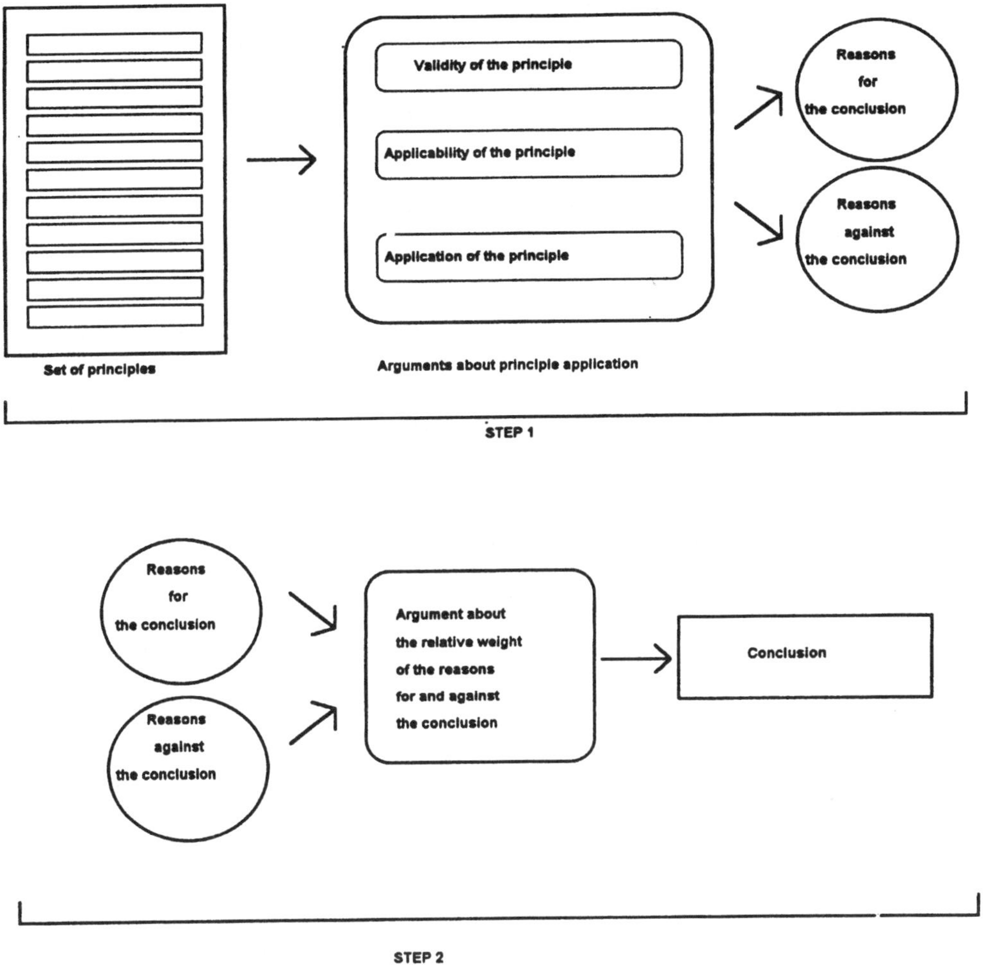

Figure 4. The two step-model of principle application.

Because many legal rules will not be perfect in the sense that they do not incorporate all factors which might be relevant for the type of case they are dealing with, reasoning with legal rules can be treated as a special kind of reasoning with legal principles, with the difference that the application of a rule excludes the application of the principles and goals which it replaces. Even this difference is not absolute, because there will also be complex legal principles, which replace more elementary principles and goals, and the application of which excludes the application of these more elementary principles and goals.*

* In [Hage Reasoning] I make a more strict distinction between principles and rules. There I assume that if a rule applies to a case, the rule's conclusion invariably follows.

For this reason, I will write primarily about principles. The discussion of principles also applies to rules, unless the contrary follows from the text. Goals differ from principles in the way they generate reasons. The reasons generated by goals function just like reasons generated by principles.

12. The Validity of Rules, Principles, and Goals

A rule, principle or goal can only generate reasons if it is a valid one. Whether a goal, principle or rule is valid or not often depends on the point of view. Legal definitions, for instance, are only valid for the legal point of view. If the validity of rules is attached to a particular point of view, this attachment also holds for the reasons based on these rules, and for the conclusions based on the reasons. The facts that somebody took away somebody else's property with the intention of appropriation are a *legal* reason, and the conclusion based on that reason is that this person is, *legally speaking*, a thief. The legal classification may or may not coincide with the same classification from other points of view, but this does neither add nor subtract from the relativization of the reasons and the conclusions to the point of view of the rule on which they are based.

Practically this means that if we are engaged in a legal discussion and we collect rules to base reasons on, these rules must be *legally* valid. Legal conclusions must be based on legal reasons, which in their turn must be based on legal rules (or legal principles, or legal goals, etc.).

This is a heavy demand, which is relaxed somewhat because intermediate conclusions, most often classifications, need not be based on legal reasons. Sometimes there are legal rules which deal with classification. More often, however, the law borrows the conditions of applicability for the terms it uses from common parlance [cf. Valente 1995, p. 57].

The issue of the validity of legal rules has also some impact on legal interpretation. Rules can be considered as consisting of a conclusion and a number of conditions. Legal rules are often based on legislation. The results of legislation are texts which are meant to contain the contents of the rules. Most often they do not exhibit a clear structure of conditions and conclusions.

If the law is to be applied to a concrete case, we must on the one hand have a legal rule and on the other hand a case description, such that the conditions of the rule match the description of the case. For instance, if a rule prescribes that vehicles are to drive on the right hand side of the road, it must be applied to a case described in terms of vehicles, rather than, for instance, cars or bicycles. In other words, the conditions of the rule and the facts of the case should be on the same level of abstraction.

Interpretation and classification deal with respectively the rule side and the case side of obtaining this match. The rule formulation is obtained by the interpretation of *legal sources*, such as statutes, social practice, and case law. The case description is obtained by classifying the most 'brute' description of the case.

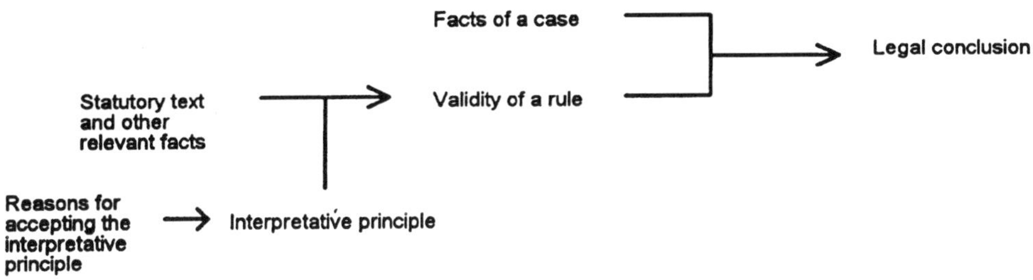

Figure 5. Interpretative principles.

To a certain extent, it is immaterial which part of the way from the texts of the legal sources to the text of the brute case description is travelled by means of interpretation, and which part by classification. It does not matter whether the rule is given a rather concrete interpretation, or whether the facts are classified rather abstractly.* For the present discussion I propose to cut the knot as follows: Issues concerning the precise conditions and conclusion of a rule are the topic of interpretation; issues concerning the denotation of these conditions and conclusion are a matter of classification. On this proposal, issues concerning syntactic ambiguity are dealt with by interpretation, while issues concerning semantic ambiguity (vagueness, open texture) are dealt with by classification.

Given this convention, different interpretations of a statute lead to different rules. Arguments for a particular interpretation of a statute can then be considered as arguments why a particular rule, rather than another one is valid on the basis of the statutory text.

Often the sources of law lend themselves to more than one interpretation. This has given rise to extensive methodological discussions, especially concerning the interpretation of statutory texts. In my opinion, the criteria to answer the question which interpretation of a text is to be preferred over another interpretation, are part of the law itself.** Sometimes they are even the object of legislation, which means that there are rules that deal with the interpretation of legal sources. Most often, however, the *principles of interpretation* – because that is what we are talking about, will be social rules. These rules or principles can be applied to generate reasons concerning the validity of (other) legal rules. In that connection, there can again be a discussion about the validity (acceptance) of these principles in turn. Cf. Figure 5.

* The distinction between interpretation and classification is legally relevant where courts are only allowed to deal with issues of the law, and not with factual issues. Classification is easily (and – in my opinion – wrongly) seen as merely a factual issue.

** Cf. [Peczenik 1989, pp. 375f.] on reasoning norms.

13. The Constitution of Reasons

The most elementary case of the constitution of a reason is where a principle or rule has one or more conditions which must all be satisfied in order for it to apply. Suppose that John took away the car of Ellen, with the intention to appropriate this car. In that case, the facts that 1. John took away the car, 2. The car belonged to Ellen, and 3. John intended to appropriate the car, *together* become a reason why John is a thief. Neither one of these facts by itself is a reason.

If a rule has alternative conditions, it can generate different reasons. Take for instance the rule 'If a person P was either physically incapable to perform his duty, or if P had a justified mental inhibition to do his duty, P acted under force majeure'. This rule has two conditions, but they are alternatives for each other. One can act under force majeure either because of physical impossibility, or because of justified mental inhibition. Both physical impossibility and justified mental inhibition constitute a reason for being under force majeure.

In addition to reasons that plead for a particular conclusion, there are also reasons that plead against a conclusion. If a rule has a negative conclusion, the facts that satisfy the rule's conditions are potential reasons against the fact that is denied in the rule conclusion.

A more subtle case is where the conclusion of a rule is not the denial of a particular thesis, but is incompatible with it. If we have the rule that somebody is a coward if, as a soldier, he flees at the approach of the enemy, the fact that soldier George's flees at the approach of the enemy is a reason against George's being a hero. It is assumed that being a hero and being a coward are incompatible, and therefore a reason for the one fact is ipso facto a reason against the other fact.

The basic mechanism by which goals generate deontic reasons is that if an action contributes to the goal, this is a reason why this action ought to be performed. Analogously, if an action detracts from a goal, this is a reason not to perform that action.

This basic mechanism can sometimes be extended from actions to states. For instance, the fact that continuation of a rent contract in case the rented house changes owners, contributes to the protection of the lessees, is a reason why the rent contract ought to be continued with the new owner.

14. The Exclusion of Rules, Principles and Goals

14.1. Scope limitations

Suppose that in the Netherlands there is a valid legal rule which says that those who murder somebody else are punishable and that in the United Kingdom a murder takes place. Suppose moreover, that both the murderer and the victim were inhabitants of the UK and that the case exhibits no connections with the Netherlands or with Dutch law at all. It is clear that the rule from the Dutch criminal law is not applicable to this case, although its conditions (which do not mention the nationality of the murderer or his victim) are satisfied.

This example illustrates that the satisfaction of a rule's conditions does not guarantee the applicability of the rule. The reason for the non-applicability of the rule in this example is that the case falls outside the scope of the rule. In addition to their conditions for applicability, rules have scope limitations which limit the application of the rule in, amongst others, time and space.

In general we must distinguish between the span of time in which a rule of law is valid, and the span of time to which it may be applicable. Normally these two time spans (more or less) coincide, but there may be exceptions. Retroactive laws are a case in point, because they are applicable to cases at a time in which the rules were not yet valid.

Usually scope limitations are not considered as part of the conditions of the rule whose scope they concern. There are several good reasons for that. First because scope limitations in the law often apply to sets of rules. It is more economical to state them in general for the whole set of rules to which they apply, rather than to add the limitations to the conditions of all concerning rules.

Second, and more importantly, the logical role of scope limitations is different from the other conditions. Often the satisfaction of the scope limitation is assumed and the non-satisfaction must be proven. The division between rule conditions on the one hand, and scope limitations on the other hand, has a corollary in the division of the burden of proof.*

Finally, if a legal rule is not applicable because its scope limitations are not satisfied, this leads to a different legal verdict than in case its normal conditions are not satisfied. In a Dutch criminal case, for instance, non-satisfaction of scope limitations leads to the dismissal of the public prosecutor or dismissal of the suspect, while non-satisfaction of conditions leads to acquittal of the suspect.

14.2. Exceptions and Rule Conflicts

Scope limitations are not the only factor that can make a rule non-applicable, even though its conditions are satisfied. Exceptions to a rule have a similar effect. Sometimes, exceptions to legal rules are just negative rule conditions. It must be shown that the exception does not apply to prove that the rule is applicable. Exceptions of this type are normally included in the formulation of the rule in the source from which the rule is derived.

Very often, however, exceptions to rules are formulated outside the provisions on which the rules are based. In these cases exceptions usually are like scope limitations in that they describe special circumstances under which the rule should not be applied. I will call these exceptions *proper exceptions*. Typical cases in

* Cf. the distinction made in [Sartor 1991] between principal and secondary facts in legal language, in particular the distinction between facts to prove and facts to which contrary prove must not be given. Cf. also Baker's views of defeasibility as described in [Baker 1977].

point are situations of force majeure in civil law, and grounds for justification or exculpation in criminal law. Proper exceptions can both be explicitly formulated in rules of law, and be implicit.*

For proper exceptions often holds the same as for (other) scope limitations. Their absence is assumed by default, and if they are present, they lead to other verdicts than the mere non-satisfaction of the rule conditions. If a crime is committed under force majeure, for instance, the verdict will be dismissal. Exceptions can apply to categories of rules (e.g. all rules of criminal law, or all laws of contract), but they can also apply to individual rules in particular cases.

Scope limitations that limit the application of a rule in time and place and proper exceptions can make a rule inapplicable although the conditions of the rule are satisfied. Their effects are absolute: if a case falls outside the scope of a rule, or if there is a proper exception to the rule, the rule is not applicable anymore with the consequence that the rule will not be applied. In the terminology of reasons, this means that scope limitations and exceptions give rise to *exclusionary reasons*. If a scope limitation is not satisfied, or if an exception applies, the application of the concerning rule is *excluded*.

In the law, a particularly important category of scope limitations derives from the phenomenon of rule conflicts. Legal ideology will have it that rules of law do not conflict. If two rules seem to conflict, at least one of them is not applicable. The scopes of conflicting rules are disjoint.

The exclusion of a rule is to be distinguished form the invalidity of the rule. If a legal rule is invalid, this means that legally it does not even exist, and as a consequence it cannot generate any reasons at all. Exclusion, on the contrary, is case-related. A rule can only be excluded if it is valid; exclusion means that the valid rule cannot be applied in the particular case(s) in which its application is excluded.

The exclusion of goals is similar to the exclusion of rules and principles. It means that even if some action or state contributes to some adopted goal, there may nevertheless be no reason for performing that action, or for the presence of this state, because the goal is irrelevant *in this particular case*.

15. Reasoning about Rule Application

The possibility that the application of rules and principles is excluded, and that goals are irrelevant illustrates the instrumental nature of goals, principles, and rules. They must be used to generate reasons. This opens the possibility to argue about whether they should be used. In the following subsections, we will study the reasons for and against rule application.

* Prakken pointed out to me that sometimes proper exceptions are mentioned in the rule to which they form an exception, as in '... unless the law indicates otherwise'.

15.1. Reasons not to apply an applicable rule

In the context of rule application, the term 'applicable' has been used as a technical term. Applicability of a rule is distinguished from the satisfaction of the rule's conditions. The latter is a necessary, but not a sufficient condition for the former. A rule is applicable to a case, if and only if its conditions are satisfied, and its application is not excluded.

In addition to the distinction between the *applicability* of a rule and the *satisfaction* of its conditions, I will distinguish between the applicability and the *application* of a rule. Applicability is a reason to apply a rule. Unless there are other reasons not to apply the rule, an applicable rule should be applied. Moreover, applicability is the major reason why a rule should be applied. The normal situation is that a rule should be applied if it is applicable, and that it should not be applied if it is not applicable.

If application of a rule would be *against the purpose* of the rule, this is a reason not to apply the rule. Fuller gave an example of a prohibition to sleep in the railway station, which was motivated by the desire to retain tramps from spending their night on the station [Fuller 1958]. It would be against the purpose of this rule to apply it to the traveller who dozed away a few minutes while waiting on a retarded late train.

If there is a 'normal' reason against the application of a rule, this reason must still be weighed against the reasons for application, the most important of which will be that the rule is applicable. This situation differs from the one in which there is an exclusionary reason against application of the rule, because exclusionary reasons against rule application are not weighed against reasons to apply the rule. The fact that the conditions of a rule are satisfied is not a reason to apply American Federal law to an ordinary Dutch case. The fact that the rule is applicable to the late traveller from Fuller's example still counts as a reason for applying the rule, although this reason may be outweighed by the reason that such application would be against the rule's purpose.

15.2. Analogous application of a rule

A rule is applied analogously if it is applied to a case in which the rule conditions are not satisfied, but that sufficiently resembles the cases in which the rule conditions are satisfied to justify the application of the rule.

Some authors argue that analogous rule application does not actually occur, but that sometimes a more abstract rule is applied to a case that does not satisfy the conditions of the original rule.* For example, a Dutch rule of law says that if a house (some good) is sold, the existing rent contract is continued with the new owner. This

* This view of analogous rule application is defended in [Tammelo and Schreiner 1977, p. 112f.], and [Prakken 1993, p. 22]. Prakken would say that the analogy is not involved in the application of the rule, but in the suggestion of the rule's new formulation. In this he follows [Soeteman 1989, p. 239].

rule appears to be applied analogously to the case where the house is not sold, but the property is transferred on the basis of some other title, say donation. According to the authors that reject analogous rule application, the seeming application of the rule about the sale of a house to other cases in which the property of the house was transferred only shows that the applied rule is actually about transfer of houses (or at least also about the donation of houses), and not only about the sale of houses. Selling and donating a house are then special cases to which the more abstract rule (or principle) can be applied in a normal fashion.

The inclination to treat analogous rule application as the application of a more abstract rule is explainable from the tendency to consider rules from a logical point of view as a kind of statements. Clearly statements cannot be applied analogously. The only way to deal with analogy in case of statements is to assume that the statements were actually more abstract than they originally seemed to be.

However, as soon as it is recognised that rules are not statements, and that they can obey a different logic than statements, analogous rule application becomes easy to explain. Rules should be considered as a kind of tools, applied by humans to structure the (legal) world. For instance, we use the rule that thieves are punishable to create a connection between the facts that somebody is a thief and that this person is punishable. This rule is normally used in the cases that somebody is a thief; these cases are the normal conditions in which the tool is used. Sometimes, however, a tool may even be used if the normal circumstances are not present, but some action is nevertheless necessary. For instance, we encounter a case in which somebody illegally copies software. This is not a real case of theft, but we need a legal tool to deal with this kind of case. Analogous rule application might be considered as such a case in which a rule is used under non-ideal circumstances. If it is applied analogously, the rule generates a reason for its conclusion, even though its conditions are not satisfied. (However, there are serious objections against applying criminal laws analogously.)

The account of the relation between legal rules and legal principles and goals that was given above makes it relatively easy to deal with analogous rule application. Let us reconsider the example about the rule that a rent contract is continued with the new owner if a rented house is sold. This rule is applied analogously to cases in which the property of the house is transferred on the basis of another title than sale.

To obtain an account of what happens, we should consider the legal goal that underlies the rule. This goal is that the persons that rent a house should be protected in their right to live in the house. This goal is elaborated in the conclusion of the rule that if the house is sold, the rent contract is continued with the new owner. Notice that the elaboration is much more specific than the goal itself. Other elaborations with a comparable effect are imaginable, such as that in order to be able to sell a rented house, the owner should offer the inhabitants an equivalent alternative.

If a rented house is sold, the legal rule generates a reason why the rent contract is continued with the new owner and excludes the application of underlying legal principles and goals such as the principle that contracts only are in force between the contracting parties, and the goal that the inhabitants of a rented house should be protected in their right of inhabitation. This principle and this goal were both taken into account in making the rule, and if the rule is applicable, the application of the principle and the goal are excluded.

What happens if a case does not satisfy the conditions of the rule? One possibility is that the rule is not applied to the case. In that case the rule does not generate a reason for the solution of the case, but neither does it generate exclusionary reasons that prevent the application of the mentioned legal goal and principle. If, for instance, the house is donated, and the rule about sale of the house is not applied, the case must be decided on the basis of the principle that contracts only are in force between the contracting parties, and the goal that the inhabitants of a rented house should be protected in their right of inhabitation. Both the principle and the goal would generate a reason, a reason why the inhabitants should be able to remain in their house, and a reason why they have no right to remain in the house at all. These reasons must be weighed to obtain a solution for the case. Notice, however, that neither reason explicitly deals with the continuation of the rent contract with the new owner. The principle and the goal are much too abstract to generate reasons against, respectively for such a specific solution.

Another possibility is that the principle and the goal generate a reason against, respectively for, application of the rule about sale of the house. The normal reason for applying a rule is formed by the facts that make the rule applicable. In the present case these facts would be that a house is sold and that this house is rented. It is not impossible, however, that there are other reasons for applying a rule, because applying a rule is a kind of acting, and there may be all sorts of reasons to act in a particular way. One reason to apply the rule about selling a house in case the house is donated is that the legal goal of protecting the rights of inhabitants of rented houses is served by applying the rule. A reason not to apply the rule is that application would be in conflict with the principle that contracts only are in force between the contracting parties. Another reason would be based on the demand for legal security.

Reasons to apply a rule even if its conditions are not satisfied, will usually be based on principles or goals that led the legislator to make the rule in the first place. Therefore the cases to which the rule is applied, although the rule conditions are not satisfied, will normally resemble cases to which the rule is applicable. That is why we normally speak of 'analogous application' of a rule, if a rule is applied to a case in which it is not applicable.

In the first way of dealing with an inapplicable rule we have direct reasons for and against measures that give the inhabitants the possibility to continue their inhabitation of the house. The conclusion of these reasons is still rather vague. In the second way, on the contrary, we obtain reasons that indirectly (namely via the intermediary of rule application) plead for and against a much more specific solution of the case, namely continuation of the rent contract. Both situations, application of a principle underlying a rule, and real application of a rule although its conditions are not satisfied, will occur in legal practice.

The reasons to apply a rule even if its conditions are not satisfied can also be interpreted as reasons to apply a more abstract rule which is directly applicable to the case at hand. This option might be preferred by the authors mentioned above, who argue that analogy is not an inference scheme, but rather a heuristic to suggest more abstract rules which can be applied 'normally'. The advantage of this option, that no deviant inference scheme is needed, is balanced by the disadvantage that the more abstract rule will not be legally valid.*

15.3. E CONTRARIO 'APPLICATION' OF A RULE

If a rule is not applicable, it may still be applied. Analogous application leads to a reason for the rule's conclusion even if the conditions of the rule are not satisfied. The opposite can, however, also happen. Sometimes it is possible to obtain a reason *against* the rule's conclusion if the rule's conditions are not satisfied. In such cases the rule is said to be used in an argument *e contrario*. According to the traditional view, an argument e contrario presupposes that the conditions of the rule not only state a sufficient condition for the rule's conclusion, but also a necessary one (e.g. [Soeteman 1989, p. 39]). The rule would express an equivalence between its conditions and its conclusion. Such a view would go too far, however. First because it leaves unexplained why of two rules which superficially seem not to differ, one states only a sufficient condition for its conclusion, while the other one states an equivalency between its conditions and its conclusion.

Second, because the conclusion of a rule that is used e contrario might follow on the basis of some other rule. For instance, the Dutch law has a rule that forbids widows to remarry within 306 days after the dead of their husbands. The ratio of this rule is to avoid confusion about who is the father of a child of which the woman might be pregnant. Clearly this prohibition is not applicable to widowers, but just as clearly it would be wrong to interpret the condition that a widow is involved as a necessary condition for the prohibition of a marriage. A woman may also be prohibited to marry because she is already married. The conditions of a rule can be a necessary condition for the *application* of the rule, but not for the *conclusion* of the rule.

E contrario 'application' of a rule can be explained by looking at the goals and principles that underlie the rule. If in a particular kind of case the conditions of a rule are not satisfied, this can have one of three causes. First, this may be because the rule has nothing to do with this kind of case. For instance, a tax rule has nothing to do with an insurance contract. In such a case the rule should completely be discarded.

* A related third option is discussed in [Verheij and Hage 1995].

A second possible cause is that the legislator overlooked this kind of case. In this situation, the case is to be solved on the basis of the underlying goals and principles, eventually leading to analogous application of the rule.

The third situation is that the kind of case we are dealing with has been considered by the legislator in drafting the rule, and that this consideration has led to a formulation of the rule conditions that made the rule inapplicable to this kind of case. Then we may assume that the legislator did not want the legal consequences of the rule to obtain in this kind of case, and this is a reason to conclude to the opposite of the rule conclusion. Of course there may still be reasons, on the basis of other rules, which plead for the conclusion of the rule.*

An example of this third case would be that the legislator made a law that says that tramps are forbidden to sleep in the railway station. By explicitly referring to tramps, the legislator made it clear that he did not want a general prohibition against sleeping in the railway station. The traveller who dozed away while waiting on a retarded late train is probably not covered by this rule. This means that such travellers are allowed to doze in the railway station, unless their behaviour falls under another prohibition.

Does this mean that in the last case the rule conditions stated both necessary and sufficient conditions for the rule conclusion? The answer is negative. The legislator did not deal with this kind of case *by means of legislation.* But we still have the underlying principles and goals, and the knowledge that the legislator decided that these principles and goals were no reason to let this kind of case fall under the rule. In combination this may lead us to the conclusion that for this kind of case we should solve the case by denying it the consequence of the rule. In other words, we 'apply' the rule e contrario. In fact, however, we do not apply the rule, but its underlying goals and principles.

16. Defeasibility of Reasoning with Rules, Goals and Principles

Rules and principles differ from statements not only in their direction of fit, but also in that they need to be applied. Application of premises does not play a rolc in traditional logic in determining whether inferences are valid. If all murderers may be punished and John is a thief, it logically follows that John may be punished, in the sense that this conclusion must be true if the premises are true. There is no need to 'apply' the premise that all murderers may be punished. The premise has a certain information content, and given this content it must be the case that John may be punished. In fact, it is not clear at all what application of a factual statement would amount to.**

* This may even have been intended by the legislator who decided to make the rule inapplicable.

** One might argue that application of a statement is the use of this statement in an argument. However, this is only relevant for the *proof* of the conclusion, not for the issue whether the conclusion logically *follows* from the premises.

Rules and principles, on the contrary, need to be applied. The principle that murderers may be punished, for example, must be applied if it is to generate a reason to punish John. Mere validity of this principle is not sufficient.

Most often, the application of this principle will be 'automatic'; it is not given much thought and as a consequence we may overlook the necessity of application. However, it is always possible to adduce reasons why a principle or rule should not be applied in a particular case, and this possibility only makes sense if application of the principle is an issue.

The fact that rules and principles need to be applied explains two characteristics of reasoning with rules that cannot be explained if rules are treated as statements. The first characteristic is that reasoning with rules (and principles) is defeasible*; the second one is that rules can be applied analogously.

Analogous rule application was already dealt with in Section 15.2. Reasoning with rules, goals and principles is also defeasible. In connection with rules and principles, defeasibility can be defined as the situation where the conditions of a valid rule or principle are satisfied, but the conclusion nevertheless does not follow.

The first reason for defeasibility is that rules and principles need to be applied in order to contribute to their conclusions. If there are decisive reasons not to apply them, they do not generate reasons for their conclusions, and these conclusions will most probably not follow.** More or less the same holds if a goal is left out of consideration because of its irrelevance in a particular case.

The second reason is that goals and principles,‡ even if they are applied, only generate reasons for their conclusions. If there are reasons against the conclusion that balance or even outweigh the reasons generated by the applied goal or principle, the conclusion does not follow, even though the goal or principle was applied.

17. Weighing Reasons

Every principle or rule with a particular fact in its conclusion is a potential generator of reasons for that fact. Conversely, every principle or rule with the negation of a particular fact in its conclusion‡‡ is a potential generator of reasons against that fact. If each of these principles and rules is checked for its application in a case, a set of zero or more reasons for, and a set of zero or more reasons against the fact obtain. The reasons from these two sets must be 'weighed', to determine whether the fact, its negation, or nothing at all follows as a conclusion.

---

* It seems that reasoning with incomplete knowledge is also defeasible, even if this knowledge consists solely of statements. This overlooks however that reasoning with incomplete knowledge involves the use of inference rules, and it is precisely this use of inference rules which causes the defeasibility.

** At least theoretically it is possible that the conclusions follow for other reasons than those based on the rule or principle involved.

‡ I have some doubts whether this also holds for rules. Cf. also the note in Section 11.

‡‡ Incompatible conclusions will also do the job; contradiction is not necessary. Cf. Section 13.

If we have no reasons why one set of reasons outweighs another set of reasons, we cannot make a rational decision. Sometimes, however, we are able to argue which sets of reasons outweighs the other set. In a legal context we can, for instance, refer to precedent: If we already had an earlier case where the same reasons obtained, and where one set of reasons was assumed (for whatever reason or cause) to outweigh the other set, we can call to the principle that similar cases are to be treated similarly, and make the same weighing as the previous time.*

In a model for reasoning with rules we should ask for reasons why a set of reasons outweighs another set. If such 'meta'-reasons are lacking, there are no rational means to obtain a conclusion. If such meta-reasons are available, it should be possible to draw the conclusion which is supported by the strongest set of reasons. One meta-reason is very obvious in this connection: If we only have reasons that plead for a conclusion, and no reasons against it, the reasons for outweigh the reasons against. Analogously, if there are only reasons against, they 'outweigh' the (non-existent) reasons for the same conclusion.

18. Summary and Recommendations

Reasoning with principles, goals and rules turns out to be a lot more complex than simple rule application according to the model of Modus Ponens. On the one hand, rules can be applied (analogously) even though their conditions are not satisfied. On the other hand, even if a rule's conditions are satisfied, it is not guaranteed that the rule will be applied: a case that satisfies the rule's conditions may fall outside the rule's scope or purpose. And finally, in the case of principles, even if a principle is applied to a case and generates a reason, there is no guarantee that its conclusion follows. Weighing reasons may lead to the result that the principle's conclusion is still not drawn. On the basis of these characteristics of reasoning with rules, goals and principles, we can draw up a list of properties we would want in a logic that deals with rules. These properties both concern the expressive power of the logical language, and the nature of the rules of inference.

Although weighing reasons will only play a role in those arguments in which there are both reasons for and against a particular conclusion, a logic for goals and principles should offer facilities to deal with the weighing of reasons. It should contain a rule of inference to the effect that a conclusion follows if the reasons that plead for it override the reasons against that conclusion.

In this connection, the logic should also offer the possibility to conclude that a particular set of facts forms a reason for or against a conclusion. As a consequence, it must be possible to refer to (sets of) facts and reasons. Since it is also necessary to reason about the facts that make up reasons, and to build on these results while arguing with the reasons, the logical connection should be maintained between the sentences that express certain facts, and the sentences that refer to these same facts as reasons. For instance, we want to be able to argue that John is a thief, to refer

* This approach to weighing reasons is extensively discussed in Section 34.

to the fact that John is a thief, and to maintain the logical relationship between the sentence 'John is a thief' and the fact that John is a thief. It should also be possible to reason about the relative weight of sets of reasons.

A rule or principle can only be applied if it is valid (accepted). An important part of legal reasoning deals with the question as to the precise conditions of legal rules, a discussion which can be seen as dealing with the validity or acceptance of rules and principles. A logic for rules should make it possible to deal with arguments about the validity of rules. As a consequence, it should allow reference to rules. Reference to rules is also necessary for arguments about the exclusion, the applicability, and the application of a rule. At the same time a logic for rules should be able to use the internal structure of rules to model the application of rules in generating reasons. All of this also holds for the adoption and the relevance of goals.

The rules of inference that deal with rule application should make the application of a rule dependent on the reasons that plead for and against application. The applicability of a rule should be an important reason for application of this rule, but there must be a possibility to have other reasons for (analogous) and against application of a rule.

B. Reason-Based Logic

In the previous sections I have offered a theory of legal reasoning as based on rules, principles and goals. This theory gives an account of reasoning with rules, etc that does not fit well in, for instance, predicate logic. In this chapter, I will introduce a logic that was especially developed to deal with the characteristics of rules, principles, goals, and reasons that we encountered above. Because reasons play a central role in this logic, the logic is called Reason-Based Logic (RBL).*

In the following sections, the essentials of RBL are exposed. In a semi-formal introduction, which takes the Sections 19 to 28, I describe some characteristics of the logic that result from the demands posed by the nature of reasoning with rules, principles and goals. Moreover, I introduce the elements of the language of RBL. Then follows a formal characterisation of the derivability relation of RBL. (Sections 29). The exposition of RBL is concluded with a number of applications of RBL to not too unrealistic examples (Sections 30 to 36).

19. Ontological Presuppositions of Reason-Based Logic

RBL uses a rich ontology, that includes principles, goals, rules, cases, states of affairs, facts, and reasons.

* RBL is the result of gradual development. This development has been laid down in a number of papers that describe different versions of this logic. Cf. [Hage 1991, 1993, and 1995; Hage and Verheij 1995]. The version described here is very similar, but not completely identical to the versions of the more recent papers. There are some differences with the version that is described in [Hage Reasoning].

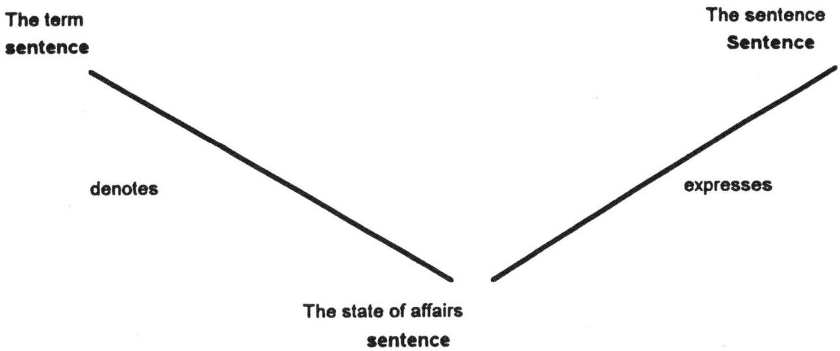

Figure 6. The relation between sentences and terms that deal with the same state of affairs.

A *state of affairs* is that part of reality that is expressed by a sentence. For instance, the sentence

```
Thief(john)
```

expresses the state of affairs that John is a thief.

A *fact* is a state of affairs that is expressed by a *true* sentence. Facts are states of affairs that actually *obtain*. False sentences express states of affairs that do not actually obtain. A *reason* is a fact that has a particular significance for a conclusion, in that it either pleads for or against it.

From a logical point of view, all states of affairs, including facts and reasons, are individuals, which means that they can be the subject of sentences. Note that this does not involve a mix up of object and meta-language, because states of affairs are not linguistic entities, although their presence presupposes language.*

RBL provides means to reason with sentences and also to reason about the states of affairs (facts, reasons) that are expressed by those sentences. Moreover, the logical connections between a sentence and the state of affairs expressed by it are maintained. To achieve this, RBL makes use of a special convention to achieve the logical connection between a sentence and the state of affairs that is expressed by it. All RBL-sentences begin with a capital and all terms (or function expressions) that denote individuals begin with a small character. Moreover, if a term is identical to a sentence, with the only difference that the term begins with a small character, this term *denotes* the state of affairs that is *expressed* by that sentence. Cf. Figure 6.

For instance, the term

```
thief(john)
```

denotes the state of affairs that John is a thief, a state of affairs that is expressed by the sentence

```
Thief(john)
```

* Cf. in this connection [Strawson 1971, pp. 193f.] on the language-dependence of facts.

Since facts and reasons are also states of affairs, the convention to denote states of affairs also applies to facts and reasons. This makes it possible to state about a particular fact that it is a reason for the presence of some other state of affairs. For instance, the following RBL-sentence expresses that the fact that John is a thief is a reason why John is punishable:

```
Reason(thief(john), punishable(john), pro)
```

The convention concerning the relationship between sentences and their corresponding terms also applies to logically compound sentences. This means that the term

```
contract(john, geraldine)& defaults(john)
  & damage(3000))
```

denotes the compound state of affairs that there is a contract between John and Geraldine, that John defaulted in this contract, and that the resulting damage is 3000 dollar. Moreover, it also holds for sentences that contain variables. The term corresponding to a sentence with free variables is a function expression.* For instance, the function expression in which *x* is a variable

killer_of(*x*, marcella)

denotes the person who killed Marcella.

20. Case-Related Facts

If we want to argue that a rule is applicable in a particular case, or that it applies or is excluded in a case, we must often refer to facts that obtain in that case or not. For instance, the fact that John is a thief in a particular case is the reason why the rule that thieves are punishable is applicable *to that case*. That is the reason why RBL needs a way to say that a particular state of affairs obtains in some case.

The RBL-sentences that say that a state of affairs obtains in a particular case have the following form:

Obtains(*state_of_affairs*, case(*c*))**

In this sentence, *state_of_affairs* stands for the state of affairs that obtains in the case denoted by case(*c*). Suppose that we have a particular case, called case(john's_theft), in which John is a thief. The fact that John is a thief in this case is expressed by the sentence:

```
Obtains(thief(john), case(john's_theft))
```

Very often when a case is described, it will be clear to which case the facts belong. In such cases, the description of the facts as belonging to a particular case is rather cumbersome. That is why the case-related notation is only used when necessary.

* This convention does not hold for variables in the conditions and the conclusion of rules.

** Italicised terms are variables. Sometimes variables are used to indicate that only the form of the sentence in which they occur is relevant. The present sentence is an example of this use of variables.

Normally facts are described by means of the sentences that express these facts without mentioning the case. For instance,

```
Obtains(thief(john), case(john's_theft))
```

will normally be replaced by

```
Thief(john).
```

21. Rules as Structured Logical Individuals

The distinction between rules and principles is reflected only indirectly in RBL. The language of RBL only has rules, which are used to represent both rules and principles.

There are many kinds of arguments in which (RBL-)rules are involved, and rules play several roles in them. Most often the rule is just applied, and generates a reason for its conclusion. However, there are also arguments about the validity of rules, and about the application of rules to particular cases. In these arguments, a rule is the topic of the argument. To formalise arguments in which rules are the topic, there should be a possibility to refer to rules.

This need to mention rules leads to a characteristic of RBL that makes it different from most other logics, namely that rules are treated as logical individuals. As a consequence, it is not possible to use a rule as a complete sentence in RBL. Rules can only be introduced into an RBL-theory by making statements about them, e.g. the statement that a rule is valid.*

Traditionally, individuals are represented in formal logics by means of an unstructured character or string. The representation of rules as logical individuals in RBL is different, however. The rules of inference of RBL must be able to distinguish between the conditions and the conclusion of an RBL-rule, and as a consequence, the representation of these logical individuals exhibits a structure.

A rule contains three elements, that are kept together by the function symbol 'rule'. These elements are an identifier, which is a kind of name, the condition-part of the rule, and the conclusion of the rule. An example of a rule-denoting expression would be:

rule(theft1, thief(*x*), punishable(*x*))

Because the identifier of a rule is unique, it is also possible to refer to the rule with the identifier *r* by means of the expression

rule(*r*)

Technically, the symbol `rule` can be seen as a function symbol that maps rule identifiers into rules.

If the rule identifier `r` is a constant, the term `rule(r)` is a function expression that denotes the rule `r`. If *r* is a variable, however, the expression rule(*r*) is

* Rules are, to a certain extent, also treated as individuals in the logics proposed by [Gordon 1994], [Sartor 1994], and [Prakken and Sartor 1995].

a logical variable. The condition-part of a rule consists of one RBL-term which denotes a state of affairs. If the natural language version of the rule has more than one condition, the term that denotes the conditions will be logically compound.

The conclusion of a rule must always be an elementary fact; it may not contain conjunctions or disjunctions.

Both the condition and the conclusion-part of a rule may contain variables, quantifiers and/or negations.

An example of a not too complex rule would be:

```
rule(rule_of_recognition,
  made_by_legislator(rule(r)) &
  ~abolished(rule(r)),
  valid(rule(r)))
```

This rule says that a rule is valid if it has been made by the legislator and has not been abolished. The name of the rule is `rule_of_recognition`. The use of variables in the rule conditions and the conclusion indicates that this rule of recognition can be applied to any rule.

Remember that a rule expression is not a well-formed RBL sentence. Well-formed sentences are for instance statements about rules. In theory, any kind of statement can be made about a rule. For instance:

```
Made_by_legislator(rule(theft1, thief(x),
  punishable(x)))
```

or, shorter,

```
Made_by_legislator(rule(theft1))
```

The statements about rules which have a special logical role in RBL are the statements that a rule is valid, that a rule is applicable, that a rule applies, and that a rule is excluded. These statements are discussed next.

VALIDITY

If a rule or principle is to be used in making a derivation, it should be valid. The statement that a rule or principle is valid has one of the following forms:

`Valid(rule(`*r*`,` *rule_conditions*`,` *rule_conclusion*`))`

or

```
Valid(rule(r))
```

The validity of a rule is expressed in a statement which can be derived in RBL like any other 'normal' statement. It can also be a premise of an argument.

APPLICABILITY

If the conditions of a rule are satisfied in a particular case, and if the rule is not excluded in that case, the rule is said to be *applicable* to that case. To state this, RBL has a special predicate `Applicable`, that has four parameters. The first parameter is meant for the rule that is applicable, the second parameter indicates the case to which the rule is applicable, while the third and fourth parameter stand for respectively the instantiated rule conditions and the instantiated rule-conclusion, which indicate respectively the facts that will be a reason on the basis of the rule and the conclusion for which these facts will be a reason.

Suppose that we have a case that consists of the facts that John is engaged in a contract with Geraldine, that John defaulted, and that the damage is $3000. The facts of the case called `contract`, are represented by:

```
Obtains(contract(john, geraldine), case(contract))
Obtains(defaults(john), case(contract))
Obtains(damage(3000), case(contract))
```

Moreover, we also have

```
Valid(rule(contractual_default,
  contract(x, y) & defaults(x) & damage(z),
  owes(x, y, z)))
```

(If x has a contract with y, x defaults, and the resulting damage amounts to z, then x owes y the amount of z.) In this case, the following statement would normally – that is, if the rule is not excluded – be true:

```
Applicable(rule(contractual_default), case(contract),
  contract(john, geraldine) & defaults(john)
    & damage(3000),
  owes(john, geraldine, 3000))
```

The statement that a rule is applicable can only be derived on the basis of a valid rule, the conditions of which are satisfied, and which is (assumed to be) not excluded. It cannot be the premise of an argument.

APPLICATION

In RBL a distinction is made between the applicability of a rule and the application of a rule. There is a special predicate `Applies`, that has the same parameters as the `Applicable` predicate, and which is used to state that a rule applies in a particular case.

The following is an example of the use of the `Applies`-predicate:

```
Applies(rule(contractual_default),
  case(contract),
  contract(john, geraldine) & defaults(john)
```

```
    & damage(3000),
  owes(john, geraldine, 3000))
```

The statement that a rule applies can only be based on the weighing of reasons and cannot be a premise of an argument.

EXCLUSION

If there is an exclusionary reason not to apply a rule in a particular case, this can be stated by saying that this rule is excluded in that case:

```
Excluded(rule(contractual_default), case(contract))
```

The statement that a rule is excluded can only be based on the weighing of reasons and cannot be a premise of an argument.

22. Goals

In RBL, goals are structured individuals, just like rules. The function symbol `goal` has two parameters. The first parameter is the identifier of the goal, the second one denotes the state of affairs that is to be pursued. This second parameter must denote a literal state of affairs. The only allowed logical operator in it is the negation.

For instance, the term

```
goal(youth_protection, youth_protected)
```

denotes the goal with the identifier `youth_protection`, and this goal-state is that the youth is protected.

Because identifiers are unique, it is possible to refer to the goal `youth_protection` by the term

```
goal(youth_protection)
```

VALIDITY OF GOALS

I will use the predicate Valid not only to represent the validity of rules, but also to represent the validity of goals. So, the fact that the goal to protect the youth is recognised can be represented in the language of RBL by

```
Valid(goal(youth_protection))
```

or, longer:

```
Valid(goal(youth_protection, youth_protected))
```

The statement that a goal is valid can be derived in RBL like any other 'normal' statement. It can also be a premise of an argument.

CONTRIBUTION TO AND DETRACTION FROM A GOAL

A goal generates a reason for a conclusion if there is some action or state that contributes to, or detracts from the goal. Suppose that the action* that John is withheld from using drugs contributes to the goal `youth_protection`. This is expressed by the predicate `Contributes_to`, which goes with two parameters. The first denotes the action that serves the goal. The second parameter denotes the particular instance of the goal that is being served by means of an instantiation of the goal state. For instance:

```
Obtains(
  contributes_to(withhold(john, using_drugs),
    youth_protected),
  case(john's_drug_addiction)
  )
```

It can also be expressed that some action detracts from a goal. To keep the language of RBL relatively simple, the fact that some action detracts from a goal is represented as the fact that this action contributes to the absence (negation) of the goal state:

```
Contributes_to(encourage(john, using_drugs),
  ~youth_protected)
```

Not only actions, but also states of affairs (if they obtain) can contribute to, or detract from a goal state. The sentences that express this have the same form as the sentences that express that action types contribute to or detract from goal states, with the difference that reference to an action type is replaced by reference to a state of affairs:

```
Contributes_to(owner(gerald),
  parties_in_good_faith_protected)
```

(If Gerald becomes the new owner, this contributes to the protection of parties who acted in good faith.)

The statement that something contributes to a goal can be derived in RBL like any other 'normal' statement. It can also be a premise of an argument.

EXCLUSION OF GOALS

A goal only generates a reason in a case, if it is not excluded in that case. The exclusion of goals is represented by the same Excluded predicate that is also used in the case of rules and principles. For instance, the sentence `Excluded(goal(privacy_protection), case(royal_divorce))` expresses the state of affairs that the goal `privacy_protection` is irrelevant in a particular case of a royal divorce.

* In this connection, actions are always action types, such as stealing, and not action tokens, such as this particular instance of John's stealing.

The statement that a goal is excluded can only be based on the weighing of reasons and cannot be a premise of an argument.

23. From the Validity to the Applicability of a Rule

The derivation of a conclusion on the basis of one or more rules takes two steps. In the first step, the sets of all reasons for, respectively against the hypothetical conclusion are collected. In the second step, the reasons in these sets are weighed against each other.

A reason for a conclusion is based on a valid rule with this conclusion as its conclusion-part. If the conditions of this rule are satisfied, and if it cannot be derived that the rule is excluded in the relevant case, the rule is said to be applicable in that case. The instantiated conditions of the rule are the facts that make the rule applicable. If the rule is applicable, this is a reason for its application.

In theory it is possible that there are more reasons to apply the rule, or that there are also reasons against application, but normally the applicability of the rule will be the only reason that is relevant for the decision to apply the rule. If the rule is actually applied, it generates a reason for its conclusion. The facts that are the reason usually are the instantiated rule conditions that make the rule applicable. Only if the rule is applied analogously, the reason will consist of other facts.

Let us have a closer look at these steps. Suppose that `facts` is an instantiation of the rule conditions, and that `iconcl` is the corresponding instantiation of the rule-conclusion. In that case, the following schematic sentences indicate the first step on the way to the generation of a reason.

If it can be derived that

`Valid(rule(`*r*`, `*conditions*`, `*concl*`))`
`Obtains(`*facts*`, case(`*c*`))`

and it cannot be derived that

`Excluded(rule(`*r*`), case(`*c*`))`

then it is possible to derive that

`Applicable(rule(`*r*`), case(`*c*`), `*facts*`, `*iconcl*`)`

In plain language: if it can be derived that a rule is valid, and that its conditions are satisfied in a case, and if it *cannot be derived* that the rule is excluded in that case, then it can be derived that the rule is applicable to that case.

Let us look at an old example. If it can be derived that:

`Valid(rule(theft1, thief(`*x*`), punishable(`*x*`)))`
`Obtains(thief(john), case(john's_theft))`

and it cannot be derived that

`Excluded(rule(theft1), case(john's_theft))`

then it can be derived that

```
Applicable(rule(theft1), case(john's_theft),
  thief(john), punishable(john))
```

Notice the important difference between the first two conditions for the derivation, and the third one. It should be derivable that the rule is valid and that its conditions are satisfied to obtain the conclusion that the rule is applicable. It need not be derivable that the rule is not excluded to obtain that conclusion. It suffices that the exclusion of the rule cannot be derived.

The third condition for the derivation is weaker than the first two, in that it is satisfied in case nothing is known about the exclusion of the rule. At the same time, this reference to what is not derivable, rather than to what is given, makes the logic non-monotonic. If a theory is extended, so that it becomes derivable that a rule is excluded, this means that the conclusion that this rule is applicable is invalidated.

24. From Applicability to a Reason for Application

If a rule is applicable, this is a reason to apply this rule. If some facts are a reason for a particular conclusion, this is in RBL expressed by means of the Reason predicate. This predicate has three parameters. First comes the (possibly compound) fact that is the reason, then follows the conclusion of the reason, and finally it is indicated whether a reason for (pro) or against (con) the conclusion is concerned. For instance:

```
Reason(thief(john), punishable(john), pro)
Reason(juvenile(john), punishable(john), con)
```

(The fact that John is a thief is a reason why John is punishable, and the fact that John is a juvenile is a reason against John's being punishable.)

The statement that some fact is a reason for or against some conclusion cannot be a premise of an RBL-theory, but must be derived on the basis of a goal or the application of a rule.

The existence of reasons can be derived from the fact that a particular rule is applicable. From

```
Applicable(rule(theft1), case(john's_theft),
  thief(john), punishable(john))
```

it may be derived that

```
Reason(
  applicable(rule(theft1), case(john's_theft),
    thief(john), punishable(john)),
  applies(rule(theft1), case(john's_theft),
    thief(john), punishable(john)),
  pro)
```

(The fact that the rule `theft1` is applicable to John's case, with its condition-part instantiated to `thief(john)` and its conclusion-part instantiated to `punishable(john)`, is a reason why this same rule, with the same instantiations, applies to John's case.)

From

```
Applicable(
  rule(juveniles_not_punishable), case(john's_theft),
  juvenile(john),
  ~punishable(john))
```

it may be derived that

```
Reason(
  Applicable(rule(juveniles_not_punishable),
  case(john's_theft), juvenile(john),
    ~punishable(john))
  Applies(rule(juveniles_not_punishable),
  case(john's_theft), juvenile(john),
    ~punishable(john)),
  pro)
```

(The fact that the rule `juveniles_not_punishable` is applicable to John's case, with its condition-part instantiated to `juvenile(john)` and its conclusion-part instantiated to `~punishable(john)`, is a reason why this same rule, with the same instantiations, applies to John's case.)

The first and the second parameter of the reason-statements are almost identical to each other, with as the only difference that the state of affairs that the rule is applicable in the first parameter is replaced by the state of affairs that the rule applies in the second parameter.

25. From the Application of a Rule to a Reason for or against Its Conclusion

If a rule applies to a case, the instantiated rule conditions become a reason for the rule's conclusion. So from

```
Applies(rule(theft1), case(john's_theft),
  thief(john), punishable(john))
```

it may be derived that

```
Reason(thief(john), punishable(john), pro)
```

(The fact that John is a thief is a reason why John is punishable.) And from

```
Applies(rule(juveniles_not_punishable),
  case(john's_theft), juvenile(john),
    ~punishable(john))
```

it may be derived that

```
Reason(juvenile(john), punishable(john), con)
```

(The fact that John is a juvenile is a reason against his being punishable.)

Notice that the rule-conclusions sometimes contain a negation, while the conclusions of reasons never contain a negation. The negation of the rule-conclusion is replaced by a reason against the conclusion. The rule `theft1` has a positive conclusion, and this is reflected in the fact that being a thief is a reason that pleads *for* (pro) the conclusion that John is punishable. The rule `juveniles_not_punishable` has a negative conclusion, and therefore the fact that John is a juvenile is a reason *against* (con) John's being punishable.

26. From Reasons to a Conclusion

The step from the presence of a reason to apply a rule to the conclusion that the rule applies is not a special one. It is like any other step from the presence of a reason for a conclusion to this conclusion. Not only this single reason has to be considered, but rather the sets of all reasons for and against the conclusion.

26.1. THE GENERAL CASE

To facilitate the discussion about the reasons for and against a conclusion, we need terms that refer to the sets of these reasons. Here we encounter a new example of structured individuals, because RBL treats sets of reasons as logical individuals.

`reasons_pro(`*state_of_affairs*`)`

and

`reasons_con(`*state_of_affairs*`)`

denote respectively the set of *derivable* reasons that plead for *state_of_affairs*, respectively against *state_of_affairs*.

In case of the theory

```
Valid(rule(theft1, thief(x), punishable(x)))
Valid(rule(juveniles_not_punishable, juvenile(x),
  ~punishable(x)))
Thief(john)
Juvenile(john)
```

it holds that

`reasons_pro(punishable(john)) = {thief(john)}`

and

`reasons_con(punishable(john)) = {juvenile(john)}`

In order to decide on the basis of reasons which conclusion is to be drawn, explicit *weighing-knowledge* is needed. This weighing-knowledge indicates which set of reasons outweighs which other set with respect to a particular conclusion.

It is not impossible that the same two sets of reasons are relevant for different conclusions, but that their relative weight differs for these different conclusions. Therefore weighing-knowledge is always relativized to a conclusion.

In the present example, the relevant weighing-knowledge is laid down in the following RBL sentence:

```
Outweighs(
  {juvenile(john)}, {thief(john)}, punishable(john))
```

which means that concerning the issue whether John is punishable, (the set of reasons containing) the fact that John is a juvenile outweighs (the set of reasons containing) the fact that John is a thief.

This sentence illustrates the general form of weighing-knowledge. Weighing-knowledge is described in a sentence formed by the Outweighs predicate. This predicate has three parameters. The first two parameters denote sets of reasons, and the third parameter denotes a state of affairs. The weighing-knowledge expresses that with respect to the state of affairs of the third parameter, the first set of reasons outweighs the second set.

Notice that the parameters do not have a fixed order in the sense that either the reasons pro, or the reasons con are mentioned first. On the contrary, by means of the order of the sets of reasons it is indicated whether the reasons pro outweigh the reasons con, or the other way round. If the first parameter refers to the reasons that plead for the state of affairs mentioned in the third parameter, the reasons pro outweigh the reasons con. In this case the sentence that expresses the state of affairs of the third parameter follows as the conclusion.

If, however, the first parameter refers to the reasons that plead against the state of affairs mentioned in the third parameter, the reasons con outweigh the reasons pro. In that case, the negation of the sentence expressing the state of affairs of the third parameter follows as the conclusion.

So, if

```
reasons_pro(punishable(john)) = {thief(john)}
```

and

```
reasons_con(punishable(john)) = {juvenile(john)}
```

and if we also have that

```
Outweighs({thief(john), juvenile(john)},
  punishable(john))
```

then it may be derived that

```
Punishable(john)
```

However, if we have

```
Outweighs({juvenile(john)}, {thief(john)},
  punishable(john))
```

then it may be derived that

`~Punishable(john)`

Notice that

`reasons_pro(`*state_of_affairs*`)`

and

`reasons_con(`*state_of_affairs*`)`

denote all the reasons for, respectively against *state_of_affairs* that are *derivable* from the theory. If a theory is extended, this can make it possible to derive more reasons both for and against a conclusion. If the extension of the theory leads to more rule exclusions or to more cases where goals are excluded, this can also lead to less reasons.

26.2. EMPTY SETS OF REASONS

To derive a conclusion on the basis of reasons, it is always necessary to have weighing-knowledge that indicates which set of reasons outweighs the other set. Normally, this weighing-knowledge is not provided by RBL, but should be incorporated in the theory from which the derivations are made. For instance, it is not the task of RBL to indicate whether the fact that John is a thief outweighs the fact that John is a juvenile as a reason concerning the punishability of John. This information should be specified by the domain theory from which the derivations are to be made.

There is, however, one important exception. RBL provides the weighing-knowledge that is necessary to weigh a non-empty set of reasons against an empty set. If there are only reasons for a conclusion, or only reasons against, it should be possible to derive the conclusion, respectively its negation, even if the theory does not say anything about the relative weight of the reasons. That is why in RBL any non-empty set of reasons outweighs an empty set.

So, if there is only a reason for a conclusion, and no reason against it, this conclusion can be derived. The other way round the same holds: if there is only a reason against a conclusion, and no reason for it, the negation of this conclusion can be derived. In practice these situations, where there is one reason that pleads for a conclusion, and no reason that pleads against it, are very important. In fact, it is the type of situation that is classically dealt with by arguments of the form Modus Ponens.

For instance, if we have the rule that thieves are punishable and the fact that John is a thief, the argument to the conclusion that John is punishable would traditionally be constructed as a case of Modus Ponens. In RBL it becomes an argument in which there is one reason why John can be punished and no reason why he cannot be punished. Since the one reason for punishability outweighs the empty set of reasons against punishability, it is possible to derive that John is punishable, even if the domain theory does not contain any relevant weighing-knowledge.

27. Deriving a Reason by Application of a Rule

It is possible to derive from

Applicable(rule(*r*), case(*c*), *iconds*, *iconcl*)

that

Reason(
  applicable(rule(*r*), case(*c*),*iconds*, *iconcl*),
  applies(rule(*r*), case(*c*), *iconds*, *iconcl*),
  pro)

Normally there will be no other reasons derivable concerning the application of the rule *r*, and then it is also possible to derive

Applies(rule(*r*), case(*c*), *iconds*, *iconcl*)

RBL makes it possible to derive from this that

Reason(*iconds*, *iconcl*, pro)

or, in case it was derived that

Applies(rule(*r*), case(*c*), *iconds*, ∼*iconcl*)

it can be derived that

Reason(*iconds*, *iconcl*, con)

This completes the derivation of a reason for the rule-conclusion from the statement that the rule is valid, and the facts that satisfy the rule conditions.

28. From the Validity of a Goal to Reasons

The reasons involved in weighing relations need not stem from rules or principles; they can also be based on goals. The derivation of a reason on the basis of a goal is relatively simple. If some action or state of affairs contributes to a valid goal, and it cannot be derived that the goal is excluded in this case, there is a reason why the action ought to be performed, respectively the state ought to be the case.

28.1. Deontic Predicates and Operators

To express that an action ought to be performed, RBL has a dedicated predicate Ought that has actors and action types as its parameters.* Ought stands for 'Ought to do'. Action types are denoted by constants or function symbols. They can

* The discussion of reasoning with goals necessitates the introduction of deontic elements in the language of RBL. It is, however, not the purpose of this text to propose a system of deontic logic. Therefore, the discussion of the deontic predicates is kept minimal.

be preceded by the sign ¬ to denote the refraining from this type of action. If `stealing` stands for an action of the type stealing, `¬stealing` stands for refraining from stealing.

The use of the Ought predicate is illustrated in the sentence

```
(x)(In_distress(person) → Ought(x, help(person)))
```

which means that everybody ought to help a person in distress.

Analogously, the sentence

```
(x)(y)((x <> y) → Ought(x, ¬hurt(y)))
```

means that nobody ought to hurt another person.

A related predicate O stands for 'It ought to be the case that'. This predicate has states of affairs as its parameter. For instance, the sentence

```
O(withheld(john, using_drugs))
```

means that the state of affairs that John is being withheld from using drugs ought to be the case.

28.2. Reasons for and against actions

The relation between accepted goals and the reasons for actions based on them is illustrated by the following. If it can be derived that

```
Obtains(
  contributes_to(withhold(john, using_drugs),
    youth_protected),
  case(john's_drug_addiction))
Valid(goal(protection_of_juveniles, youth_protected))
```

and it cannot be derived that

```
Excluded(goal(protection_of_juveniles),
  case(john's_drug_addiction))
```

then it can be derived that

```
Reason(
  contributes_to(withhold(john, using_drugs),
    youth_protected),
  ought(x, do(withhold(john, using_drugs))),
  pro)
```

(From the sentences that the goal `protection_of_juveniles` is valid and that withholding John from using drugs contributes to this goal, it can be derived that one ought to withhold John from using drugs, if it cannot be derived that the goal `protection_of_juveniles` is excluded in the case of John's drug addiction.)

If a type of action detracts from a goal, this leads to a reason against this action. If it is derivable that

```
Obtains(
  contributes_to(smoke, ~lives_long(x)),
  case(alice's_smoking))
Valid(goal(long_smokeless_life, lives_long(x))
```

and it is not derivable that

```
Excluded(goal(long_smokeless_life),
  case(alice's_smoking))
```

then it can be derived that

```
Reason(
  contributes_to(smoke, ~lives_long(alice)),
  ought(alice, ¬smoke),
  pro)
```

Notice that the fact that the smoking of Alice detracts from her long living is a reason *for* the conclusion that Alice ought to *refrain from* smoking, and not *against* the conclusion that Alice ought to smoke.

28.3. Reasons for and against states of affairs

If a state of affairs contributes to a goal-state, this leads to a reason why this state of affairs ought to be the case. If it can be derived that

```
Valid(goal(protection_of_parties_in_good_faith,
  parties_in_good_faith_protected))
Obtains(contributes_to(owner(gerald, clock),
  parties_in_good_faith_protected),
  case(transfer_clock))
```

and it is not derivable that

```
Excluded(goal(protection_parties_in_good_faith),
  case(transfer_clock))
```

then it can be derived that

```
Reason(contributes_to(owner(gerald, clock),
  parties_in_good_faith_protected),
  o(owner(gerald, clock)), pro)
```

Analogously, if a state of affairs detracts from a goal-state, this is a reason why this state of affairs ought not to be the case. If it can be derived that

```
Valid(goal(crime_prevention, less_crime))
Contributes_to(abolished(crime_prevention_team),
  ~less_crime)
```

and it cannot be derived that

```
Excluded(goal(crime_prevention), case(prevention_team))
```

then it can be derived that

```
Reason(
  contributes_to(abolished(crime_prevention_team),
    ~less_crime)
  o(~abolished(crime_prevention_team)), pro)
```

29. Derivability in Reason-Based Logic

After the informal discussion of RBL in the previous sections, I will now propose a definition of the derivability relation of RBL. Let T be an RBL-theory, that is a set of well-formed RBL-sentences which are allowed as premises for an argument. It then holds that:

> A sentence can validly be derived from an RBL-theory T, if and only if this sentence is an element of the intersection of all extensions of T.

29.1. EXTENSIONS OF RBL-THEORIES

Extensions of RBL-theories are defined as follows:*

Let T be an RBL-theory, let Th(T) be the deductive closure of T, let E be a set of sentences, and let $T_0 \ldots T_\infty$ be a sequence of sets of sentences such that:

1. T_0= Th(T ∪
   `{(`*reasonset*`)(`*state*`)`
   `(`*reasonset* `<> ∅ → Outweighs(`*reasonset*`, ∅, `*state*`) ),`
   `(`*state*`)(∃c)(case(`*c*`) & Obtains(`*state*`, case(`*c*`)) → `*state*`) })`
   T_0 is intuitively the original theory with the additional information that every non-empty set of reasons outweighs the empty set, and that if a state of affairs obtains in some case, this state of affairs obtains, and everything which can be deduced from this.
2. T_{m+1} = Th(T_m ∪ Δ(T_m)), where Δ(T_m) is the smallest set of sentences such that:
   Assume that the sentence `Facts` minimally entails** the sentence Condition under some substitution , and that the term iconcl is the instance of the term conclusion under σ. Then the following holds:
   a. If `Valid(rule(`*rid*`, `*condition*`, `*conclusion*`))` ∈ Tm, and
      `Obtains(`*Facts*`, case(`*c*`))` ∈ Tm, and not
      `Excluded(rule(`*rid*`), case(`*c*`), `*facts*`, `*iconcl*`)` ∈ E, then
      `Applicable(rule(`*rid*`), case(`*c*`), `*facts*`, `*iconcl*`)` ∈ (Tm).

* The following definition of extensions of an RBL-theory is an adaptation of the second way in which [Reiter 1980] defines extensions of default-theories.

** A sentence A minimally entails a sentence C, if and only if C is true in all models of A, and there is no sentence B such that B is true in all models of A, while it is not the case that A is true in all models of B, and C is true in all models of B.

b. If `Applicable(rule(`*rid*`), case(`*c*`),` *facts*`,` *atom*`)` ∈ Tm, then `Reason(applicable(rule(`*rid*`), case(`*c*`),` *facts*`,` *atom*`), applies(rule(`*rid*`), case(`*c*`),` *facts*`,` *atom*`), pro)` ∈ Δ(Tm).
c. If `Applies(rule(`*rid*`), case(`*c*`),` *facts*`,` *atom*`)` ∈ Tm, then `Reason(`*facts*`,` *atom*`, pro)` ∈ Δ(Tm).
d. If `Applies(rule(`*rid*`), case(`*c*`),` *facts*`,` *~atom*`)` ∈ Tm, then `Reason(`*facts*`,` *atom*`, con)` ∈ Δ(Tm).
e. If `Valid(goal(`*gid*`,` *state*`))` ∈ Tm, and `Obtains(contributes_to(`*action*`,` *state*`), case(`*c*`))` ∈ Tm, and not `Excluded(goal(`*gid*`), case(`*c*`))` ∈ E then `Reason(contributes_to(`*action*`,` *state*`), ought(`*x*`, action), pro)` ∈ Δ(Tm).
f. If `Valid(goal(`*gid*`,` *state2*`))` ∈ Tm, `Obtains(contributes_to(`*state1*`,` *state2*`), case(`*c*`))` ∈ Tm, and not `Excluded(goal(`*gid*`), case(`*c*`))` ∈ E then `Reason(contributes_to(`*state1*`,` *state2*`), o(`*state1*`), pro)` ∈ Δ(Tm).
g. If `Valid(goal(`*gid*`,` *state*`))` ∈ Tm, and `Obtains(contributes_to(`*action*`,` *~state*`), case(`*c*`))` ∈ Tm, and not `Excluded(goal(`*gid*`),case(`*c*`))` ∈ E then `Reason(contributes_to(`*action*`,` *state*`), (`*x*`)ought(`*x*`,(¬action), pro)` ∈ Δ(Tm).
h. If `Valid(goal(`*gid*`,` *state2*`))` ∈ Tm, `Obtains(contributes_to(`*state1*`,` *~state2*`), case(`*c*`))` ∈ Tm, and not `Excluded(goal(`*gid*`),case(`*c*`))` ∈ E then `Reason(contributes_to(`*state1*`,` *state2*`), o(`*~state1*`), pro)` ∈ Δ(Tm).

Let `reasons_pro(`*atom*`)` be {*s*`: Reason(`*s*`,` *atom*`, pro)` ∈ E} and let `reasons_con(`*atom*`)` be *s*`: Reason(`*s*`,` *atom*`, con)` ∈ E}

i. If `Outweighs(reasons_pro(`*atom*`), reasons_con(`*atom*`),` *atom*`)` ∈ Tm, then *Atom* ∈ Δ(Tm).
j. If `Outweighs(reasons_con(`*atom*`), reasons_pro(`*atom*`),` *atom*`)` ∈ Tm, then *~Atom* ∈ Δ(Tm).

3. E is an extension of T iff E = $\bigcup_{i=0}^{\infty}$ Ti

Intuitively this definition of an extension of the theory T comes down to the following. Starting with a set of sentences (T_0), that consists of the original theory T and two axioms of RBL, a series of ever increasing sets of sentences ($T_0 \ldots T_\infty$) is defined. Every set contains the sentences of the previous set plus what 'immediately follows' from that set (Δ(Tm)). Normally, at some moment there are no new conclusions possible anymore ($T_{m+1} = T_m$) The set E which is achieved at that moment is an extension of T.

A complication in this definition is that the sentences that can be added to a set to obtain the new set (Δ(Tm)) do not only depend on the first set (T_m), but

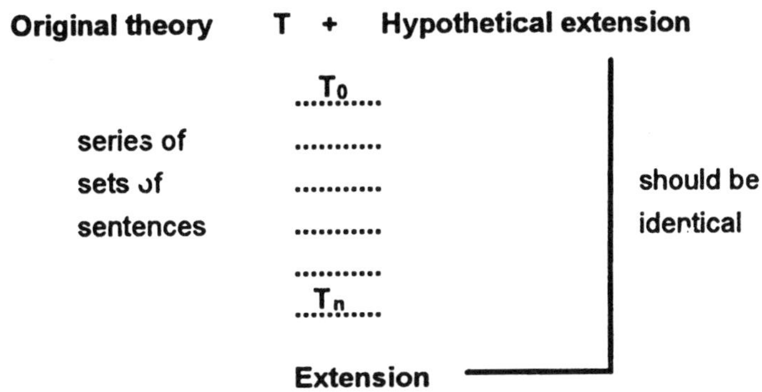

Figure 7. From the original theory to its extension.

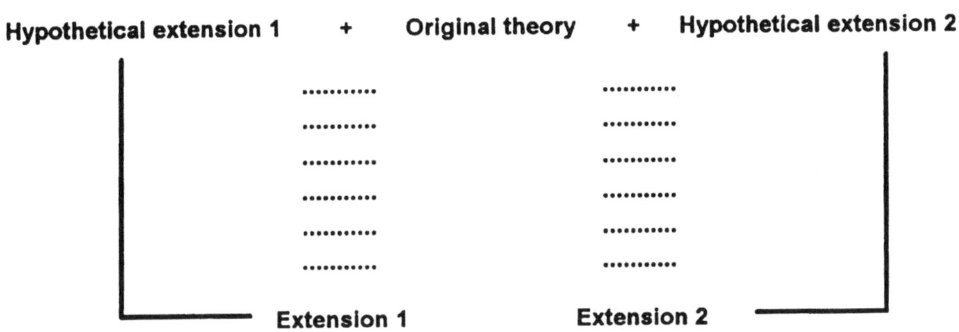

Figure 8. Multiple extensions.

also on the final set E that will be achieved. That this is the case follows from the conditions sub a, e, f, g, h, i, and j, which refer to the exclusions or the reasons which are present in the final extension of the theory.

This complication has at least two consequences. The first consequence is that it is not possible to generate the series of sets of sentences just by starting with the original theory. In addition to the original theory, an 'hypothesis' concerning the final extension is needed to generate the series of sets. An hypothesis concerning the extension of a theory is correct if the series of sets based on the original theory and the hypothetical extension ends with the hypothetical extension. Cf. Figure 7.

29.2. THE NUMBER OF EXTENSIONS OF A THEORY

The second consequence is that a theory can at least in theory have more than one extension. That is because there may be more than one combination of the original theory and a hypothetical extension that fulfils the demand that the resulting series of sets of sentences ends up with the hypothetical extension on which the series was based. Cf. Figure 8.

Moreover, it is also possible that a theory has no extension at all. Let me give an example of a theory which has no extension:

```
Obtains(a, case(1))
Valid(rule(1, a, excluded(rule(1), case(1)))
```

This theory has no extension, because if an extension contains the sentence

```
Excluded(rule(1), case(1))
```

it should for this very reason not contain that sentence, and the other way round. (If rule 1 is not excluded in case 1, it can be derived that it is excluded in that case. If, however, it is excluded, the very reason why it should be excluded, that is derivation on the basis of rule 1, does not obtain anymore.)

The following theory has two extensions:

```
Obtains(a, case(1))
Obtains(b, case(1))
Valid(rule(1, a, excluded(rule(2), case(1)))
Valid(rule(2, b, excluded(rule(1), case(1)))
```

The one extension contains, amongst others, the sentences

```
Applicable(rule(1), case(1), a,
  excluded(rule(2), case(1)))
Excluded(rule(2), case(1))
```

and not the sentences

```
Applicable(rule(2), case(1), b,
  excluded(rule(1), case(1)))
Excluded(rule(1), case(1))
```

The other extension contains, amongst others, the sentences

```
Applicable(rule(2), case(1), b,
  excluded(rule(1), case(1)))
Excluded(rule(1), case(1))
```

and not the sentences

```
Applicable(rule(1), case(1), a,
  excluded(rule(2), case(1)))
Excluded(rule(2), case(1))
```

Otherwise than in other logics, in RBL multiple extensions cannot be the result from inconsistencies, because RBL does not strive after consistency maintenance. It appears from the examples above that the occurrence of multiple extensions or the lack of any extension is the consequence of circularities in a theory.

As may be seen in the first example, if a rule directly refers to itself, this may block the existence of extensions. If the self-reference is indirect (one rule refers to another rule and vice versa), the result is that there are multiple extensions (cf. the second example).

If this hypothesis is correct, the intuitively correct conclusions from a theory can be obtained by not applying the rules which are involved in the self-reference. In the case of multiple extensions, the present definition of valid conclusions obtains this result by using the intersection of all extensions to define derivable sentences.* In this way, any rule that cannot be applied in some extension does not lead to conclusions in that extension. Its conclusion will therefore not be derivable from the theory.

30. Simple Rule Application

In the following sections I will illustrate how RBL can be put to use for legal applications. This involves a series of examples of how legal arguments can be cast in the form of reasons for and against particular conclusions. As a consequence, this part of the paper is particularly relevant for those who read this text with an interest in how RBL can be used for legal knowledge representation.

First I will show how the standard cases such as simple rule application and the weighing of reasons for and against a particular classification are handled. Then follow three extended examples that show how RBL deals with complex legal reasoning. These examples concern arguments about the relative weights of sets of reasons, arguments about the validity of legal rules, and an argument about the relative importance of conflicting case law where the interpretation of a statutory provision is concerned.

Most often, when we apply a rule, there are no complications at all. The conditions of the rule are satisfied and the rule conclusion follows just like that. A theory about reasoning with rules should be able to handle this situation without problems. This section deals with simple rule application and illustrates how RBL functions if there are no special circumstances that must be dealt with.

Suppose we have the rule that thieves ought to be punished, and the fact that John is a thief. From this information we want to derive that John ought to be punished.

This information can be represented by the following RBL-sentences:

```
Valid(rule(theft2, thief(x), o(punished(x))))
Obtains(thief(john), case(john's_theft))
∴ O(punished(john))
```

By following the definition of an extension of an RBL-theory in Section 29, it can be seen that the deductive closure of the following sentences is an extension of the theory given above:

* Notice that the use of the intersection of extensions in RBL is inspired by the need to avoid the complications of indirectly self-referring theories, and not to obtain a skeptical inference relation. RBL is skeptical because it demands explicit weighing knowledge in the case of colliding reasons.

```
Valid(rule(theft2, thief(x), o(punished(x))))
Obtains(thief(john), case(john's_theft))
(reasonset)(state)
  (reasonset <> ∅ → Outweighs(reasonset, ∅, state))
Thief(john)
Applicable(rule(theft), case(john's_theft),
  thief(john), o(punished(john)))
Reason(
  applicable(rule(theft), case(john's_theft),
    thief(john), o(punished(john))),
  applies(rule(theft), case(john's_theft),
    thief(john), o(punished(john))),
  pro)
Applies(rule(theft), case(john's_theft),
  thief(john), o(punished(john)))
Reason(thief(john), o(punished(john)), pro)
O(punished(john)
```

Moreover, unless there are extensions which contain reasons not included in this extension, all sentences of this extension will be derivable. By inspecting the theory that consists of the two premises, it can easily be seen that there is no information which can underlie other reasons, because reasons must be based on valid rules or goals, and no other rules or goals than the rule `theft2` occur in the theory. Therefore, the sentence `O(punished(john))` will occur in the intersection of all extensions of the theory and is therefore derivable.

Notice that this argument makes use of meta-level reasoning. Presently there is no constructive proof theory for RBL.

31. The Exclusion of Rules

RBL uses the mechanism of exclusionary reasons to model exceptions that block the application of a rule. The law knows several situations in which such exceptions occur (cf. Section 14). Sometimes the exception only makes it impossible to apply a rule. At other occasions the exception not only blocks the application of a rule, but also provides a reason for an incompatible conclusion. In the following two subsections I will discuss the prescription of punishable facts as an example of the first situation, and the rule that governs force majeure in contract law as an example of the second situation.

31.1. UNDERCUTTERS

Reasons that only block the application of a rule, without having any other impact on the case at hand are sometimes called 'undercutters'.* The scope limitations of legal rules form the basis for several kinds of undercutters. One of these scope limitations concerns the scope of legal rules in time. In the case of criminal law, this means that a criminal law may not be applicable anymore, if the crime occurred sufficiently long ago. This situation is illustrated in our old example about John, the thief. Although John is a thief, he is not punishable, because his crime is prescribed.**

Let us formulate the relevant rules in an RBL-theory:

```
Valid(rule(theft1, thief(x), punishable(x)))
Valid(rule(prescription,
  criminal_law(rule(r)) &
    crime_type(rule(r), crime_type) &
    type(crime, crime_type) &
    prescribed(crime, case(c)),
  excluded(rule(r), case(c)) ))
```

The rule `prescription` boils down to the fact that if a particular rule is a rule of criminal law, if this rule is about a particular type of crime, and if a crime of this type is in a particular case prescribed, then the application of this rule is excluded in that case.

The facts

```
Criminal_law(rule(theft1))
Crime_type(rule(theft1), stealing)
Type(theft, stealing)
Prescribed(theft, case(john's_theft))
```

make the rule `prescription` apply to the theft of John's with as a consequence that it can be derived that

```
Excluded(rule(theft1), case(john's_theft))
```

and as a consequence it is not anymore possible to derive that

```
Applicable(rule(theft1), case(john's_theft),
  thief(john), punishable(john))
```

nor that

```
Reason(thief(john), punishable(john), pro)
```

* The term stems from [Pollock 1987], and was also adopted in [Prakken 1993]. [Sartor 1991] distinguishes between exceptions to norms and exceptions to effects, where the former are undercutters, and the latter 'rebutters'.

** In Dutch law, the prescription of crimes is actually regulated in a more complex way, namely through the non-admissibility of the public prosecutor. An adequate analysis of this phenomenon demands for a procedural approach. Cf. [Hage et al. 1994].

As a further consequence, the sentence

```
Punishable(john)
```

cannot be derived anymore.

Notice that the facts that the rule `theft1` is a rule of criminal law, and that the crime was prescribed only block the application of the rule `theft1`, and have no other implication for the punishability of John whatsoever.

Notice also how the treatment of rules as logical individuals in RBL makes it possible to formulate general rules about when rules are excluded.

31.2. REBUTTALS

Some exceptions to rules do not only block the application of the rule, but also provide the case with a legal consequence that is incompatible with the conclusion of the rule. Such exceptions are also called 'rebutters' [Pollock 1987].

In Dutch criminal law, theft is punishable with a fine of the third category, but burglary is punishable with a fine of the fourth category. Obviously, since burglary involves theft, application of the rule about burglary blocks application of the rule about theft. This can be formalised as follows:*

```
Valid(rule(theft3, thief(x),
  punishable(x, fine_type_3)))
Valid(rule(burglary1, burglar(x),
  punishable(x, fine_type_4)))
Valid(rule(burglary2,
  obtains(burglar(x), case(c)),
  excluded(rule(theft3), case(c)))
Thief(gerald) & Burglar(gerald)
```

Because Gerald is a burglar, both the rules `burglary1` and `burglary2` are applied. The first application leads to the conclusion that Gerald is punishable with a fine of the fourth category, while the second application leads to an exclusionary reason for rule `theft3`. As a consequence it cannot be derived that that Gerald is punishable with a fine of the third category.

Notice that the original rule that in the case of burglary, one is punishable with a fine of the fourth category has been translated into two RBL rules. The reason for this is that the application of this rule has two effects. First that the application of the rule theft is blocked, and second that there the burglar is punishable with a fine of the fourth category. RBL rules can (for historical reasons) only have one conclusion, and therefore two rules are needed to express the two effects of force majeure.

* Another formalisation which makes use of the Lex Specialis rule would be less ad hoc, but also a less clear example. Cf. [Hage and Verheij 1995] for this more principal approach.

32. Elementary Goal-Based Reasoning

An important legal goal in most Western countries is to protect the possibility for every citizen to express his or her opinion. Let us call this goal Freedom of Expression. Clearly, having a free press contributes to this goal. As a consequence of the goal Freedom of Expression, there should be a free press.

This simple argument, based on the application of a goal, would be expressed in RBL as follows:

```
Valid(goal(freedom_of_expression), freedom_to_express)
Obtains(
  contributes_to(free_press, freedom_to_express),
  case(press_freedom))
```

The extension of this theory contains the following sentences:

```
Reason(contributes_to(free_press, freedom_to_express),
  o(free_press), pro)
Outweighs(
  {contributes_to(free_press, freedom_to_express)},
  ∅, o(free_press))
O(free_press)
```

and they would not contain the sentence:

```
Excluded(goal(freedom_of_expression),
  case(press_freedom))
```

Therefore, from this theory it can be derived that:

```
O(free_press)
```

Imagine, however, that a particular country is in war, and that there are serious reasons to assume that freedom of expression can be misused by the enemy for spreading unnecessary anxiety. Under these circumstances there is reason to restrict the goal to have freedom of expression. The goal is not completely abandoned; its effects are only temporarily suspended. Under these circumstances, the following sentence will be derivable:

```
Excluded(goal(freedom_of_expression), case(free_press))
```

This exclusion blocks the generation of the reason that a free press contributes to the freedom of expression, which would plead for the conclusion that there ought to be a free press. As a consequence, there is no reason left for the conclusion that there ought to be a free press, and this conclusion can therefore not be drawn anymore.

33. Weighing Reasons

In legal reasoning, weighing reasons most often occurs when there are no legal rules to apply. Classification springs to mind as a field that is not always governed by rules of law and where reasons for and against a particular classification have to be weighed. Another situation where weighing reasons is important, is where legal decision makers have discretion. In the Netherlands, determining the measure of punishment (within certain limits) belongs to this field.

I will adapt an earlier example to show how weighing reasons in the field of criminal law can be represented in RBL. We have already met with the case of John, the thief. That he is a thief is a reason why John ought to be punished. Suppose, however, that John is a child of thirteen. This is a reason not to punish him. In some legal systems the age of John may even block the application of the normal rule about the punishment of thieves. In that case it should be represented by means of an exclusionary reason. If the age does not completely block the application of the rule `theft2`, and if the judge has discretion to determine whether the crime will be punished, the age of John will at least form a reason against punishing him.

The situation can then be represented as follows:

```
Valid(rule(theft2, thief(x), o(punished(x))))
Valid(rule(child, child(x), ~o(punished(x))))*
Thief(john) & Child(john)
```

On the basis of this theory we have:

```
reasons_pro(o(punished(john))) = {thief(john)}
reasons_con(o(punished(john))) = {child(john)}
```

However, to derive a conclusion regarding whether John ought to be punished, we need to know which set of reasons outweighs the other set. On the basis of the present theory, which contains no information concerning the relative weight of the reasons, it is not possible to derive whether John ought to be punished or not.

Suppose, however, that the information is added that being a child outweighs being a thief as a reason concerning punishment:

```
Outweighs( {child(x)}, {thief(x)}, o(punished(x)))
```

On the basis of this information, it is possible to derive that it is not the case that John ought to be punished:

```
~O(punished(john))
```

Suppose, moreover, that John is not only a thief, but also a mistreator, and that mistreators ought to be punished:

```
Valid(rule(mistreatment, mistreator(x),
```

* Arguably, this rule should be replaced by a goal. For the purpose of the example, however, I have chosen for a rule (principle) that children ought not to be punished. For the same purpose, I have chosen to let the conclusion of the rule run that it is not the case that the child ought to be punished, rather than that it is the case that the child ought not to be punished.

```
  o(punished(x))))
Mistreator(john)
```

This information can be combined with the following additional weighing knowledge:

```
Outweighs( {child(x)}, {mistreator(x)},
  o(punished(x)))
Outweighs( {mistreator(x) & thief(x)}, {child(x)},
  o(punished(x)))
```

(Concerning the issue of punishment, being a child outweighs being a mistreator, but the combination of being a mistreator and a thief outweighs being a child.)

Here we encounter an important characteristic of RBL, that is the *accrual of reasons*. Two or more reasons that are individually outweighed by another reason, may together outweigh that other reason. So if John is both a thief, a mistreator and a child, the conclusion will be that John ought to be punished, because the facts that John is a mistreator and a thief together outweigh the fact that he is a child:

```
Outweighs(
  {mistreator(john) & thief(john)},
  {child(john)},
  o(punished(john)))
```

34. Reasoning about Weights

Whether one set of reasons outweighs the other set, or just the other way round, needs not solely depend on the reasons themselves and the conclusion for or against which they plead. It is also possible that there are other facts which, although they are not reasons for or against a particular conclusion themselves, influence the relative weight of the concerned sets of reasons.

34.1. AN EXAMPLE

Such a situation is illustrated by the following real life example [Kantongerecht Rotterdam, June 12th, 1985]. A small supermarket had to dismiss one of its employees for financial reasons. For such a dismissal, the allowance of a judge is necessary. One of the employees, called Mary, has been longer in service, and this is a reason for the judge not to permit to dismiss her.*

```
Reason(longer_in_service(mary),
  permitted(x, dismiss(mary)), con)
```

The other employee, called Richard, on the other hand, has better papers for the job, and this is a reason not to dismiss him either.

* In the formalisation of this example, I make use of the Permitted-predicate, which is the counterpart of the Ought-predicate.

```
Reason(better_papers(richard), permitted(x,
  dismiss(richard)), con)
```

Since it is clear that one of the employees has to be dismissed for financial reasons, a reason against permitting the dismissal of the one is also a reason for permitting the dismissal of the other:*

```
(reason)
  (Reason(reason, permitted(x, dismiss(richard)), con)
  → Reason(reason, permitted(x, dismiss(mary)), pro))
```

To determine what has to be decided, we will focus on the reasons that plead for and against permitting to dismiss Mary. We have the following two sets of reasons:

```
reasons_pro(permitted(x, dismiss(mary)))
  = {better_papers(richard)}
reasons_con(permitted(x, dismiss(mary)))
  = {longer_in_service(mary)}
```

The judge decided that, although Richard had better papers for the job, Mary was still sufficiently qualified, so that the better papers did not count for much. The fact that Mary had been longer in service should therefore tip the balance of reasons:

```
Reason(
  suitable_for_job(mary),
  outweighs(
    {longer_in_service(mary)}, {better_papers(richard)},
     permitted(x, dismiss(mary)),
  pro)
```

Notice that the fact that Mary was suitable for the job was not considered as a reason no to dismiss her, but only as a reason why the seniority of Mary should outweigh the better papers of Richard.

34.2. CASE-BASED REASONING AS A WAY TO REASON ABOUT RELATIVE WEIGHTS

One important function of case law is to indicate how sets of reasons are to be weighed against each other. A case that has already been decided can be seen as containing both a set of reasons that pleads for a particular decision, a set of reasons that pleads against this decision, and the decision about the issue, which is also a decision about which set of reasons outweighs the other set. (Of course, this only holds for cases in which the weighing of reasons was involved.) In this connection the following functions may be used:

```
reasons_for(decision, case(c)) =
```

* Strictly, the following sentences would be better represented as RBL-rules. To keep the example relatively simple, I have to chosen to use material implications.

```
  {f: obtains(f, case(c)) & reason(f, decision, pro)}
reasons_against(decision, case(c)) =
  {f: obtains(f, case(c)) & reason(f, decision, con)}*
```

If we can find a case in which some decision was taken, this is a reason why the reasons in that case that pleaded for this decision, outweigh the reasons in that case that pleaded against that decision:

```
Valid(rule(case_based_reasoning,
  (∃c)(case(c) & decision(case(c)) = d &
    reasons_for(d, case(c)) = pro_reasons &
    reasons_against(d, case(c)) = con_reasons),
  outweigh(pro_reasons, con_reasons, d)))
```

Intuitively, a decided case can provide a reason why the reasons in a new case have to be weighed in the same manner.

In this connection we can distinguish five situations. In all of them I assume that the issue at stake is the same for the case that was already decided, and the new case. I will use the following abbreviations:

`reasons_for(issue, case(old))`

stands for the set of reasons in the decided case that pleaded for the thesis `issue`.

`reasons_against(issue, case(old))`

stands for the set of reasons in the decided case that pleaded against the thesis `issue`.

`reasons_for(issue, case(new))`

stands for the set of reasons in the new case that plead for the thesis `issue`.

`reasons_against(issue, case(new))`

stands for the set of reasons in the new case that plead against the thesis `issue`.

`decision(issue, case(old))`

stands for the decision on the issue that was taken in the decided case, that is either `issue`, or `~issue`.

`decision(issue, case(new))`

stands for the decision on the issue that should be taken in the new case, that is either `issue`, or `~issue`.

Given these abbreviations, the following situations and their consequences can be distinguished:**

---

* These functions should not be confused with the functions `reasons_pro` and `reasons_con`. Cf. Section 26.1.

** The distinctions between the situations and the consequences attached to the distinctions were inspired by the HYPO-system for case-based reasoning. Cf. [Ashley 1991]. The parallel with the HYPO-system can even be increased if the presence to a higher degree of a reason for a conclusion is treated as an additional reason for the conclusion, if presence to a lesser degree of a reason for a

Situation 1

`reasons_pro(issue, old)` = `reasons_pro(issue, new)`
`reasons_con(issue, old)` = `reasons_con(issue, new)`

Then there is a reason why `decision(issue, old)` = `decision(issue, new)`, because the situations are completely identical insofar as the reasons are concerned. **Situation 2**

`reasons_pro(issue, old)` $\subset$ `reasons_pro(issue, new)`
`reasons_con(issue, old)` $\supseteq$ `reasons_con(issue, new)`
`decision(issue, old)` = `issue`

Then there is a reason why `decision(issue, new)` = `issue`, because in the new case there are even more reasons that plead for `issue`.

Situation 3

`reasons_pro(issue, old)` $\subseteq$ `reasons_pro(issue, new)`
`reasons_con(issue, old)` $\supset$ `reasons_con(issue, new)`
`decision(issue, old)` = `issue`

Then there is a reason why `decision(issue, new)` = `issue`, because in the new case there are only less reasons that plead against `issue`.

Situation 4

`reasons_pro(issue, old)` $\supset$ `reasons_pro(issue, new)`
`reasons_con(issue, old)` $\subseteq$ `reasons_con(issue, new)`
`decision(issue, old)` = `~issue`

Then there is a reason why `decision(issue, new)` = `~issue`, because in the new case there are only less reasons that plead for `issue`.

Situation 5

`reasons_pro(issue, old)` $\supseteq$ `reasons_pro(issue, new)`
`reasons_con(issue, old)` $\subset$ `reasons_con(issue, new)`
`decision(issue, old)` = `~issue`

Then there is a reason why `decision(issue, new)` = `~issue`, because in the new case there are even more reasons that plead against `issue`.

34.3. General rules to reason about the weights of reasons

These different situations are based on an underlying style of reasoning. If we know that a set of reasons outweighs another set, and the stronger set is only

conclusion counts as a reason less for the conclusion, and if reasons against a conclusion are treated analogously. The presence of facts in degrees is discussed in [Hage Reasoning].

strengthened by adding new reasons, the result will also outweigh its unchanged (or even weakened) rival. And analogously, if a set of reasons is outweighed by another set, and this set is weakened by deleting one or more reasons from it, the resulting set will also be outweighed by the other set that remained the same or was even strengthened.

Formally these rules look as follows:

```
Valid(rule(strengthening_reasons,
  outweighs(reasons1, reasons2, conclusion) &
    (reasons1 ⊆ reasons3),
  outweighs(reasons3, reasons2, conclusion)))
```

If a set of reasons outweighs another set, this is a reason why a superset of the first set will also outweigh the last set.

```
Valid(rule(weakening_reasons,
  outweighs(reasons1, reasons2, conclusion) &
    (reasons3 ⊆ reasons2),
  outweighs(reasons1, reasons3, conclusion) ))
```

If a set of reasons outweighs another set, this is a reason why a subset of the last set will also be outweighed by the first set.

These rules assume that reasons are independent of each other. Therefore, in a case where reasons are not independent, the application of these rules is excluded.

35. Reasoning about the Validity of Rules

Since, from an RBL-point of view, rules are individuals, and not sentences, they cannot stand on their own in a theory of RBL. Moreover, only a valid rule can be used in a derivation to create reasons. These two facts together are the reason why rules are introduced into arguments by means of the statement that they are valid. This has the additional advantage that it becomes possible to 'derive rules', because to derive a rule it is only necessary to derive the statement that it is valid.

RBL does not specify from which premises it can be derived that a rule is valid. In fact, it completely depends on the domain which criteria are used to determine the validity of rules (cf. [Toulmin 1958, pp. 36f. and 104] on the field dependence of backings). In the following subsections, I will discuss a number of examples.

35.1. Rules of Recognition

According to Hart, a rule is a valid rule of law, if it is identified as such by a rule of recognition [Hart 1961, pp. 92f.]. An example of such a rule of recognition would be that a rule is a valid rule of law if it was made by the legislator. In RBL such a rule of recognition is expressed as follows:

```
Valid(rule(legislation,
  adopted_by_legislator(rule(r)),
```

```
  valid(rule(r))))
Adopted_by_legislator(rule(statutory_rule))
```

From these two sentences it is possible to derive (the validity of) the rule called `statutory_rule`:

```
Valid(rule(statutory_rule))
```

35.2. Interpretation

Another way to argue about the validity of a rule has to do with the interpretation of a legal source. Take for instance the rule that women and children under sixteen are not allowed to partake in the rodeo. This rule formulation is syntactically ambiguous, because at first sight it is not clear whether women over fifteen are allowed to partake. There are two possible interpretations of the rule formulation, only one of which expresses a valid rule (`P` is a predicate for permitted to be, analogous to the `O`-predicate):

```
rule(rodeo1,
  woman(x) v
    (child(x) & under_sixteen(x)),
  ~p(partakes_in_rodeo(x)))
rule(rodeo2,
  (woman(x) v child(x)) &
    under_sixteen(x),
  ~p(partakes_in_rodeo(x)))
```

Clearly the second interpretation `(rodeo2)` does not make much sense, because on this interpretation the condition that somebody is a woman is completely superfluous. This is a reason why the second interpretation does not expresses a valid rule.

```
Reason(
  superfluous(condition_woman_x), rule(rodeo2)),
  valid(rule(rodeo2)),
  con)
```

On the basis of this reason it can be derived that the rule `rodeo2` is not valid. Moreover if there are only two seemingly acceptable interpretations, the rejection of interpretation 2 forms a reason to accept interpretation 1:

```
Reason(
  ~valid(rule(rodeo2)),
  valid(rule(rodeo1)),
  pro)
```

This leads to the final conclusion that the rule expressed in the first interpretation (rodeo1) is a valid one:

```
Valid(rule(rodeo1))
```

35.3. Principles of Interpretation

The law knows a number of traditional reasons that can be adduced in arguments about the interpretation of statutory rules [cf. MacCormick and Summers 1991]. These reasons are connected to 'maxims of interpretation', such as that the law should be interpreted according the normal meaning of its wordings, according to the historical intention of the legislator, according to the interests of society, or according to the system of the law. These maxims can in RBL be represented as rules that generate reasons why particular rules are valid ones. Take, for instance, the following rule that says that a rule is correctly interpreted if the interpretation is in accordance with the intentions of the legislator as they become clear from the preparatory works:

```
Valid(rule(genetic_interpretation,
  interpretation_of(text, rule(r)) &
    in_accordance_with(rule(r), intention_legislator),
  correct_interpretation_of(text, rule(r)) ))
```

Moreover, the correct interpretation of a legal source is a valid rule:

```
Valid(rule(source_validity,
  legal_source(text) &
    correct_interpretation_of(text, rule(r)),
  valid(rule(r)) ))
```

Historical interpretation and systematic interpretation can be dealt with by similar principles of interpretation.

35.4. Case-based Interpretation

Case law is an important source of reasons for and against interpretations of legal texts. If in a case a particular interpretation of a statutory regulation has been adopted, this is a reason why this interpretation is the 'correct' one. Analogously, the rejection of an interpretation is a reason against this interpretation. So we have the principle of legal precedent:

```
Valid(rule(legal_precedent,
  (∃c)(case(c) &
    decision(case(c)) =
     correct_interpretation_of(source, rule(r))),
  correct_interpretation_of(source, rule(r)) ))
```

If there is a case in which it is decided that the correct interpretation of a particular source is some rule, then this rule is the correct interpretation of that source.

Remember that this is no more than a principle that generates reasons which may be outweighed by other reasons. If there is only one relevant case, it leads to only one reason concerning the interpretation of the legal source, and this one reason will probably be decisive in the sense that the interpretation of the previous case is a sufficient reason to adopt this interpretation for future cases.*

However, it is possible that in different cases, different interpretations of a source have been adopted:

```
decision(case(1))
  = correct_interpretation_of(source, rule(rule_1))
decision(case(2))
  = correct_interpretation_of(source, rule(rule_2))
```

If we also have

```
Incompatible(
  correct_interpretation_of(source, rule(rule_1)),
  correct_interpretation_of(source, rule(rule_2)) )
```

we must make a decision which court decision concerning the interpretation of source is to be preferred.

To facilitate the reading of the rest of this example, I introduce the following abbreviations:

```
d1 = (decision(case(c1)) =
  correct_interpretation_of(source, rule(rule_1)))
d2 = (decision(case(c2)) =
  correct_interpretation_of(source, rule(rule_2)))
e1 = (court_of(decision(case(c1))) = court1)
e2 = (court_of(decision(case(c2))) = court2)
```

One good reason in this connection is that recent cases prevail over old ones:

```
Valid(rule(old_and_recent_cases,
  recent(decision(case(c1))) & old(decision(case(c2))),
  outweighs({d1}, {d2},
    correct_interpretation_of(source, rule(rule_1))) ))
```

Another good reason is that decisions of superior courts prevail over decisions of inferior courts:

```
Valid(rule(superiority_of_courts,
  e1 & e2 & superior_to(court2, court1),
  outweighs({d2}, {d1}),
    correct_interpretation_of(source, rule(rule_1))) ))
```

If only one of these (or other) reasons is present to prefer a particular court decision above another one, this decision will provide us with the reason to prefer a particular interpretation of the source. For instance, if one court is superior, while

* Of course there may be reasons against a particular interpretation that have nothing to do with precedents.

both decisions are approximately equally recent, the decision of the superior court will be preferred and the interpretation of this court will be chosen.

If, however, one court is superior, while the decision of the other court is more recent, we must weigh reasons about which court decision to adopt. Suppose that if there have been changes in society that are relevant for the issue at stake, the most recent decision is to be preferred, while if there were no such changes, the superiority is decisive. In that case, we will have the following reasons:

```
Reason(relevant_changes,
  outweighs(
    {recent(decision(case(c1))) &
     old(decision(case(c2)))},
  {e1 & e2 & superior_to(court2, court1)},
    outweighs({d2}, {d1},
     correct_interpretation_of(source, rule(rule_1))) )
  pro)
```

(If there have been relevant changes in society, the fact that one decision is more recent than another outweighs the hierarchical relation between the courts as a reason concerning the correct interpretation of a source.)

```
Reason(~relevant_changes,
  outweighs(
    {e1 & e2 & superior_to(court2, court1)},
    {recent(decision(case(c1))) &
     old(decision(case(c2)))},
    outweighs({d1}, {d2},
     correct_interpretation_of(source, rule(rule_1))) )
  pro)
```

(If, however, there have been no relevant changes in society, the hierarchical relation between the courts outweighs the fact that one decision is more recent than another as a reason concerning the correct interpretation of a source.)

Suppose that there have been relevant changes. In that case, the more recent case will be adopted as authoritative for the interpretation:

```
Outweighs({d1}, {d2},
  correct_interpretation_of(source, rule((rule_1)))
```

This leads us to the conclusion that the interpretation of the more recent decision (decision(case(*c1*))) is the correct one:

```
Correct_interpretation_of(source, rule(rule_1))
```

This extended example not only shows how cases can serve as the justification for preferring one interpretation above another one, but also how it is possible to weigh reasons about the issue how reasons (for some other conclusion) ought to be weighed, and – in general – how RBL deals with what would in other logics be meta-level arguments.

C. Some Logico-Philosophical Reflections on Reason-Based Logic

The examples of the previous sections illustrated how RBL matches the model of legal reasoning that was exposed in parts A of this paper.

Since RBL is closely tied to First Order Predicate Logic, one may ask whether RBL is really a logic, rather than a formalisation of a model of legal reasoning in terms of FOPL. For instance, in one sense, RBL is no more than an extension of FOPL. All deductive arguments are valid in RBL. Moreover every well-formed sentence of FOPL is a legal sentence of RBL and the other way round. RBL 'only' adds a number of inferential possibilities to those of FOPL.

Nevertheless, the 'spirit' of RBL is completely different from that of FOPL. RBL is a non-monotonic logic, because the part that is added to FOPL is non-monotonic. Moreover, the central notions in RBL-inferences are those of a reason and of the weighing of reasons, not that of a deductive argument.

The difference between the two logics is most prominent where the use of the material implication is concerned. Most real-life arguments will be represented in FOPL as arguments of the form Modus Ponens, where the relation between one sentence and another sentence that is derived from it is represented by a material implication. In RBL, most of these arguments will be represented as the application of a rule. As a consequence, almost all real life arguments – and not only legal ones or those which make explicitly use of rules – will be dealt with by the part of RBL that is built on top of FOPL. Where RBL is technically spoken only an extension of FOPL, it is for practical purposes an alternative.

In the line of the question after the difference between RBL and FOPL lie some other ones: Why does RBL deviate from other logics in that it assigns such a central place to the notion of a reason? And why does RBL not contain some more derivational possibilities which seem very natural? These and related questions are the topic of the final part of this paper. Of necessity, the discussion of these question leads the argument into philosophical waters, away from the more down to earth approach of legal knowledge engineers.

36. Why Reason-Based Logic is a Logic

An argument is said to be deductively valid if it is not possible that the premises of the argument are true, while the conclusion of the argument is false [Copi 1978, p. 32]. I will leave the difficult question of what kind of possibility is involved here, only to notice that defeasible arguments based on the application of rules, goals and principles, are certainly not deductively valid. Of course it is possible to reconstruct them in a way that is deductively valid, but only at the cost of replacing the original argument by another one (cf. the first note on p. 203). The defence of the use of non-monotonic logics in the field Artificial Intelligence and Law shows that many authors are convinced that deductive logic is not the ideal means to evaluate reasoning with rules, etc.

Still there are arguments based on the application of rules, and within these arguments one can distinguish between good and bad ones. To make this distinction, we need a standard that is to be applied to arguments in order to classify them as either good or bad. Clearly, different arguments can be good or bad for different reasons, but it seems attractive to have a standard that is sufficiently abstract to encompass all arguments. The standard of deductive logic has turned out to be too specifically made for arguments which are not based on rules and has therefore to be rejected as the general standard for the evaluation of arguments. As an alternative I propose the following standard:

> An argument from a set of premises to a conclusion is good, and the conclusion of such an argument is justified, if the reasons that can be based on the premises which plead for the conclusion outweigh the reasons that can be based on the premises and which plead against the conclusion.

Notice that this is a very abstract standard which leaves it to domain theories to specify what counts as a reason, when a reason can be based on a set of premises, and when one set of reasons outweighs another set. RBL can be seen as an elaboration of this standard by specifying how reasons relate to rules etc, and which reasons can be based on a set of premises. RBL does not specify under which circumstances one set of reasons outweighs another set, with the exception of when one set of reasons is empty and the other one is not.

Because RBL is so closely related with a general theory of what counts as a good argument and as a justified conclusion, I would say that RBL is a kind of logic, rather than a mere formalisation of the notions reason, rule, etc., and their mutual relations.

37. Reasons Instead of Arguments

A reason in RBL has some similarity with an argument in other logics.* Why replace the familiar notion of an argument with the relatively unfamiliar one of a reason? To answer this question we must take a closer look to the notion of a reason and the argument form of Modus Ponens to which it is related.

Suppose we have the rule that thieves are punishable and the fact that John is a thief. In FOPL the following argument leads to the conclusion that John is punishable:

---

* This becomes very clear if the notion of a reason in my definition of a good argument is replaced by the notion of an argument, and the outweigh-relation is replaced by the defeats-relation. Cf. [Prakken and Sartor 1995] and the discussion in Section 40.

[Pollock 1987] also assigns a central place to the notion of a reason. He distinguishes between decisive reasons and defeasible ones. His defeasible reasons are rather similar to the reasons of RBL. Pollock pays relatively little attention to the relation between principles and rules on the one hand, and reasons on the other hand, however.

```
(x)(Thief(x) → Punishable(x))
Thief(john)
∴ Punishable(john)
```

In this argument there are two premises which logically have the same function: they are both necessary for the application of the rule of derivation that allows Modus Ponens arguments (Detachment). That the premises have different logical structures is irrelevant for their identical logical roles.

In RBL, on the contrary, rules and facts have different logical roles. The rule is used to give the fact some additional value: the fact is made relevant for the conclusion. This is reflected in the two step-procedure of RBL, where the first step concerns the 'transformation' of brute facts into reasons, and the second step concerns the derivation of a conclusion on the basis of reasons. The argument (in an abbreviated form) would run:

```
Valid(rule(r, thief(x), punishable(x)))
Thief(john)
∴ Reason(thief(john), punishable(john), pro)
∴ Punishable(john)
```

In this way the difference between the two causes of defeasibility can be made clear. Pure undercutters operate only in the first step, where a fact is prevented from becoming a reason. Rebutters can operate in two ways. First they can solely consist of colliding reasons which have to be weighed. In that case their only function lies in the second step. Second, they can function in both steps, as is the case of conflicting rules. In that case the presence of a rebutter excludes the operation of the competing rule in the first step, and provides a reason for an incompatible conclusion which decides the matter in the second step.

A second advantage is that the division of arguments in two steps makes it easier to recognise goals as the basis of reasons. We have seen that goals fulfil a role in legal reasoning which is very similar to that of principles. Yet, because goals do not have a structure that resembles that of the material implication, their function in legal reasoning has hardly been recognised in logical theories. Goals simply do not fit in the classical model of arguments.* As soon as the attempt to model legal reasoning as a kind of detachment is given up, there comes room for the logical role of goals. We have seen in Section 32 how RBL can give goals a logical role which is similar to that of principles.

38. Argument-Based Logics

RBL has some important characteristics in common with argument-based logics. Argument-based logics are built on the idea that given a set of premises, there can be a number of arguments which possibly lead to conflicting conclusions. It is also

* Of course, it is always possible to give them a place by adding the necessary premises, or by rewriting them as principles. Cf. Section 8.

possible that one argument has as its conclusion that a subargument of another argument does not hold. In such cases, these arguments are not compatible and they need to be compared in order to determine which argument 'survives'. In the end a number of arguments survive, and the conclusions of these arguments are justified on the basis of the original set of premises. Other arguments are defeated, and their conclusions are not justified. Finally some conflicts of arguments may end undecided, and the conclusions of these arguments so to speak 'hang in the air'.

A recent version of an argument-based logic is the logic proposed in [Prakken and Sartor 1995] (PS-logic for short). RBL and PS-logic can to a large extent be translated into each other. There is, however, one essential difference. RBL takes the notion of a reason as central, which almost automatically leads to the result that the comparison takes place between *sets* of reasons in the form of weighing reasons. Almost all argument-comparison logics compare arguments one by one*, and as a consequence have difficulties if larger sets of reasons (arguments) have to be weighed.

In the following subsections I will compare RBL to PS-logic to show both how similar they are in some respects, and to argue why the reason-based approach is still to be preferred.**

38.1. ARGUMENTS

The central notion in PS-logic is that of an argument. An argument is a tree of rules, where the conclusion of the one rule is one of the conditions of the following rule.‡ Premises are rules without conditions.

Reasons in RBL are comparable to the joint conditions of the last rule in a chain. This means that an argument in PS-logic corresponds to one reason in RBL, with the difference that an argument contains its conclusion, while a reason in RBL does not contain its conclusion yet, although it is known for which conclusion a reason pleads. Take for instance the argument a $\rightarrow$ b $\rightarrow$ c. In RBL-terminology, b would be a reason for c.

In PS-logic there are two kinds of rule conditions, strong and weak ones. Strong conditions are the ones which must be shown to be satisfied to apply the rule. Weak ones are assumed to be satisfied unless their contrary is shown; they are satisfied by default. The weak conditions which are part of an argument, are called the assumptions of this argument.

* By reconstructing an argument, so as to include two or more reasons into one argument, this characteristic of argument-based logics can be circumvented. Reconstruction of arguments to obtain more attractive logical results has some disadvantages, which are discussed extensively in [Hage Reasoning].

** I will omit some technical details which are not essential for the comparison between PS-logic and RBL. This means that the description of PS-logic is not sufficiently precise to evaluate PS-logic on its own. I expect, however, that it is sufficiently precise for the comparison with RBL.

‡ The terminology used here is not that of [Prakken and Sartor 1995], but that of the present paper. However, this should not make an important difference.

In the terminology of PS-logic, one might say that each RBL rule has two weak conditions, namely that the rule is not excluded, and that if there are reasons against the application of the rule, they do not outweigh the reason for application based on the rule's applicability.

38.2. Conflicts of arguments

In PS-logic arguments can conflict. There are two kinds of conflict. One argument is said to *rebut* another argument if the conclusions of the two arguments are complementary. One argument *undercuts* another argument if the conclusion of the former argument is the complement of one of the assumptions of the latter argument. An argument which undercuts or rebuts another argument is said to *attack* that other argument.

In RBL-terminology, two arguments rebut each other if they plead for and against the same conclusion. An argument undercuts another argument, if the conclusion of the former is that some rule which occurs in the latter cannot be applied.

If an argument undercuts another argument, the former is said to *defeat* the latter. In case of two arguments which rebut each other, the *stronger* argument of the two defeats the other one. (If both arguments are equally strong, they both defeat the other argument.) Which argument is the stronger is determined by another argument, which has as its conclusion that some argument is stronger than another argument. This argument with a conclusion concerning the relative strength of other arguments is comparable to weighing information in RBL.

38.3. Three categories of arguments

A conflict between two arguments cannot be solved by looking only at the arguments involved in that conflict. It is possible that some argument A1 is invalidated by an argument A2, and therefore cannot invalidate the argument A3 anymore. A3 'survives' because it is saved from defeat through the help of A2.

This is comparable with the situation in RBL where the reason R1 which pleads for a conclusion C does not have competition from a reason R2 which pleads against C, because the rule which would lead to R2 is excluded.

Because it can only be determined which arguments survive by considering all arguments at once, the definition of justified arguments, the ones which win and justify their conclusions, can only be defined in terms of sets of arguments.

Given a set of rules (including rules without conditions) it is possible to construct a number of arguments. These arguments are divided into three categories, the *justified* ones, the *overruled* ones, and the *defensible* ones.

The justified arguments are those arguments which are not attacked at all, or are only attacked by arguments which are defeated by a(nother) justified argument. The overruled arguments are the ones which are defeated by a justified argument. The defensible arguments are the arguments which are neither justified, nor overruled. In RBL, overruled arguments would not lead to reasons at all.

Defensible arguments would in RBL fall in one of two subcategories. If the unsolved conflict, which makes that the arguments are not justified, belongs to a subargument which leads to a reason, the argument does not generate a reason. If the unsolved conflict concerns the reasons that plead directly for or against the conclusion, the arguments lead to reasons, but the necessary weighing information to decide the collision of reasons is lacking.

Take for instance the following arguments:

A1: $a \rightarrow b \rightarrow c \rightarrow d$
A2: $e \rightarrow {\sim}b \rightarrow f \rightarrow {\sim}d$

A1 is attacked by the argument $e \rightarrow {\sim}b$ and A2 is attacked by the argument $a \rightarrow b$. Assuming that there is no argument that determines whether the argument for or against b is stronger, the arguments A1 and A2 would merely be defensible in PS-logic. In RBL it would be impossible to derive either b or ~b, and consequently the reasons c and f, respectively for and against d, would not be derivable.

If, however, we take the arguments:

A3: $a \rightarrow b$
A4: $e \rightarrow {\sim}b$

the situation becomes different in RBL. We have two reasons, one which pleads for b, and one which pleads against b. Without additional weighing information it is impossible to decide which reason wins.

In both cases PS-logic and RBL lead to the same final conclusion, namely that the final conclusions of the arguments cannot be derived. The constructions used are somewhat different, however.

In the case of justified arguments, PS-logic and RBL are rather similar. A justified argument in PS-logic is one where the chain of reasons that leads to a conclusion is uninterrupted and where the final reason is stronger than any reason against the same conclusion. The main difference with RBL is that in PS-logic a justified argument justifies its conclusion on the basis of one single reason. This reason is stronger than any other reason which pleads in a different direction, but the conclusion is still based on one reason. In RBL, however, every conclusion is based on the weighing of the *sets of reasons* for and against that conclusion. Very often one set will consist of only one reason, and the other set of at most one reason, but this does not subtract from the principle that in RBL it is sets of reasons which determine the conclusions, and not single reasons. As a consequence, the weighing information in RBL deals with sets of reasons, rather than with pairs of reasons.

It would be relatively easy to modify PS-logic so that the relation of strength which now holds between individual arguments, would hold for sets of arguments. With that modification, PS-logic would lead to the same results, and along essentially the same line as RBL.* The only remaining difference would be the way in which arguments are conceptualised. In RBL the notion of a reason takes the central place, and there is a two step-procedure that consists of collecting and weighing reasons. In PS-logic the notion of an argument plays the central role, and the two step-procedure consists of collecting and comparing all arguments. The main differences are first that in RBL reasons are weighed setwise, while in PS-logic arguments are compared individually, and second that the exclusion of rules plays in RBL its role in the first phase of collecting reasons, while in PS-logic it plays its role in the second phase of comparing arguments. The first difference leads to other differences, but can easily be remedied in PS-logic. The second difference makes in the end no difference at all.

38.4. FINAL REMARKS REGARDING THE RELATION BETWEEN PS-LOGIC AND RBL

PS-logic and RBL have a different conceptualisation of arguments, but despite this difference they are rather similar. There is one fundamental difference, namely that PS-logic compares arguments one by one, while RBL weighs reasons setwise. This difference is a natural consequence of the difference in conceptualisation. The notion of a reason almost automatically leads to the idea of weighing, while weighing is not confined to one item pro scale. The notion of an argument, on the contrary, is strongly related to that of a proof. Traditionally a proof guarantees the truth of its conclusion. In a non-monotonic logic, this is not possibly anymore, because there can be arguments for incompatible conclusions. The natural suggestion in that case is that the strongest argument wins, which is precisely the approach adopted in PS-logic.

We have seen in the first part of this paper that reasoning with rules and goals can adequately be modelled by means of reasons that are weighed setwise. The comparison of arguments is less suitable because this approach cannot account for the accrual of reasons that plead for (or against) the same conclusion. That is why a reason-based conceptualisation of legal arguments seems more attractive than an argument-based conceptualisation. It is, however, possible to enhance the argument-based approach to allow setwise comparison of arguments. Then it also becomes possible in argument-based approaches to deal with the weighing of reasons, although the reason-based conceptualisation remains more attractive, precisely because the weighing of sets of reasons is a natural consequence of it.

Some other differences are that PS-logic has a proof-theory, which RBL presently has not, while on the other hand, RBL at this moment has more extensive facilities to reason about rules. I will not discuss these differences here, however.

* This may not be fully correct for some deviant arguments in which rules are used that refer to themselves and to each other. Cf. section 29.2. For those cases, PS-logic might offer a slightly different solution than RBL.

39. Possible Extensions of RBL

In this section I will discuss some possible extensions of RBL. One other extension has already been mentioned in Section 34.3, where general rules for case-based reasoning were presented.

39.1. Reasons for Incompatible Conclusions

Suppose that I receive a postcard from England which was signed by Tracey, and in which she writes me that she spends some weeks with her uncle there. This is a reason to assume that Tracey is in England. Suppose, moreover, that when I spoke Tracey a few weeks ago, she told me that she would leave for Australia and would stay there for a couple of months. This is a reason to assume that Tracey is in Australia.

Strictly spoken, the reasons why Tracey is in England and why she is in Australia have no logical relationship with each other. Still it seems that if I have reason to assume that Tracey is in Australia, this is also a reason to assume that she is not in England, and the other way round. This predicament can be solved by assuming that if two states of affairs are incompatible, a reason why the one state of affairs obtains is ipso facto a reason why the other state of affairs does not obtain:

$$(state\_1)(state\_2)(\texttt{Incompatible}(state\_1,\ state\_2) \rightarrow \\ (\texttt{Reason}(reason,\ state\_1,\ \texttt{pro}) \rightarrow \\ \texttt{Reason}(reason,\ state\_2,\ \texttt{con})))$$

This cannot be turned around to the assumption assuming that if two states of affairs are incompatible, a reason why the one state of affairs does not obtain is a reason why the other state of affairs obtains, because this would commit the fallacy of the excluded middle.

It remains to be specified when two states of affairs are incompatible. The most obvious case is when they are each others opposite:

$$(state\_1)(state\_2) \\ (\Box(State\_1 \equiv \sim State\_2) \rightarrow \texttt{Incompatible}(state\_1,\ state\_2))^{*}$$

For instance, the states of affairs that John is a thief and that he is not a thief are complementary and therefore also incompatible.

The lightest form of incompatibility of two states of affairs is when they happen not to obtain both:

$$(state\_1)(\ state\_2) \\ ((State\_1 \equiv \sim State\_2) \rightarrow \\ \texttt{Incompatible}(state\_1,\ state\_2))$$

A special form of incompatibility deals with the relative weights of sets of reasons:

$$(set\_1)(set\_2)$$

* □ stands here for the traditional operator for logical necessity. Cf. [Chellas 1980, p. 4].

```
Incompatible(
  outweighs(set_1, set_2, conclusion),
  outweighs(set_2, set_1, conclusion)
))
```

Sentences like these about incompatibility and its effects might be added a axioms to RBL.

39.2. Epistemic rules

Some ways to derive rules seem so natural that it may seem strange that these ways to derive rules are not built into RBL. For instance if A is a reason for B, and if B logically entails C, then surely A must be a reason for C. Still, this cannot be derived in pure RBL. From the theory

```
Reason(a, b, pro)
□(B → C)
```

it cannot be derived that

```
Reason(a, c, pro)
```

Analogously, from

```
Valid(rule(r1, a, b))
□(B → C)
```

it is not possible to derive

```
Valid(rule(r2, a, c))
```

Why is this not possible? The answer is that the conclusion of this latter argument is a statement about the validity of a rule. It depends on the domain, under which circumstances a rule is said to be valid, and domain dependent knowledge is not part of RBL. Clearly, in a domain that contains the rule `r1`, there will normally be a reason to adopt the rule `r2`, but this need not be the case. That is why RBL does not allow the inference that leads to the conclusion that rule `r2` can be derived from the given theory.

However, this is not the whole story. If the rules `r1` and `r2` are epistemic rules, it is very attractive* to make it possible to derive

```
Valid(rule(r2, a, c))
```

from

```
Valid(rule(r1, a, b))
□(b → c)
```

To this purpose the following rule might be added to RBL theories, which makes it possible to derive a more specific from a more general rule:

* The reasons why this is so attractive are discussed extensively in [Hage Reasoning].

```
Valid(rule(limited_transitivity_of_epistemic_rules,
  epistemic_rule(rule(r1)) &
    valid(rule(r1, cond, concl1)) &
    □(concl1 → concl2),
  valid(rule(r2, cond, concl2)) ))
```

One can even imagine that the following inference relation between rules is allowed:

```
Valid(rule(extended_transitivity_of_epistemic_rules,
  epistemic_rule(rule(r1)) &
    epistemic_rule(rule(r2)) &
    valid(rule(r1, condition, conclusion1)) &
    valid(rule(r2, conclusion1, conclusion2)),
valid(rule(r3, condition, conclusion2)) )).
```

40. Summary

In this paper I have argued for a particular way of conceptualising legal reasoning and for a logic that is based on this conceptualisation. The picture of legal reasoning defended here has two main characteristics. First it assigns a central place to the notion of a reason, rather than to the notion of an argument. In the line of this, rules, principles and goals are strictly distinguished from statements, which have a different logical role to play. And second, the picture of legal reasoning distinguishes two layers in the law, the interaction of which to a large extent determines the nature of legal arguments.

Not coincidentally, the conceptualisation of legal reasoning as reason-based, with its distinction between rules etc. and statements, makes it easy to deal with the interaction between the two layers of law. On the one hand, normally the applicability of a rule that replaces principles and goals excludes the application of these principles and goals. On the other hand, in exceptional cases, the application of a rule can be blocked by the violation of one of its underlying goals or principles.

Traditional logics, such as first order predicate logic, are not very suitable to deal with legal arguments as they are modelled in the picture of reasoning that is proposed here. That is why I proposed a special logic which assigns a central place to the notion of a reason: Reason-Based Logic. Although RBL is not a special logic for legal reasoning, it was nevertheless developed with the demands of legal reasoning in mind. By means of a number of simple and not so simple examples it was shown how RBL can be used to model familiar patterns of legal reasoning.

Finally some philosophical reflections on the nature of RBL were given, with the threefold purpose to argue why RBL is a logic and not merely a formal description of a model of legal reasoning, to compare RBL with its main competitor, the approach based on the comparison of arguments, and to explain why RBL is not extended with some natural-seeming additions.

Acknowledgements

The author wishes to thank Henry Prakken and Giovanni Sartor for their suggestions and criticisms which have improved this paper. Bart Verheij deserves credit for helping develop the formalism of RBL.

The author thankfully recognises the cooperation of the Maastricht Law Faculty in giving him exemption from part of his teaching tasks during 1993 and 1994.

The research for this paper was partly made possible by a grant of the Dutch Foundation for Knowledge Based Systems.

References

Alexy, R. (1978). *Theorie der juristischen Argumentation*. Suhrkamp Verlag, Frankfurt am Main.

Alexy, R. (1985). *Theorie der Grundrechten*, Nomos Verlagsgesellschaft, Baden-Baden.

Anscombe, G.E.M. (1957). *Intentions*, Blackwell, Oxford.

Ashley, K.D. (1991). Reasoning with cases and hypotheticals in HYPO. *International Journal of Man-Machine Studies* 34, 753–796.

Baker, G.P. (1977). Defeasibility and Meaning. P.M.S. Hacker and J. Raz (eds.) *Law, Morality and Society*. Clarendon Press, Oxford, pp. 26–57.

Chellas, B.F. (1980). *Modal logic; an introduction*. Cambridge University Press, Cambridge e.a.

Copi, I.M. (1978). *Introduction to Logic*. 5th ed. MacMillan Publishing Co., New York.

Dworkin, R. (1978). *Taking Rights Seriously*, 2nd ed., Duckworth, London.

Fuller, L.L. (1958). Positivism and Fidelity to law: A Reply to Professor Hart, *Harvard Law Review* 71, 630–672.

Gordon, Th. F. (1994): The Pleadings Game: An Exercise in Computational Dialectics, *Artificial Intelligence and Law* 2, 239–292.

Hage, J.C. (1991). Monological reason based reasoning. (J.A. Breuker, R.V. de Mulder and J.C. Hage eds.) *Legal Knowledge Based Systems. Model-based reasoning*, Koninklijke Vermande BV, Lelystad, pp. 77–91.

Hage, J.C. (1993). Monological Reason Based Logic. *Proceedings of the Fourth International Conference on Law and Artificial Intelligence*, ACM-press, Amsterdam, pp. 30–39.

Hage, J.C. (1995). Teleological reasoning in reason-based logic. *Proceedings of the Fifth International Conference on Artificial Intelligence and Law*, ACM, New York, pp. 11–20.

Hage, J.C. (Reasoning), *Reasoning with rules*, to be published by Kluwer Academic Publishers in the Law and Philosophy series.

Hage, J.C., R. Leenes, and A. Lodder (1994). Hard cases; a procedural approach. *Artificial Intelligence and Law* 2, 113–167.

Hage, J.C. and H.B. Verheij (1995). Reason-Based Logic: a logic for reasoning with rules and reasons. *Law, Computers and Artificial Intelligence* 3, nrs. 2/3, 171–209.

Hare, R.M. (1952). *The Language of Morals*. Oxford University Press, Oxford.

Hare, R.M. (1963). *Freedom and Reason*, Oxford University Press, Oxford e.a.

Hart, H.L.A. (1961). *The Concept of Law*. Clarendon Press, Oxford.

MacCormick, D.N. (1978). *Legal Reasoning and Legal Theory*, Clarendon Press, Oxford.

MacCormick, D.N. and O. Weinberger (1987), *An Institutional Theory of Law*, Reidel, Dordrecht etc.

MacCormick, D.N. and Summers, R.S. (1991). *Interpreting statutes: a comparitive study*, Darthmouth Publishing Company Limited, Hants and Brookfield.

Peczenik, A. (1989). *On Law and Reason*, Kluwer Academic Publishers, Dordrecht e.a.

Pollock, J.L. (1987). Defeasible Reasoning. *Cognitive Science* 11, 481–518.

Prakken, H. (1993). *Logical tools for modelling legal argument*, Ph.D.-thesis Amsterdam.

Prakken, H. and G. Sartor (1995). On the relation between legal language and legal argument: assumptions, applicability and dynamic priorities, *Proceedings of the Fifth International Conference on Artificial Intelligence and Law*, ACM, New York, pp. 1–10.

Raz, J. (1975). *Practical Reason and Norms*, Hutchinson, London.

Raz. J. (1979). *The Authority of Law; Essays on Law and Morality*, Clarendon Press, Oxford.
Reiter, R. (1980). A logic for default reasoning. *Artificial Intelligence* 13, 81–132.
Sartor G. (1991). The Structure of Norm Conditions and Nonmonotonic Reasoning in Law, *Proc. of the Third International Conference on Artificial Intelligence and Law*, ACM Press, p. 155–164.
Searle, J. (1983). *Intentionality; An essay in the philosophy of mind*, Cambridge University Press.
Searle, J. (1995). *The construction of social reality*. The Free Press, New York.
Soeteman, A. (1989). *Logic in Law. Remarks on Logic and Rationality in Normative Reasoning, Especially in Law*. Kluwer Academic Publishers, Dordrecht e.a.
Soeteman, A.(1991). Hercules aan het werk; over de rol van rechtsbeginselen in het recht. Dolman e.a. (eds.) *Rechtsbeginselen*, Ars Aequi, Nijmegen, pp. 41–56.
Strawson, P. (1971). *Logico Linguistic Papers*, Methuen, London.
Tammelo, I. and Schreiner, H. (1977). *Grundzüge und Grundverfahren der Rechtslogik*, Verlag Dokumentation Saur KG, München.
Toulmin, S.E. (1958). *The Uses of Argument*, Cambridge University Press, London, New York.
Valente, A. (1995). *Legal Knowledge Engineering. A modelling approach*. Thesis. IOS Press, Amsterdam.
Verheij, H.B. and J.C. Hage (1994). Reasoning by analogy; a formal reconstruction. H. Prakken, A.J. Muntjewerff and A. Soeteman (eds.), *Legal knowledge based systems; the relation with legal theory*, Koninklijke Vermande, Lelystad, pp. 65–78.

Artificial Intelligence and Law **4:** 275–296, 1996.

Abstract Argumentation

ROBERT A. KOWALSKI AND FRANCESCA TONI
Department of Computing, Imperial College of Science, Technology and Medicine 180, Queen's Gate, London SW7 2BZ, UK

Received and accepted 5 September 1996

Abstract. In this paper we explore the thesis that the role of argumentation in practical reasoning in general and legal reasoning in particular is to justify the use of defeasible rules to derive a conclusion in preference to the use of other defeasible rules to derive a conflicting conclusion. The defeasibility of rules is expressed by means of non-provability claims as additional conditions of the rules.

We outline an abstract approach to defeasible reasoning and argumentation which includes many existing formalisms, including default logic, extended logic programming, non-monotonic modal logic and auto-epistemic logic, as special cases. We show, in particular, that the 'admissibility' semantics for all these formalisms has a natural argumentation-theoretic interpretation and proof procedure, which seem to correspond well with informal argumentation.

In the admissibility semantics there is only one way for one argument to attack another, namely by undermining one of its non-provability claims. In this paper, we show how other kinds of attack between arguments, specifically how rebuttal and priority attacks, can be reduced to the undermining of non-provability claims.

Key Words: argumentation, default reasoning, priority

1. Introduction

The purpose of this paper is to outline a formal theory of argumentation, which promises to have relevance for practical reasoning in general and for legal reasoning in particular. We will argue that the role of argumentation is to justify the use of certain defeasible rules deriving a conclusion in preference to the use of other defeasible rules deriving conflicting conclusions.

We explore the thesis that defeasible reasoning with rules of the form

P if Q.

can be understood as 'exact' reasoning with rules of the form

P if Q and S can not be shown.

containing one or more defeasible 'non-provability claims' of the form

S can not be shown, for some sentence *S*.

In many cases, the sentence *S* is the 'contrary', *not P*, of the conclusion, *P*, of the rule. In other cases, *S* may state that the rule itself is 'defeated' by another rule.

With this understanding of defeasibility, argumentation is a dialectic process whereby a proponent presents an 'exact' argument for a conclusion, which is based, however, upon defeasible non-provability claims of the form *S can not be shown*. Such a claim, and the argument it helps to support, can be defeated if an opponent undermines the claim by presenting an argument for S. Like the proponent, the opponent can also base her/his argument upon non-provability claims.

The argumentation process can be viewed, therefore, as a game in which the proponent moves first. In the 'credulous' version of the game, which we study in this paper, by moving first, the proponent has the advantage of being able to use his/her previously used claims of non-provability to defeat the opponent's counter-claims. Such credulous argumentation can be used to justify more than one point of view. If the opponent moves first, the opponent can use her/his previously used claims to defeat the proponent. In the 'sceptical' version of the game, which we do not explore in this paper, the proponent can use only undisputed claims of non-provability to defeat the opponent's counter-claims.

A similar view of defeasible reasoning and argumentation has been put forward by several authors, e.g. [Pollock, 1987; Prakken & Sartor, 1996; Gordon, 1993]. Our approach differs, however, in several respects. The most important of these are:

1. Our approach to argumentation focuses on the acceptability of the non-provability claims of an argument, rather than on the acceptability either of the argument or of the conclusion of the argument. This concentrates attention, therefore, on the contentious parts of the argument and avoids being distracted by those parts of the argument that are beyond dispute.
2. We reduce all forms of defeasibility to that of non-provability claims. As a consequence, the only way to defeat an argument is by undermining one of its claims, namely by presenting an argument for a sentence *S* which is claimed to be unprovable. Indirect defeat (also called 'rebutting' [Pollock, 1987; Prakken & Sartor, 1995] or 'reductio-ad-absurdum' [Dung, 1993]), showing that a rule

   P if Q.

   leads to contradiction, is transformed into undermining defeat, by rewriting the rule in the 'exact' form

   P if Q and not P can not be shown.

   making explicit in the conditions of the rule that the contrary, *not P*, of its conclusion, *P*, can not be shown.
3. Our semantics is credulous rather than sceptical. A sceptical semantics can be obtained from credulous semantics by regarding a conclusion as justified if and only if it can be derived from any credulously 'acceptable' set of claims.
4. Our methodology deals with priorities between rules by introducing explicit rule names into the language and adding conditions to the rules expressing that the rules are not defeated by other higher priority rules. This approach avoids the need to deal with priorities in the semantics.

5. Our approach does not require the introduction of a new language or of a new semantics. On the contrary, we base our formalisation upon a variant of an abstract approach to defeasible reasoning [Bondarenko et al., 1996] which has been shown to include many existing formalisms, including (extended) logic programming, default logic [Reiter, 1980], non-monotonic modal logic [McDermott, 1982] and autoepistemic logic [Moore, 1985] as special cases. Thus the approach taken in this paper is abstract and can be formalised in any one of these and other formalisms. Although all these formalisms use the 'stability' semantics, we argue that the 'admissibility' semantics is more adequate.

The paper is organised as follows. In section 2, we illustrate our approach by means of examples, which are used elsewhere in the paper. In section 3, we describe the abstract framework for defeasible reasoning, and present the stability semantics. In section 4, we show how default logic, extended logic programming, non-monotonic modal logic, and auto-epistemic logic can all be considered special cases of the framework. Thus our approach to defeasible reasoning and argumentation can be formulated in any one of these and other formalisms for default reasoning. In section 5, we define the admissibility semantics and its argumentation proof procedure. In section 6, we show how our approach reduces rebutting attacks to undermining attacks. In section 7, we show how the approach reduces priorities to non-provability conditions. In section 8, we conclude.

We assume the reader is already familiar with the general subject of argumentation and its relevance to legal reasoning. In particular, we recommend the article by Prakken and Sartor in this issue [1996] for an overview of related work.

The framework we use in this paper is a variant of one we have developed elsewhere [Bondarenko et al., 1996]. The reader will find formal definitions and results in [Bondarenko et al., 1996]. The main technical contribution of this paper, therefore, is the methodology we present for eliminating rebuttal attacks and priorities from the semantics. The main general contribution is our use of the methodology for argumentation which is abstract and language-independent.

2. Examples°

EXAMPLE 2.1. Consider the following statement of the principle that, by default, a person accused of a crime should be assumed innocent unless the person can be shown to be not innocent.

(1) *A person is innocent of a crime*
if the person is accused of committing the crime
and it can not be shown that the person is not innocent of the crime.[1]

The inclusion in the rule of the explicit non-provability condition transforms a defeasible rule

(1') A *person is innocent of a crime*
if the person is accused of committing the crime.

° These and all other examples in this paper can easily be formalised using the techniques described in [Kowalski, 1995].

[1] We use the phrases '*S can not be shown*' and '*it can not be shown that S*' interchangebly.

which might be subject to argument, into an 'exact' rule, which is beyond dispute. Any dispute about the defeasible rule is transformed, instead, into a dispute about the non-provability condition.

In contrast, the 'exact' rule

(2) *A person is not innocent of a crime*
if the person was observed committing the crime.

does not contain any non-provability conditions and consequently does not represent a defeasible rule.

Suppose now that we are given the fact

(3) *John is accused of theft.*

We can justify the conclusion that John is innocent by the following argument.

> Proponent: *John is innocent of theft,*
> because (although *John is accused of theft*)
> *it can not be shown that John is not innocent of theft.*

The proponent's claim, *it can not be shown that John is not innocent of theft*, is upheld, because the only way to defeat it, by using rule (2), fails to apply, given the lack of any 'fact' ('exact' rule) recording an observation of his having committed the crime. The claim can be defeated, however, if such information becomes available at a later time. It is because of this that such logic is often said to be 'non-monotonic', in contrast to the case in 'monotonic' logic, where once a conclusion is established it continues to hold no matter what further information is added.

Although the two rules, (1) and (2) above, are both 'exact', the inclusion of the extra condition in (1) can be understood as giving the defeasible rule, (1'), that (1) represents, a lower priority than (2). We shall argue more generally, in section 7, that priorities involving defeasible rules can be represented by explicit non-provability conditions of 'exact' rules.

EXAMPLE 2.2. Consider the two defeasible rules

> *A person inherits an estate*
> *if he/she is the beneficiary of a valid will.*

> *A person does not inherit an estate*
> *if he/she murders the owner of the estate.*

and the facts

> *John is the beneficiary of Henry's valid will.*
> *John has murdered Henry.*

Everything else being equal, in a credulous approach to defeasible reasoning, there are two equally 'acceptable' arguments: one concluding that John inherits Henry's estate because he is the beneficiary of Henry's valid will; the other that he does not inherit the estate because he has murdered Henry. In a sceptical approach (which we do not discuss in this paper, but which we do discuss in [Bondarenko et al., 1996]) neither conclusion holds.

In this paper, we will consider two kinds of 'acceptable' arguments, namely 'stable' (section 3) and 'admissible' (section 5). The two arguments above, one concluding that John inherits Henry's estate and the other concluding that he does not inherit the estate, are 'acceptable' in both senses.

In our analysis of defeasibility and argumentation, we justify the credulous reasoning of this example in the following way:

To say that the first two rules are defeasible is to say that they have implicit conditions to the effect that the contrary of their conclusions can not be shown. We make these conditions explicit by rewriting the rules in the 'exact' form

A person inherits an estate
if he/she is the beneficiary of a valid will
and it can not be shown that the person does not inherit the estate.
A person does not inherit an estate
if he/she murders the owner of the estate
and it can not be shown that he/she inherits the estate.

We can now justify the conclusion that John inherits the estate by the following dialogue game.

Proponent: *John inherits the estate,*
because *John is the beneficiary of a valid will*
and because
it can not be shown that John does not inherit the estate.

Opponent: On the contrary,
it can be shown that *John does not inherit the estate*
because *John murdered the owner of the estate*
and because
it can not be shown that John inherits the estate.

Proponent: But, on the contrary,
it can be shown that *John inherits the estate,*
as I have already argued.

The rules of the game are designed to be liberal about the arguments that are 'admissible'. An argument is 'admissible' if its non-provability claims can be defended against any counter-claims of an opponent. By being the first player, the proponent has the advantage of being able to use his/her earlier claims to defeat the opponent's counter-claims. This enables the proponent, in this example, to have the last word and to win the argument. If the opponent is allowed to move first, then the opponent's argument will be equally 'admissible'.

It is also possible to design a conservative version of the game, which is sceptical about what conclusions can be established.

EXAMPLE 2.3. (Adapted from [Prakken & Sartor, 1995])
Consider the following general principle of European Community law:

A product can be sold in a country
if the country is part of the EC
and the product can be sold in another country
and the other country is part of the EC
and it can not be shown that
the selling of the product in the country endangers public health
and it can not be shown that
the selling of the product in the country prejudices the consumer.

This principle potentially conflicts with the following rule of Italian law:

A product can not be sold in Italy
if the product is called 'pasta'
and the product is not made of durum wheat.

The potential conflict becomes real, when we are given only the following facts:

Italy is part of the EC.
BDR is part of the EC.
alpha is sold in BDR.
alpha is called 'pasta'.
alpha is not made of durum wheat.

If the two rules above are understood as 'exact' rules, then it is possible to derive the inconsistent conclusion that *alpha* can be sold in Italy and *alpha* can not be sold in Italy. This derivation is based upon the two non-provability claims of the first rule, neither of which can be undermined, using the given rules and facts.

However, if the two rules are understood as defeasible, then in our methodology for representing defeasibility we would transform them into 'exact' rules by adding extra non-provability conditions to both, rewriting them as:

A product can be sold in a country
if the country is part of the EC
and the product can be sold in another country
and the other country is part of the EC
and it can not be shown that
the selling of the product in the country endangers public health
and it can not be shown that
the selling of the product in the country prejudices the consumer
and it can not be shown that
the product can not be sold in the country.

A product can not be sold in Italy
if the product is called 'pasta'
and the product is not made of durum wheat
and it can not be shown that the product can be sold in the country.

As in example 2.2, it would now be possible to construct two separate 'admissible' arguments, each of which undermines the other, rather than one 'admissible' argument with an inconsistent conclusion.

However, if, as is the case, we want to give higher priority to European Community law than to Italian law, then we would simply retain the original formulation of the European Community law without an extra non-provability condition, following the lead of example 2.1.

Thus, by adding appropriate non-provability conditions to rules, expressing that the contrary of their conclusions can not be shown, we obtain the same result as Prakken and Sartor [1995], who, in addition to using undermining attacks, also employ indirect rebutting attacks and deal with priorities in the semantics. We will see later in section 7 that the treatment of priorities in this example can be seen as an optimised version of a more general approach that can handle more complex priorities, like those of Prakken and Sartor [1995], which can be defined by means of rules. This approach is illustrated by the following example.

EXAMPLE 2.4. (Adapted from [Hage, 1995])
Consider the principles:

> r_1: Except as provided for by r_2, all thieves should be punished.
> r_2: Except as provided for by r_3, thieves who are minors should be rehabilitated and not punished.
> r_3: Any thief who is violent should be punished.

These can be represented by the defeasible rules

> r_1: *A person should be punished*
> *if the person is a thief.*
> r_2: *A person should not be punished*
> *if the person is a thief*
> *and the person is a minor.*
> r_3: *A person should be punished*
> *if the person is a thief*
> *and the person is violent.*

where rule r_3 has higher priority than rule r_2, and r_2 higher priority than rule r_1 ($r_3 > r_2$ and $r_2 > r_1$).

Given the facts

> f_1: *John is a thief.*
> f_2: *John is a minor.*

rules r_1 and r_2 conflict. Intuitively, the priority $r_2 > r_1$ can be used to derive the conclusion *John should not be punished* of the second rule, in preference to the conclusion of the first. If we are given the additional fact

f_3: John is violent.

then rules r_1, r_2 and r_3 now conflict. Intuitively, the priority $r_3 > r_2$ can be used to derive the conclusion *John should be punished* of the third rule.

In the previous example 2.3 we used a simple method to represent defeasible rules as 'exact' rules while taking into account the priorities between them. The method consists of adding non-provability conditions, that the contrary of their conclusions can not be shown, to defeasible rules with lower priority, without adding similar conditions to the higher priority rules. This method can not be used in this example, since rule r_2 has higher priority than rule r_1 but lower priority than rule r_3.

In such an example, we need to distinguish the different ways a conclusion can be established, and add non-provability conditions to defeasible rules with lower priority stating that no higher priority rule applies. In this way, using this more refined methodology, we obtain the following representation of the example.

A person should be punished
if the person is a thief
and it can not be shown that r_1 is defeated for the person.

r_1 is defeated for a person
if the person is a thief
and the person is a minor
and it can not be shown that r_2 is defeated for the person.

A person should not be punished
if the person is a thief
and the person is a minor
and it can not be shown that r_2 is defeated for the person.

r_2 is defeated for a person
if the person is a thief
and the person is violent
and it can not be shown that r_3 is defeated for the person.

A person should be punished
if the person is a thief
and the person is violent
and it can not be shown that r_3 is defeated for the person.

Now, given the facts f_1 and f_2, there is only one 'admissible' argument for the conclusion *John should not be punished*, supported by the non-provability claim *it can not be shown that r_2 is defeated for John*. However, given the facts f_1, f_2 and f_3, there is only one 'admissible' argument for the conclusion *John should be punished*, supported by the non-provability claim *it can not be shown that r_3 is defeated for John*. This argument undermines the conflicting claim *it can not be shown that r_2 is defeated for John*, supporting the conclusion that *John should not be punished*.

3. An Abstract Framework for Representing Defeasibility

All the examples above have been formulated in a form of English which can be represented directly in many existing (and also in many presently uninvestigated) formalisms for default reasoning. Indeed, to formalise such examples, we need only to choose a logic of 'exact' (i.e. monotonic, non-defeasible) reasoning (such as classical first-order logic) and extent it, if necessary, by adding a non-provability operator. We then need to define a semantics and proof theory for the extended language, which appropriately interprets the intended meaning of the non-provability operator. More precisely

1. We assume an underlying **monotonic** (or **exact**) **logic** with a logical connective representing implication (to which modus ponens applies) and a universal quantifier (to which universal quantifier elimination applies).
2. We extend the language of the underlying logic, if necessary, by means of a **non-provability operator**, to express statements of the form.

   S can not be shown

   where *S* names a sentence of the language of the underlying logic. We restrict the occurrence of these non-provability statements to conditions of implications.
3. Defeasible rules can then be represented in the extended language by transforming them into (exact) universally quantified implications with non-provability conditions.
4. Defeasible reasoning from a set *T* (called a **theory**) of sentences in the extended language, is reduced to exact reasoning in the underlying logic, from an extended set of sentences $T \cup N$, where *N* is an 'acceptable' set of non-provability claims of the form

   S cannot be shown.

Since, in most cases[2], the underlying language does not contain non-provability formulae, we have to explain how, in such cases, the underlying logic can be used to derive conclusions from the extended theory $T \cup N$. For this purpose, we assume that sentences in *N* are treated as atomic propositions. We also assume that instantiation can be applied to universally quantified implications representing defeasible rules, obtaining instantiated implications with atomic non-provability conditions. Modus ponens can then be applied to such instantiated implications and sentences in *N*, obtaining sentences of the original underlying language.

It remains to specify, given a theory *T*, when a set of non-provability claims *N* is 'acceptable'. Almost all existing logics for default reasoning solve this problem in the same way, by means of a requirement that *N* be 'stable', i.e.

> A candidate set *N* of sentences of the form *S can not be shown* is said to be **stable** if and only if for every *S* in the underlying language,
> *S can not be shown* is in *N* if and only if
> *S* is not derivable from $T \cup N$ in the underlying logic.

[2] As we will see later, non-monotonic modal logic and autoepistemic logic are exceptions.

Different logics for default reasoning formulate this stability requirement in different ways, which are all, nonetheless, equivalent [Bondarenko et al., 1996].[3]

Despite its being the dominant semantics for default reasoning, stability semantics has a number of drawbacks, the most obvious being that to verify the acceptability of a claim *S can not be shown* necessitates determining an entire stable set N to show that S is not derivable from $T \cup N$. This is computationally infeasible in most interesting cases. There are also cases where a stable set does not exist because of local paradoxical sentences in T, but where an intuitively acceptable argument can be constructed from other parts of T which are not affected by the paradox.

Consider again the theory T consisting of the set of sentences (1), (2) and (3) of example 2.1. Intuitively, the set N consisting of the single sentence

(4) *John is not innocent of theft can not be shown*

is acceptable, because there is no way to show, given only T and N that *John was observed committing theft.*

The conclusion that *John is innocent of theft* then follows from $T \cup N$ in the underlying logic, by instantiating (1), obtaining the variable-free implication

John is innocent of theft
if John is accused of theft
and John is not innocent of theft can not be shown.

and then applying modus ponens, using (3) and (4).

Intuitively, in this example it is unnecessary to consider the set of all sentences unprovable from $T \cup N$ to be convinced that the single sentence in N is unprovable. Similarly, even if T is extended to a much larger set of sentences T', the same argument presented above continues to hold, provided T' does not contain any new sentences which can be used to derive either that *John was observed committing theft* or to derive more directly that *John is not innocent of theft.* Even a paradoxical sentence of the form

P if P can not be shown

in T' need not affect the correctness of the argument.

In section 5, we will show that these drawbacks of the stability semantics can be overcome by means of the more liberal 'admissibility' semantics [Dung, 1993], which has an argumentation-theoretic interpretation, as illustrated informally already in examples 2.1 and 2.2. The 'admissibility' semantics is compatible with stability semantics, in the sense that whenever a stable extension exists it is 'admissible'. Moreover, in many cases an 'admissible' set can be extended to a stable set [Bondarenko et al., 1996].

First, we show how a number of existing formalisms for default reasoning can be understood as instances of the abstract framework.

[3] In non-monotonic modal logic and autoepistemic logic, non-provability sentences not in N may be derivable from $T \cup N$. In such cases, for N to be stable, N must also be **closed** in the sense that it contains all non-provability sentences derivable from $T \cup N$.

4. Special Instances

4.1. DEFAULT LOGIC

1. The underlying logic is first-order classical logic, augmented with domain-specific inference rules. These inference rules can equivalently be formulated as sentences of the form

   P *if* Q_1 *and*... *and* Q_n.

   where $P, Q_1, \ldots, Q_n$ are all first-order formulae of the underlying language, $n \geq 0$, and *if* is a new implication sign, for which the inference rule of modus ponens applies. Notice that in this formulation there are two logical connectives for implication, the new implication symbol and the material implication of classical logic.
   Any variables in these new implications which are not explicitly quantified are implicitly universally quantified, with scope the entire implication. The rule of instantiation applies to such variables.
2. Non-provability is expressed by means of a logical operator, M, where the intended meaning of $M\ P$, where P is a sentence of first-order logic, is that the contrary of P, namely *not* P, can not be shown. $M\ P$ can be interpreted equivalently as expressing that P is consistent.
3. Thus defeasible rules are expressed in default logic by translating them into exact sentences of the form

   P *if* Q_1 *and*... *and* Q_n *and* $M\ P_1$ *and*... *and* $M\ P_m$.

   where $n \geq 0$, $m > 0$ and apparently free variables are implicitly universally quantified. Statements of the form $M\ P$ are interpreted as atoms in the underlying first-order language.
4. The standard semantics of default logic [Reiter, 1980] has been shown [Bondarenko et al., 1996] to be a special case of the stable semantics defined in the previous section for abstract frameworks in general.

4.2. EXTENDED LOGIC PROGRAMMING

1. The underlying language consists of implications of the form

   P *if* Q_1 *and*... *and* Q_n.

   where $P, Q_1, \ldots, Q_n$ are literals, i.e. atomic formulas A or the 'classical' negation *not* A of an atomic formula, $n \geq 0$ and *if* is an implication sign. Variables in implications are implicitly universally quantified with scope the entire implication. The only inference rules are modus ponens for *if* and instantiation for the implicit universal quantifiers.
2. Non-provability is expressed by means of a logical operator, *naf* (negation as failure), where the intended meaning of *naf* P, where P is a literal, is that P can not be shown. Therefore, *naf not* P expresses that the contrary of P can not be shown, i.e. that P is consistent.

3. Thus defeasible rules are expressed in extended logic programming by translating them into exact sentences of the form

   P *if* Q_1 *and... and* Q_n *and naf* P_1 *and... and naf* P_m.

   where $n \geq 0$, $m > 0$ and apparently free variables are implicitly universally quantified. Statements of the form *naf P* are interpreted as atoms in the underlying language.
4. The answer set semantics of extended logic programming [Gelfond & Lifschitz, 1990] has been shown [Bondarenko et al., 1996] to be a special case of the abstract stable semantics, where the theory corresponding to an extended logic program is understood as implicitly containing all implications of the form

   P if Q and not Q.

   where P is any literal and Q is any atomic formula of the underlying language.

Normal logic programs can be understood as extended logic programs without any occurrence of 'classical' negative literals of the form *not P*. Normal logic programming is the minimal language that is an instance of the abstract framework. The stable model semantics of normal logic programming [Gelfond & Lifschitz, 1988] has been shown [Bondarenko et al., 1996] to be a special case of the abstract stable semantics.

As argued in [Kowalski, 1995; Sartor, 1991; Prakken & Sartor, 1995], extended logic programming is better suited for legal knowledge representation than normal logic programming, due to the presence of both 'classical' negation (*not*) and non-provability (*naf*).

4.3. NON-MONOTONIC MODAL LOGIC AND AUTOEPISTEMIC LOGIC

1. In non-monotonic modal logic, the underlying logic can be any modal logic with a modal operator, L, which can be interpreted as representing provability. Clearly, some modal logics are not appropriate for this purpose. However, all modal logics incorporate an inference rule, called necessitation, which sanctions deriving $L\, P$ from P.

   One of the most frequently advocated modal logics for this purpose is K45, which contains the axiom schemata

   (K) $L\,\psi$ *if* $(L\,(\psi$ *if* $\phi)$ *and* $L\,\phi)$.
   (4) $L\,L\,\phi$ *if* $L\,\phi$.
   (5) L *not* $L\,\phi$ *if not* $L\,\phi$

   where *if* is material implication. Non-monotonic modal logic with K45 as underlying logic is equivalent to autoepistemic logic [Shvarts, 1990].
2. The underlying logic is already sufficiently expressive to represent non-provability. Non-provability is represented by means of formulae of the form *not L P*, expressing that P can not be shown. Therefore, *not L not P* expresses that the contrary of P can not be shown, i.e. that P is consistent. The first version of non-monotonic modal logic was defined in terms of a modal operator M, standing for consistency. Obviously, the two modal operators, L and M, are interdefinable.

3. Defeasible rules are expressed in non-monotonic modal logic by translating them into exact sentences of the form

   P *if* $L\ Q_1$ *and... and* $L\ Q_n$ *and not* $L\ P_1$ *and... and not* $L\ P_m$.

   prefixed by explicit universally quantified variables, where $n \geq 0$ and $m > 0$.
4. The fixed point semantics of non-monotonic modal logics [McDermott, 1982] has been shown [Bondarenko et al., 1996] to be a special case of the abstract stable semantics defined in section 3.

Arbitrary non-monotonic modal logics are more expressive than default logic and extended logic programming, because they allow the expression of complex modal sentences, with nested modal operators. However, Konolige [1994] has shown that in propositional K45 any theory T can be reformulated equivalently as a theory in which all sentences have the form

P *if* $L\ Q_1$ *and... and* $L\ Q_n$ *and not* $L\ P_1$ *and... and not* $L\ P_m$.

where the Q_i, P_j and P are non-modal, and $n, m \geq 0$.

5. Admissibility Semantics and Argumentation

Like the stability semantics, the admissibility semantics specifies that a conclusion C follows from a theory T if and only if C follows from $T \cup N$ in the underlying logic, where N is an acceptable set of non-provability claims. However, to be 'admissible', N need only contain enough non-provability claims to derive C, supplemented by sufficiently many additional non-provability claims needed to defend itself against any arguments which attack it.

Thus, the admissibility semantics can be understood in argumentation-theoretic terms. Given a theory T, an **argument** is simply a derivation in the underlying logic of some conclusion C from $T \cup N$, where N is some set of non-provability claims. In such a case, we also say both that N **supports the argument** and that the **argument is based on** N. One argument, based on N', is said to **attack** (or **undermine**) another argument, based on N, if, for some claim *S can not be shown* in N, the first argument derives the conclusion S. In such circumstances, we also say that N' is an (undermining) attack against N and that N' attacks (or undermines) the claim *S can not be shown*.

A candidate set N of non-provability sentences is said to be **admissible** if and only if

for every (undermining) attack N' against N, N attacks $N' - N$.[4]

Thus, an argument is admissible if and only if it is based upon an admissible set of non-provability claims.

Note that the stability semantics can also be understood in argumentation-theoretic terms, i.e. a set of non-provability claims is stable if and only if it does not attack itself and it attacks every non-provability claim it does not contain [Bondarenko et al., 1996].

[4] In non-monotonic modal logic and some other logics, where non-provability sentences not in N may be derivable from $T \cup N$, the sets N and N' in the definition of admissibility should be closed (see footnote 3).

The definition of admissibility is a semantics in the sense that it specifies what is admissible, without indicating how such admissible sets of claims and arguments are to be constructed. For this latter purpose, we have developed an abstract proof procedure [Toni & Kakas, 1995; Dung et al., 1996], which applies to any instance of the framework.

The proof procedure is initiated by a proponent presenting an argument based upon sufficiently many non-provability claims N_0 to derive a desired conclusion C. The proponent then needs to defend N_0 against any attack N'_0 that an opponent might make. For this purpose, the proponent extends N_0 to a possibly larger set N_1 which, for every such attack N'_0 attacks $N'_0 - N_0$. The proponent then similarly needs to defend any new claims in $N_1 - N_0$ against all attacks. The process continues with the proponent generating an increasingly larger set of supporting claims $N_0, N_1, \ldots, N_n$.

The process terminates with a win for the proponent, with $N = N_n$, if N_n successfully counter-attacks all attacks by the opponent on the set of non-provability claims $N_n - N_{n-1}$. It terminates with a win for the opponent, if, for every sequence of moves $N_0, N_1, \ldots, N_n, \ldots$ by the proponent, there is an n for which the opponent has an attack against $N_n - N_{n-1}$ and the proponent has no defence.

The formal definition of the proof procedure and a formal proof of its correctness and completeness, relative to the admissibility semantics, are given in [Dung et al., 1996].

6. Reduction of Rebuttal Attacks to Undermining Attacks

The abstract admissibility semantics and its dialectic proof procedure reduce all attacks to undermining attacks. In contrast, starting from [Pollock, 1987], a number of argumentation-based frameworks [Dung, 1993; Prakken & Sartor, 1995] allow, not only undermining attacks ('ground attacks' in [Dung, 1993]), but also – **rebutting attacks** ('reductio-ad-absurdum attacks' in [Dung, 1993]), between arguments which derive contradictory conclusions.

Examples of such contradictory conclusions are *John is innocent of theft* and *John is not innocent of theft* in example 2.1 and *John inherits Henry's estate* and *John does not inherit Henry's estate* in example 2.2.

Undermining and rebutting attacks do not have equal status: undercutting attacks are stronger than rebutting attacks. Dung [1993] motivates the difference in status between the two kinds of attack by an example (example 1 in [Dung, 1993]) which has the form of the following variant of our example 2.2.

EXAMPLE 6.1. Consider the following two rules:

r_1: *A person inherits an estate*
if he/she is the beneficiary of a valid will
and it can not be shown that r_1 *is defeated for the person.*

r_2: *A person does not inherit an estate*
if he/she has murdered the owner of the estate
and it can not be shown that r_2 *is defeated for the person.*

The additional, third rule

r_1 is defeated for a person
if it can not be shown that r_2 is defeated for that person.

expresses the priority of the second rule (r_2) over the first (r_1). This rule might be justified, for example, by the general principle that no one should benefit from committing a crime. (In the next section, 7, we will show how to obtain this rule by compiling explicit priorities into non-provability claims.)

Suppose that, as in example 2.2, the facts

John is the beneficiary of a will.
John has murdered Henry.

are also given. Consider now the two conflicting arguments

Arg_1, based upon the set N_1 consisting of the single claim
it can not be shown that r_1 is defeated for John,
deriving the conclusion *John inherits an estate*, and

Arg_2, based upon the set N_2 consisting of the single claim
it can not be shown that r_2 is defeated for John,
deriving the conclusion *John does not inherit an estate.*

Arg_1/N_1 and Arg_2/N_2 attack each other via a rebutting attack. In addition, Arg_2/N_2 attacks Arg_1/N_1 via an undermining attack. If undermining attacks were not stronger than rebutting attacks, then the two alternative arguments would be equally admissible, and the priority given by the third rule would fail to be taken into account. Instead, if undermining attacks are stronger than rebutting attacks, then only Arg_2 is admissible.

In our argumentation framework only undercutting attacks are considered. In this example 6.1 we obtain the same intuitively correct result, as the more complicated frameworks, namely that only Arg_2 is admissible, since there is no undermining attack against Arg_2/N_2. On the other hand, Arg_1 is defeated, not by Arg_2, but by the third rule using the claims N_2 upon which Arg_2 is based.

The viability of our reduction of rebutting attacks to undermining attacks depends upon adopting a specific knowledge representation methodology, which introduces explicit non-provability conditions into rules. We will describe the full methodology, taking priorities into account, in the next section.

7. Reduction of Priorities to Non-Provability Conditions

Several authors, in particular Prakken and Sartor [1995] and Dimopoulos and Kakas [1995], have investigated extended logic programming with priority relations between rules. Other authors, such as Brewka [1989], have studied the problem of assigning priorities to default rules more generally. Here, we present a methodology for dealing with priorities by adding extra non-provability conditions to rules, without changing the semantics. This methodology has been illustrated already, in condensed form, in examples 2.4 and 6.1.

For every rule which might be defeated by other rules we introduce a new predicate, which can be understood as naming the rule. The new predicate can also be interpreted as introducing a new concept standing for the way in which the rule establishes its conclusion.

For example, given several rules all of which imply that a particular person is a British citizen, the methodology introduces new predicates for each such rule. These new predicates can be thought of as representing new concepts, such as British citizenship by acquisition at birth, British citizenship by descent, or British citizenship by naturalisation, associated with different rules, all of which imply British citizenship. Arguably, the introduction of such predicates simply enables a more exact statement of the meaning of the originally given rules.

Thus each defeasible rule of the form

P(X) if Q.

where X is a tuple of variables, is rewritten as two exact rules

P(X) if holds(rule(X)).
holds(rule(X)) if Q and defeated(rule(X)) can not be shown.

where *rule(X)* can be understood both as the name of the original rule and as a more precise name for the conclusion of the rule.

Notice that if we do not need to establish separate conclusions of the form *holds(rule(X))*, then the two rules can be condensed into one

P(X) if Q and defeated(rule(X)) can not be shown.

as in examples 2.4 and 6.1.

A rule is defeated if there is a conflicting rule which holds and has higher priority:

defeated $(R_1(X))$
  if $R_2(Y) > R_1(X)$
  and conflicting$(R_1(X), R_2(Y))$
  and holds$(R_2(Y))$.

The priority relation can be defined by means of facts or by means of rules such as

$r_1(X) > r_2(Y)$ *if R.*

Similarly, the predicate *conflicting* can be defined by means of facts or by means of rules such as

conflicting$(R_1(X), R_2(X))$
  if conclusion$(R_1(X), P(X))$
  and conclusion$(R_2(X), \text{not } P(X))$

conflicting$(R_1(X, Y), R_2(X, Y))$
if conclusion$(R_1(X, Y), R_3(X) > R_4(Y))$
and conclusion$(R_2(X, Y), R_4(Y) > R_3(X))$.

where *conclusion*(R, P) holds when R is a rule of the form P *if* Q.

Notice that, given two rules

$r_1(X)$: *P if Q.*
$r_2(X)$: *not P if R.*

with priority

$r_2(X) > r_1(X)$

the definition of defeated can be simplified to

defeated$(r_1(X))$ *if R and defeated*$(r_2(X))$ *can not be shown.*

as in examples 2.4 and 6.1.

Our treatment of priority is illustrated by the following example, adapted from [Prakken & Sartor, 1995].

EXAMPLE 7.1.
Consider the following set of defeasible rules, including priority defining rules, before our transformation:

$r_1(X)$: *X's exterior may not be modified if X is a protected building.*
$r_2(X)$: *X's exterior may be modified if X needs restructuring.*
$r_3(X, Y)$: $R_1(X) > R_2(Y)$ *if* $R_1(X)$ *concerns artistic buildings*
and $R_2(Y)$ *concerns town planning.*
$T(X, Y)$: $R_1(X) > R_2(Y)$ *if* $R_1(X)$ *is later than* $R_2(Y)$.

and the following facts/exact rules:

$r_1(X)$ *concerns artistic buildings.*
$r_2(X)$ *concerns town planning.*
$r_2(X)$ *is later than* $r_1(X)$.
$r_3(X, Y)$ *is later than* $T(X, Y)$.

villa is a protected building.
villa needs restructuring.

After the transformation, and after simplifying the transformed rules by eliminating (using modus ponens) conditions that match the facts, we obtain

villa's exterior may not be modified if holds$(r_1(villa))$.

villa's exterior may be modified if holds$(r_2(villa))$.

$r_1(villa) > r_2(villa)$ *if holds*$(r_3(villa, villa))$.

r_2(villa) > r_1(villa) if holds(T(villa, villa)).

r_3(X, Y) > T(X, Y) if holds(T((X, Y), (X, Y))).

holds(r_1(villa)) if defeated(r_1(villa)) can not be shown.

holds(r_2(villa)) if defeated(r_2(villa)) can not be shown.

holds(r_3(villa, villa)) if defeated(r_3(villa, villa)) can not be shown.

holds(T(villa, villa)) if defeated(T(villa, villa)) can not be shown.

holds(T((X, Y), (X, Y))) if defeated(T((X, Y), (X, Y))) can not be shown.

Using these rules, the definition of *defeated* can be simplified first to

defeated(r_1(villa)) if holds(r_2(villa)) and holds(T(villa, villa)).

defeated(r_2(villa)) if holds(r_1(villa)) and holds(r_3(villa, villa)).

defeated(T(villa, villa)) if holds(r_3(villa, villa))
and holds(T((villa, villa), (villa, villa))).

After further simplification, eliminating the predicate *holds*, the original problem reduces to:

villa's exterior may not be modified
if defeated(r_1(villa)) can not be shown.
villa's exterior may be modified
if defeated(r_2(villa)) can not be shown.
defeated(r_1(villa))
if defeated(T(villa, villa)) can not be shown
and defeated(r_2(villa)) can not be shown.
defeated(r_2(villa))
if defeated(r_3(villa, villa)) can not be shown
and defeated(r_1(villa)) can not be shown.
defeated(T(villa, villa))
if defeated(T((villa, villa), (villa, villa))) can not be shown
and defeated(r_3(villa, villa)) can not be shown.

We can now justify the conclusion that *villa's exterior may not be modified* by the following dialogue game.

Proponent: *villa's exterior may not be modified*
because *defeated(r_1(villa)) can not be shown.*

Opponent: On the contrary, *defeated(r_1(villa))* can be shown
because *defeated(T(villa, villa)) can not be shown*
and because *defeated(r_2(villa)) can not be shown.*

Proponent: But, on the contrary, *defeated(r_2(villa))* can be shown

because *defeated*(r_3(*villa, villa*)) *can not be shown*
and because *defeated*(r_1(*villa*)) *can not be shown*,
as I have already argued.

Alternatively, *defeated(T(villa, villa))* can be shown
because
defeated(T((villa, villa), (villa, villa))) can not be shown
and because *defeated*(r_3(*villa, villa*)) *can not be shown*.

Note that the proponent has two alternative ways to defeat the opponent. The second argument is 'more conclusive' than the first because it does not rely on its own claims to defeat the opponent. This argument can also be shown to be justified via a sceptical semantics as defined in [Bondarenko et al., 1996].

The general methodology presented in this section applies also to the case of rules having contradictory conclusions where priorities are not given explicitly, as in example 2.2. In such cases, we treat each rule as having higher priority than every other rule with a contradictory conclusion. Applying the general transformation and simplifying the transformed rules in the manner of the discussion of this section, we obtain the same result as that illustrated in example 2.2.

For example, given the two defeasible rules

P(X) if Q.
not P(X) if R.

with contradictory conclusions, the general transformation introduces rule names, say $r_1(X)$ and $r_2(X)$, for the two rules and replaces the defeasible rules by four exact rules

P(X) if holds($r_1(X)$).
holds($r_1(X)$) *if Q and defeated*($r_1(X)$) *can not be shown.*
not P(X) if holds($r_2(X)$).
holds($r_2(X)$) *if R and defeated*($r_2(X)$) *can not be shown.*

Using the two priorities

$r_1(X) > r_2(X)$.
$r_2(X) > r_1(X)$.

the definition of *defeated* simplifies to

defeated($r_1(X)$) *if holds*($r_2(X)$).
defeated($r_2(X)$) *if holds*($r_1(X)$).

Further simplifying, by removing some of the *holds* conditions, we obtain

P(X) if Q and defeated($r_1(X)$) *can not be shown.*
holds($r_1(X)$) *if Q and defeated*($r_1(X)$) *can not be shown.*
not P(X) if R and defeated($r_2(X)$) *can not be shown.*

holds(r_2(X)) if R and defeated(r_2(X)) can not be shown.
defeated(r_1(X)) if holds(r_2(X)).
defeated(r_2(X)) if holds(r_1(X)).

But now the conclusions *holds(r_1(X))* and *P(X)* are interchangeable, as are *holds(r_2(X))* and *not P(X)*. Therefore, rewriting *holds(r_1(X))* as *P(X)* and *holds(r_2(X))* as not *P(X)*, we obtain

P(X) if Q and defeated(r_1(X)) can not be shown.
not P(X) if R and defeated(r_2(X)) can not be shown.
defeated(r_1(X)) if not P(X).
defeated(r_2(X)) if P(X).

Eliminating the predicate *defeated* gives

P(X) if Q and not P(X) can not be shown.
not P(X) if R and P(X) can not be shown.

which is exactly the result of the simplified transformation needed to convert defeasible rules into exact rules, when no priorities are explicitly given. This simplification can be generalised to the general case where there are several rules having conclusion *P(X)* or *not P(X)*.

In all the examples considered up until now, we obtain the same results as those obtained by Prakken and Sartor [1995] (but we employ a credulous semantics while they employ a sceptical one). In general, however, our treatment of priorities gives different results from those of Prakken and Sartor [1995], as illustrated by the following example.

EXAMPLE 7.2. (Taken from [Prakken and Sartor, 1995])
Consider the defeasible rules

r_1: *A.*
r_2: B *if A.*
r_3: *not A if B can not be shown.*

with $r_3 > r_1$. Then, according to [Prakken and Sartor, 1995], the derivation consisting of r_1 and r_2 is a justified argument, while the derivation consisting of r_3 and the claim *B can not be shown* is not justified. Therefore, they derive *A* but not *not A*. Instead, our method produces three admissible arguments:

Arg_1 concluding *A*,
based upon the set of claims N_1 consisting of
defeated(r_1) can not be shown and *defeated(r_2) can not be shown*,

Arg_2 concluding *not A*,
based upon the set of claims N_2 consisting of
B can not be shown and *defeated(r_3) can not be shown*,

Arg_3 concluding *not A*,
based upon the set of claims N_3 consisting of
B can not be shown, defeated(r_3) *can not be shown* and
defeated(r_2) *can not be shown*.

Note that our approach takes into account the given priority, while their approach does not.

8. Conclusion

We have argued that our abstract framework for defeasible reasoning, with the admissibility semantics and its dialectic proof procedure, is adequate for the formalisation of many aspects of practical reasoning. We have outlined a methodology for transforming inexact, defeasible rules into exact rules with explicit non-provability conditions; and we have argued that this transformation eliminates the need for rebuttal attacks and for dealing with priorities in the semantics. Our transformation is an elaboration of transformations [Kowalski & Sadri, 1990; Toni & Kowalski, 1995] we have developed earlier.

Because our approach is abstract, it can be formalised in any one of the many formalisms, including default logic, extended logic programming, non-monotonic modal logic, and auto-epistemic logic, which are special cases of our framework.

It needs to be noted, however, that our representation of priorities uses metapredicates, such as 'holds' and 'defeated', in the manner of meta-logic programming. In this respect, our approach bears many resemblances to that of Hage [1995], who uses similar meta-predicates. However, his approach differs form ours in his introduction of a new formalism for this purpose, while our approach can be employed with many existing formalisms. Moreover, as we saw in several examples and in one general case, in our simple use of them, these meta-predicates can generally be eliminated in favour of simpler non-provability conditions.

In this paper, we focussed entirely on the credulous admissibility semantics. However, as has been shown elsewhere [Bondarenko et al., 1996], the abstract framework also admits sceptical semantics and proof procedures.

Although we have given several examples to show how our methodology eliminates the need for rebuttal attacks and for dealing with priorities in the semantics, we do not have any formal results proving that the methodology is always adequate. This remains to be done for future work.

Acknowledgements

This research was partially supported by Fujitsu Research Laboratories. The authors are grateful to Phan Minh Dung and Henry Prakken for many helpful discussions, and to the referees and Henry Prakken for helpful suggestions.

References

A. Bondarenko, P. M. Dung, R. A. Kowalski, F. Toni (1996) An abstract, argumentation-theoretic framework for default reasoning. To appear in *Artificial Intelligence*, Elsevier.

G. Brewka (1989) Preferred subtheories: an extended logical framework for default reasoning. *Proceedings of the 11th International Joint Conference on Artificial Intelligence*, Detroit, Mi Morgan Kaufmann (N. Sridharan, ed.) 1043–1048

Y. Dimopoulos, A. C. Kakas (1995) Logic programming without negation as failure. *Proceedings of the International Logic Programming Symposium*, Portland, Oregon MIT Press (J. Lloyd, ed.) 369–384

P. M. Dung (1993) The acceptability of arguments and its fundamental role in non-monotonic reasoning and logic programming. *Proceedings of the 13th International Joint Conference on Artificial Intelligence*, Chambery, France Morgan Kaufmann (R. Bajcsy, ed.) 852–857

Dung, P. M. (1993) An argumentation semantics for logic programming with explicit negation. *Proceedings of the 10th International Conference on Logic Programming*. Paris MIT Press (K. Furukawa, ed.)

P. M. Dung, R. A. Kowalski, F. Toni (1996) Argumentation-theoretic proof procedures for non-monotonic reasoning. *Proc. 6th Logic Programming Synthesis and Transformation* (J. Gallagher ed.)

M. Gelfond, V. Lifschitz (1988) The stable model semantics for logic programming. *Proceedings of the 5th International Conference on Logic Programming*, Washington, Seattle MIT Press (K. Bowen and R. A. Kowalski, eds.) 1070–1080

M. Gelfond, V. Lifschitz (1990) Logic programs with classical negation. *Proceedings of the 7th International Conference on Logic Programming*, Jerusalem MIT Press (D. H. D. Warren and P. Szeredi, eds.) 579–597

T. F. Gordon (1993) The pleadings game: an exercise in computational dialectics, *Artificial Intelligence and Law* 2(4), Kluwer Academic Publishers 239–292

J. Hage (1995) Teleological reasoning in reason-based logic. *Proceedings of the 5th International Conference on Artificial Intelligence and Law*, College Park, MD ACM Press, 11–20

K. Konolige (1994) Autoepistemic logic. *Handbook of Logic in Artificial Intelligence and Logic Programming* 3, Oxford University Press (D. Gabbay, C. Hogger, J. A. Robinson, eds.)

R. A. Kowalski (1995) Legislation as logic programs. *Informatics and the Foundations of Legal Reasoning*, Kluwer Academic Publishers (Z. Bankowski et al., eds.) 325–356

Kowalski, R. A., Sadri, F. (1990) Logic programs with exceptions. *Proceedings of the 7th International Conference on Logic Programming*, Jerusalem MIT Press (D. H. D. Warren and P. Szeredi, eds.) 598–613

D. McDermott (1982) Nonmonotonic logic II: non-monotonic modal theories. *Journal of ACM* 29(1) 33–57

R. Moore (1985) Semantical considerations on non-monotonic logic. *Artificial Intelligence* 25, Elsevier 75–94

J. L. Pollock (1987) Defeasible reasoning. *Cognitive Science*, 11 481–518

H. Prakken, G. Sartor (1995) On the relation between legal language and legal argument: assumptions, applicability and dynamic priorities. *Proceedings of the 5th International Conference on Artificial Intelligence and Law* College Park, MD ACM Press, 1–10

H. Prakken, G. Sartor (1996) A dialectical model of assessing conflicting arguments in legal reasoning. In this issue.

R. Reiter (1980) A logic for default reasoning. *Artificial Intelligence* 13, Elsevier 81–132

G. Sartor (1991) The structure of norm conditions and non-monotonic reasoning in law. *Proceedings of the 3th International Conference on Artificial Intelligence and Law*, Oxford ACM Press, 155–164

G. Shvarts (1990) Autoepistemic modal logics. *Proc. 3rd Conference on Theoretical Aspects of Rationality and Knowledge*, Pacific Grove, CA Morgan Kaufmann (R. Parikh, ed.) 97–110

F. Toni, A. C. Kakas (1995) Computing the acceptability semantics. *Proceedings of the 3rd International Workshop on Logic Programming and Non-monotonic Reasoning*, Springer Verlag LNAI 928 (V. Marek, A. Nerode, M. Truszczynski, eds.) 401–415

F. Toni, R. A. Kowalski (1995) Reduction of abductive logic programs to normal logic programs. *Proceedings of the 12th International Conference on Logic Programming*, Japan MIT Press (Leon Sterling, ed.) 367–381

Artificial Intelligence and Law **4:** 297–329, 1996.

Jumps and Logic in the Law

What Can One Expect from Logical Models of Legal Argumentation?

ALEKSANDER PECZENIK
Juridiska Institutionen, Juridicum, Universitetet i Lund, Box 207, 22100 Lund, Sweden

Abstract. The main stream of legal theory tends to incorporate unwritten principles into the law. Weighing of principles plays a great role in legal argumentation, inter alia in statutory interpretation. A weighing and balancing of principles and other prima facie reasons is a jump. The inference is not conclusive.

To deal with defeasibility and weighing, a jurist needs both the belief-revision logic and the nonmonotonic logic. The systems of nonmonotonic logic included in the present volume provide logical tools enabling one to speak precisely about various kinds of "rules about rules", dealing with such things as applicability of rules, what is assumed by rules, priority between rules and the burden of proof. Nonmonotonic logic is an example of an extension of the domain of logic. But the more far-reaching the extension is, the greater problems it meets. It seems impossible to make logical reconstruction of the totality of legal argumentation.

The lawyers' search for reasons has no obvious end point. Ideally, the search for reasons may end when one arrives at a coherent totality of knowledge. In other words, coherence is the termination condition of reasoning. Both scientific knowledge and knowledge of legal and moral norms progresses by trial and error, and that one must resort to a certain convention to define what "error" means. The main difference is, however, that conventions of science are much more precise than those of legal scholarship.

Consequently, determination of "error" in legal science is often holistic and circular. The reasons determining that a legal theory is "erroneous" are not more certain than the contested theory itself. A strict and formal logical analysis cannot give us the full grasp of legal rationality. A weaker logical theory, allowing for nonmonotonic steps, comes closer, at the expense of an inevitable loss of computational efficiency. Coherentist epistemology grasps even more of this rationality, at the expense of a loss of preciseness.

Key words: coherence, defeasibility, nonmonotonic logic, principles, weighing

1. Introductory Remarks

The present author has in many years worked with legal reasoning from the internal point of view of a jurist. A lesson derived from this work is that orthodox logical analysis leaves out many problems the lawyers perceive as important. Another lesson is that clear-cut philosophical positions tend to fit rather badly into a jurist's intuitions. For example, neither consistent emotivism nor consistent value-objectivism are able to make sense of the everyday juristic talk. For legal evaluations are obviously something more than mere expression of a subject's emotions, yet they are so to say less objective than statements of fact. The solution the author finds the best one (or more correctly, the least objectionable) need not be restated here. Let it suffice to say that the keywords are weighing and coherence. But a reconstruction of legal argumentation from a jurist's point of view faces a risk of amateurism. It is a well-known fact that law professors tend to have their own philosophy, psychology, sociology, and what not, more or less reasonable but certainly not professionally sophisticated. A medicine against this deficiency is to attempt at finding a link between jurisprudential analysis and contributions of professional logic and philosophy. Not that the former should be a slave of the latter ones. For example, only a confusion results from mechanical application of recent philosophical fashion to the law. Rather, one must start from the law, go into philosophy and then go back to the law. For the present author, two such excursions seem most promising: coherentist epistemology and artificial-intelligence research. Hence this paper.

I am grateful to Henry Prakken and Giovanni Sartor for valuable comments to the present paper. The comments resulted in very important improvements of the text.

2. Legal Principles

Most present-day law-theorists are not extreme legal positivists; this means, that they no longer reduce the law to enacted rules. The main stream of legal theory tends instead to follow such philosophers as *Ronald Dworkin* and *Robert Alexy* and to incorporate unwritten principles into the law. Each legal rule may be presented as a result of a weighing and balancing of principles, performed by the lawgiver. Moreover, weighing of principles plays a great role in legal argumentation, inter alia in statutory interpretation. A principle in the sense used in this context, let me call it a value-principle, establishes an ideal. The ideal can be carried into effect to a certain degree, more or less. Each principle expresses a value (cf. Alexy 1985, 133). The principles make the law coherent (cf., e.g., MacCormick 1984, 235 ff.). Similarly, Hage's paper included in the present issue (Section 2) develops "a picture of the law which focuses on two layers. In the first layer . . . more fundamental . . . the law consists of a number of principles and goals . . . The second layer consists of legal rules . . . Normally, the content of these rules reflect the relevant factors that are identified by legal rules and principles". Furthermore, if one intends to say what ought to be done – without exclusive reliance upon authority – one must pay attention to all relevant *moral* principles (cf. Alexy 1992, 128) and values.

> For Alexy, principles correspond closely to values. Indeed they express values in a normative manner. But other ways of see the relationship of values and principles are also plausible. Hage (1997, III.10) disagrees with Alexy, and makes an interesting contrast between principles on the one hand and goals on the other hand: apart of another difference which I am ignoring here, "the second difference is that that a goal by itself does not make it clear for which conclusion it generates reasons. The nemo plus-principle, for example, will

always generate reasons for the conclusion that somebody does not obtain a particular right. The goal to protect the economically weak by itself does not indicate for which actions it will generate reasons ... (V)alues are also a kind of goals, just as interests.

Not surprisingly, Hage's view can be contested, too. One can say that the goal to protect the weak does indicate an action, to protect the weak. What Hage has in mind must be that this action is described too vaguely. But no principle indicates an action described 100% precisely either. It is a matter of degree: principles are more precise from a point of view (which one??) than goals and values.

Fortunately, this controversy does not matter in our context, because weighing such principles as nemo plus and weighing goals face similar logical problems.

3. The Idea of "Prima Facie"

The principles and general value judgements do not stipulate *definitively* that an action ought to be performed. They are only moral reasons; they have the *prima facie* character. They do not determine definitive moral duties; the latter must result from weighing and balancing of all morally relevant general values, principles and rules in the particular case (cf. Peczenik 1995, 444 ff. and 484 ff., to some extent inspired by Ross 1930, 27 ff.). The definitive moral duty results from a weighing and balancing between many such reasons.

A difficult problem concerns the possibility of priority orders among principles. Priority orders vary from case to case, as a result of contextual weighing. When principles collide, the relevant question is not, What principle is to be eliminated from the system?, but, How to optimise both principles within the system? The only possible answer is to establish definitive priority relations in a particular case and prima facie priority orders of general principles (cf. Alexy 1985, 516 ff.; Alexy 1985b, 25 ff. and Alexy 1993 *passim*). A definitive duty is thus a duty based on weighing and balancing of "all relevant things", "an all-things-considered duty" (cf. Peczenik 1989, 76–77). The weighing is contextual, i.e. depending on the total context of the discussed (actual or hypothetical) case, including all applicable moral considerations. *Ceteris paribus*, a definitive weighing and balancing is better, the greater number of relevant *prima facie* reasons is considered. In such a weighing, the weight of any considered reason is affected by all the other reasons.

The idea of "*prima facie*" is most often used in moral theory. But it is applicable in general epistemology, as well. For example, common sense provides *prima facie* justification for certain sorts of beliefs when one is in certain mental states. We are justified in accepting that things are the way they look when there is no reason to think that something has gone wrong. But if there is such a reason, justification is "defeated". Thus justification is fallible, defeasible (cf., e.g., Chisholm 1966, 48). The leading advocate of "semantic foundationalism",

John Pollock (1986, 147) states, similarly to Chisholm, that it is part of the meaning of the word "red" that "x's looking red to S is a *prima facie* reason for S to believe that it is red."

4. "Jumps" in the Law

A weighing and balancing of *prima facie* reasons is a jump: one has premises, the conclusion and a gap between. The inference is not conclusive. One performs a weighing of reasons, in spite of not having a precise knowledge as to how much they do "weigh".

In legal argumentation, such jumps occur in various contexts (cf. Peczenik 1989, 284 ff.). Not all of them concern outright weighing of values. Sometimes it is difficult to tell what is weighed, or even if there is a weighing involved in the jump.

A good example is a legal *interpretative* jump which occurs, when one through a jump derives conclusions concerning interpretation of a norm from a set of premises containing a statement about the wording of a source of the law, e.g., a statute or a precedent. Such jumps result in legal interpretative transformations. The lawyer transforms knowledge of the wording of the sources of the law into knowledge of interpreted law. Interpretation involves weighing of reasons, including moral ones.

The jump into the law, from the criteria of law to legal validity, is more difficult to detect, yet important for a legal philosopher. The jump results in what I have called the transformation into the law. The legal mind transforms knowledge of some simpler facts into cognition of valid law. Metaphorically speaking, it transforms these facts into valid law. From the psychological point of view, there is no doubt that the lawyers spontaneously, without argumentation, recognise a normative system as a system of socially established law. From a normative point of view (in the context of justification) one can, nevertheless, ask the lawyer why he does it. The concept of valid law is not fully precise. Upon reflection, one can proffer reasons for and against the conclusion that a certain normative system is valid law and thus ought to be observed.

More precisely, one may state that the following facts, *inter alia*, constitute such criteria of law.

Some facts concern the content of the norms. A legal system consists of several levels; a certain norm is valid if it was created in accordance with a norm of a higher level. A legal system includes not only norms of conduct but also constitutive rules which enable us to speak about institutional facts, such as contracts, promises, marriage, citizenship etc. A legal system includes some norms claiming, what follows: the law is the supreme system of norms in the society; it has the sole right to authorise exercise of physical force in its territory; it has authority to regulate any type of behaviour.

Other facts concern various kinds of action. A legal system includes certain norms intentionally created by a complex of various actions jointly constituting the legislation process. A legal system is highly efficacious in the following sense. The most important norms of conduct belonging to it are always or nearly always observed in the practice of ordinary people, performing everyday actions like buying, paying taxes, marrying, etc.; other norms of conduct included in this system are by and large thus observed; most of them are at least not systematically violated. A legal system is also highly efficacious another sense. Some important norms of conduct belonging to it are always or nearly always observed in the practice of officials, thus applying them to affect actions of others. Some of the officials, e.g. judges, prosecutors, police, execution officers etc., participate in the exercise of a legally authorised force. The law is often published and applied openly; it is also frequently interpreted by professional lawyers, using established and noticeably advanced methods and doctrines.

Moreover, it is plausible to assume that a system of valid law may not be too immoral, since it is morally better for a society to allow an individual to decide all cases according to his moral judgement than to establish a normative order that too often leads to morally wrong decisions. Assume now, that the "legal" system in question contains very many extremely immoral provisions. It is plausible to assume that this "legal" system is not even a *prima facie* valid law.

In uncontroversial cases, like the present Swedish law, the legal system in question fulfils all of these criteria. In borderline cases, some criteria are fulfilled, others are fulfilled to a small degree only, or perhaps not at all, and a weighing becomes necessary to answer the question whether one has to do with a system of valid law. For example, was the normative system of Pol Pots Cambodia valid law in spite of its grave immorality? Or is the normative system of Liberia valid law in spite of its inefficiency?

5. Derogation and Belief Revision

Jumps are relatively less problematic when they are enthymemes. A gap in the argumentation can then be filled up by an additional premise. After such an addition is performed, the inference becomes deductively correct. Jumps are, however, more problematic when they result in changes of the originally assumed premises.

> "Relatively less problematic" does not mean "unproblematic". In fact, there is the need of moving from deduction to argumentation because we do not find a ready set of consistent and certain premises allowing us to deduce our conclusion. This is obvious when our premises are inconsistent since in this case deduction would lead us to every arbitrary conclusion. Furthermore, when our set of incontrovertible premises is insufficient to establish the desired conclusion, the logic alone does not prevent us from keeping into consideration every plausible new relevant premise which may fill the gap. In this way, we obtain again inconsistency. Therefore logic is not enough while facing jumps (both when the jump is determined by an excess and by a lack of premises): we

need to make and justify choices among inconsistent premises (or inconsistent arguments).

To be sure, change of normative systems has been analysed by ordinary (monotonic) logical means. Mention must be made here of Carlos Alchourrón's and David Makinson's already classical works.

> Alchourrón and Makinson (1982) have analysed precisely defined functions, serving as reasonable approximations of the intuitive processes of contraction and revision of theories and normative codes. The authors distinguish two natural ways in which one might try to define functions to serve as formal analogues to the process of contraction: by intersection ("meet") and by choice. The authors show that meet contraction and revision throw out far too much to be of interest for the representation of the intuitive processes, thus leaving us with sets that are too small. On the other hand, choice contraction or revision leaves us with a set that must in general be considered as too large (p. 19). The authors explain these difficulties by the fact that the propositions in the analysed theory A will in general not be all of equal epistemological status, and that some tend to be used as reasons for others (p. 20). Thus, they admit that there are severe limitations on the use of choice contraction and revision. They show, however, that these functions are useful as applied to irredundant bases of theories. They suggest further that when applied to bases that are "close to irredundant" these functions serve as "reasonable approximations" to the intuitive processes of contraction and revision (p. 21). The authors thus work with irredundant axiomatic bases of theories and use a monotonic logic.
>
> Moreover, subsequent contributions of Alchourrón Makinson and Gärdenfors have allowed them to overcome some of the difficulties unsolved in their paper of 1982. For example in their contribution of 1985, they show how they can build partial meet contractions, in which the result of the contraction is defined as the intersection of just the best alternative theories not implying the contracted conclusion (the result is therefore an intermediate step between meet contraction and choice contraction).

Such an approach is a suitable means to formulate consequences of a derogation, a removal of a rule from the system. However, it is not of much help when one has to analyse consequences of a changed weight of rules which stay in the system. The authors simply assume that the "wrong" statements must be thrown away. This does not allow for their subsequent reinstatement, when the weigh changes. This is not an adequate reconstruction of legal argumentation. When facing a contradiction of valid legal rules, a lawyer often feels compelled to keep the inconsistent premises while modifying the status of the arguments which can be built with them. For example, a judge may recognise inconsistency of the "wording" of statutory provisions and then go beyond this wording and propose an interpretation which avoids inconsistency. Although such an interpretation may gain wide approval, the inconsistent provisions will stay in the statute until the legislator changes it.

6. Nonmonotonic Logic as a Theory of Default Argumentation

To deal with defeasibility and weighing, one may use a nonmonotonic logic. Nonmonotonic logic is an example of the trend to enlarge of the area of application of logic (cf., e.g., von Wright's remarks, 1957, vii: "Logic, so to speak, has a wider reach then truth"). Hage (this issue, p. 262) thus discusses the question whether his "RBL is really a logic, rather than a formalisation of a model of legal argumentation in terms of FOPL". He subscribes to Quine's view that there is no clear boundary between logic and in particular those parts of domain theory that are 'farthest from observation'. Then, he concludes, what follows: "An argument is said to be deductively valid if it is not possible that the premises of the argument are true, while the conclusion of the argument is false ... The standard of deductive logic has turned out to be too specifically casted for arguments which are not based on rules ... As an alternative I propose the following standard: An argument from a set of premises to a conclusion is good, and the conclusion of such an argument is justified, if the reasons that can be based on the premises which plead for the conclusion outweigh the reasons that can be based on the premises and which plead against the conclusion". This is a very good program, indeed.

The "nonmonotonicity of a logic means that the addition of new information to a theory can make sentences underivable which used to be derivable on the basis of the smaller theory" (Hage, this issue, 199, second note). Notice that the old information is not removed, it stays in the theory. In a nonmonotonic logic, an extension of the set of premises can lead to a contraction of the set of conclusions. One sees clearly that nonmonotonic logic does not deal with truth, only with justification. For example, the locution "before the extension, the old theory made p justified, after the addition p is no longer justified" sounds plausible, but "before the addition, the old theory made p true, after the addition p is no longer true" is not plausible. The essential point is that the premises are defeasible. "Nonmonotonicity, or defeasibility, arises from the fact that arguments can be defeated by stronger counterarguments" (Prakken and Sartor). The new ones defeat some old ones. In a monotonic logic this would mean that the new set of premises is inconsistent, and thus anything can be derived from it (*ex falso quodlibet*). But all default argumentation means that *ex falso quodlibet* is no longer regarded as a logical rule. Moreover (cf. Hage, 1997, IV.1), nonmonotonic logic makes it possible to extend a theory in such a way that it becomes possible to derive more reasons both for and against a conclusion.

However, the notion "nonmonotonic" is ambiguous. The systems included in the present volume (possibly with the exception of Hage's) are not systems of nonmonotonic logic in strict sense. The latter would propose a nonmonotonic notion of inference. This is not exactly the case for the formalisms developed in this volume which preserve a monotonic notion of inference, and add, on the top of it, a mechanism (which Prakken and Sartor call argumentation framework) for selecting best (justified) arguments. In other words, in the formalisms here presented the set of arguments always monotonically increases, while the set of justified ones does not necessarily.

Those formalisms are therefore not so different from the Alchourrón-Gärdenfors-Makinson (AGM) theory: also in this theory a form of nonmonotonic reasoning is obtained, by merging monotonic inference and a revision operator: some consequences of A may not be contained in A+p since those consequences have been discarded when revising A (assuming that A is a deductive closure, that is a set including all its consequences). Therefore, the difference with the AGM model is not determined by the fact that argumentation uses a nonmonotonic logic, but by a different technique for obtaining nonmonotonicity: in AGM by revising the original belief set (i.e. by selecting the beliefs which can be consistently maintained), in argumentation by selecting the justified arguments.

7. Change and Justification in the Law: The Use of the Belief-Revision Logic and the Use of Nonmonotonic Logic

Now, it seems that a jurist needs both the belief-revision logic and the nonmonotonic logic. Whereas the former elucidates consequences of a change of the law, the latter elucidates some rationality behind the change. The following examples show this "division of labour".

Theses about valid law can be almost always justified on the basis of a legal norm valid at an earlier moment. So is the case even if the previously valid norm already lost its validity. The old constitution can, e.g., decide how the new one, perhaps radically different, may be enacted (cf., e.g., Luhmann 1993, 109–110). The law changed, yet the change is justifiable on the basis of the situation which existed before the change.

Furthermore, improvement of the law by means of analogy and precedents is based on essential similarities between (actual or hypothetical) cases. The judgement of essentiality must be justifiable by recourse to the legal tradition of the society, including established rules and principles of legal argumentation. But, at the same time, the improvement may lead to a change of the legal tradition.

Another example regards the so-called legal doctrine (*Rechtswissenschaft*, "science of law", legal dogmatics), consisting of professional legal writing, whose task is to systematise and interpret valid law. The tradition of this "science" implies that argumentation should not only be used to derive justified conclusions from conflicting information, but also to support justified (=more coherent) modification of this information. To be sure, the jurists make a distinction between a cognitive inquiry into the law as it is (*de lege lata*), and justified recommendations for the lawgiver, *de lege ferenda*. But as every legal scholar knows, the distinction between *de lege lata* and *de lege ferenda* is not clear-cut. A radical reworking of the law "as is" is hardly distinguishable from a proposal of new "professor-made" law. In brief: the legal doctrine is a good example of a practice of rational reasoning, aimed at a cognitive refinement of the law, yet in many cases leading to a change of it.

> Doctrine has been of varying importance in the history of law. In Rome, Augustus gave to certain prominent jurists the right to answer questions of law by authority of the Emperor, *ius publicae respondendi ex auctoritate principis*. Other emperors, too, gave a similar right to certain jurists. The courts regarded the views of these jurists as valid law. Certain statutes of 4th and 5th centuries A.D. regulated the order in which these jurists should be cited, if their views were incompatible. The so-called citation-statute from A.D. 426 accorded binding force to books of Papinian, Paulus, Ulpian, Gaius and Modestinus, and regulated in detail the relative authority of these jurists. In Medieval Europe the legal *communis opinio doctorum*, based on Roman sources and embraced by the majority of celebrated legal writers, mostly French or Italian, had a dominating influence. Opinions of the "doctors" were often used in the canonical process. After a long history of successes and failures, doctrine made a comeback in the 19th century. Great scholars, such as C. F. von Savigny, influenced the German legal development of this period. The German *Pandektenwissenschaft*, based on sophistication of Roman law, achieved a uniquely high level, influenced the final codification of civil law (BGB of 1896) and was highly influential even outside the boundaries of Germany. At the end of 19th century, the standing of doctrine in Sweden was strong (cf. Sundberg 1978, 177–186.). In the present-day Sweden, some jurists are afraid of the risk of a significant decrease of the role of doctrine (cf. Sundberg 1978, 262 ff.).

8. Logic of Arguments or Logic of Extensions?

A jurist can thus profit of both the beliefs-revision logic and nonmonotonic logic. Within the latter, he can also profit of different approaches, reported in this volume. For example, Kowalski and Toni propose a model in which the emphasis is on extensions, that is on maximal sets of premises implying a certain result, rather than (like Sartor and Prakken) on arguments, that is minimal sets of premises directly justifying the intended result (although at the end of their article they also discuss the relation between extensions and arguments). Extension-based approaches provide a different model of legal problem-solving: the problem to be solved does not concern just premises relevant for the specific debated questions, but the maximal sets of beliefs (the point of view, or the view of the world) in which the conflicting premises may be included.

> Kowalski and Toni use logic to construct arguments which derive conclusions from agreed facts extended by means of assumptions. Their system evaluates alternative extensions and therefore the arguments they support, by comparing their relative ability to defend themselves under attack. It differs from popular

conceptions of logic in that it does not aim to determine a unique collection of truth that follow deductively from a given set of axioms. It allows the possibility that several alternative, but mutually incompatible extensions and the arguments they support may be equally acceptable.

Now, this shift of emphasis is interesting for a jurist. Extension-based models are less adequate for reconstructing a particular legal dispute before a court of law. Neither the parties nor the judge care very much of such things as the view of the world, or a total belief system. What matters is, so to say, local coherence. Attention must be paid to the legal provisions and circumstances directly relevant to the solution of the case, and in some cases to the effect the solution may have upon similar cases in future (in the context of precedent-creating judgements of the supreme court of the country etc.). On the other hand, the extension approach seems to be very valuable in the context of the so-called "legal science" (doctrine, see above). In this "science", the legal scholars attempt at presenting the legal system as a whole as coherent (cf. Peczenik 1995, 278 ff. referring, among others, to *Hans Kelsen*). Nota bene, this postulate of coherence of the law as a whole, and the abstract "legal science" in general, is much less respected in, for instance, Anglo-Saxon countries than in the European continent. It has also become fashionable in some circles, not the least in Scandinavia, to preach for the inevitable split of the "legal science", and indeed of the law itself, into incoherent fragments (cf. critical remarks of Peczenik 1995, 276). Though this fashion will probably be over soon, the important problem will remain: In some branches of the law, such as legal procedure or torts, different "points of view" seem to compete with each other, each one characterised by its own rough priority order of the sources of the law, principles, values, interests and policies, its own terminology, its own theories and techniques, perhaps developed under influence of interdisciplinary research (such as, e.g., law and economics) and so on; cf., e.g. Zahle 1986 and 1992. It may be profitable to conceptualise these "points of view" as extensions in Kowalski and Toni's sense.

9. Cumulating of Arguments and Chains of Arguments

There are also other examples of the fact that different systems, included in this volume, give a jurist different kinds of help.

For example, Prakken and Sartor pay much attention to the step-by-step nature of argumentation: conflicts about conclusions or assumptions earlier in the chain are dealt with before 'later' conflict. They thus deal with chains of arguments, whereas Hage focuses on sets of reasons and weighing of such sets of reasons. Hage (this issue, Section 38.1) summarises it, as follows: "The central notion in Prakken-Sartor-logic is that of an argument. An argument is a tree of rules, where the conclusion of the one rule is one of the conditions of the following rule. Premises are rules without conditions. Reasons in [Hage's system of] RBL are comparable to the joint conditions of the last rule in a chain ... Take for instance the argument

$a \to b \to c$. In RBL-terminology, b would be a reason for c." A question occurs whether a law-theorist has any ground to prefer one of these approaches before the other. Isn't it so that we need both sets and chains of reasons?

Hage's logic is plausibly applicable to weighing principles. A definitive ordering of principles is possible in a particular case only, where all the relevant circumstances of the case serve as auxiliary arguments. Strictly speaking, a lawyer does not perform weighing of principles but weighing of complex sets of arguments, each including a principle.

> On the other hand, a cumulation of arguments is confronted with logical paradoxes. There can exist reasons, each individually pulling in one direction and jointly pulling in the opposite direction. Prakken and Sartor give an example. A person can consistently endorse the following set of reasons: If it is hot, it is a reason not to jog. If it is raining, it is another reason not to jog. But if it is hot and raining, it is a reason to jog, because the combination is pleasant. To avoid such problems, Prakken and Sartor prefer not to deal with combinations of reasons. A lesson to be learned from this is that logical problems can force a theoretician to chose the next best theory of legal argumentation. Another lesson is that the best theory would, instead, solve such problems. It is no criticism, since I do not know how the best theory would look like. But it may be a starting point of further research.

A jurist may thus use Hage's system for some purposes, but he also needs an analysis of the chain of reasons. Under impact of legal practice, Alexy and Peczenik stated generally that coherence of a theory depends among other things on how long chains of reasons belong to it (*see below*).

On the other hand, Hage (1997, VI.6), quoting Verhey, considers the possibility that the justification for the conclusion of an argument can become weaker, depending on the length of the chain of the argument which leads to it. This is like the chain evidence in a court. In a libel case, it is obviously a stronger evidence that a witness heard the defendant to say the libel than that the witness heard someone else to say that the defendant had said it.

Yet, when one thinks about the depth of argumentation, it is the other way around. Compare the following dialogues, each containing a chain of reasons:

> A: x is guilty of libel. B: why? A: because y has heard x calling z a thief.
>
> A: x is guilty of libel. B: why? A: because y has heard x calling z a thief. B: So what? A: y is a reliable witness. B: why? A: because he is a trained police officer.

The chain 2 seems to be stronger than the chain 1. Why? Because it is longer? This is not the whole story. The length of the chain strengthens the argument only because the reasons for reasons add something to the first-order reasons. The chain is a kind of cumulation of reasons, and this cumulation is structured. The first-order reason "... because y has heard x calling z a thief" has already a weight. The information "y is a reliable witness" adds a little more weight to it. The information "y is a trained police officer" adds even more. Can one then explicate the chain of this kind as a conjunction: "y has heard x calling z a thief and y is a reliable witness and y is a trained police officer"? Intuitively, a chain of reasons of this kind gives us more information than a conjunction would.

In general, the length of a chain (constituting an argument) is in fact an indication of the strength of the argument. By building longer arguments we usually minimise the number of assumptions upon which conclusions are based. The chain "p because of q because of r" is stronger than cumulation "p and q and r". In cumulation three reasons are unsupported: p, q and r. In chain "p because of q because of r" only one is unsupported, that is r. More technically, the conclusion p derived by using $q \rightarrow p$ and q is stronger then the simple affirmation of p by the speciality criterion, since the rule $q \rightarrow p$ relativises the conclusion p to the condition q, so making it stronger. Moreover, in some cases, we can use more basic and less disputable assumptions, for example r can be more basic and less disputable than p and q.

> No doubt, a longer argument may be attacked in more ways (since attacks can be directed against every ring of the argument). But in any case, by extending a rule base $\{q, q \rightarrow p\}$ with the additional rule $r \rightarrow q$, and "fact" r, you do not lose anything since you get three arguments: $\{q, q \rightarrow p\}$, and moreover $\{r, r \rightarrow q\}$ and $\{ r, r \rightarrow q, q \rightarrow p\}$. The second argument (which is a subargument of the third) may be useful in order to counter to an argument for non q, which could defeat the assumption $\{q\}$ included in the first argument. Obviously, and argument for non r could defeat the third argument, while leaving untouched the first.

Also: the longer the chain deciding on whether the reason holds, the weaker the holding-quality of the reason. But – at the same time – the longer the chain determining the weight of the reason, the stronger the weight of the reason.

10. A Few Words about Philosophy Behind the Choice of Logic. Hage about the Concept of "Legal Rule"

A lawyer has thus great difficulties to make a choice between the proposed logical systems. He rather needs all of them, each for a different purpose. Instead, a choice may perhaps be made on a philosophical basis. Let me show this on the example of Hage's use of the concept "legal rule".

Hage (this issue, Section 14.1) discusses "scope conditions that limit the application of a rule in time and space and proper exceptions can make a rule inapplicable although the conditions of the rule are satisfied". Let me give an example. The legal rule "whoever kills another person ought to be sentenced to prison" is not applicable if the killer acted in self-defence. This way of speaking about legal rules may be contrasted with the terminology used by many law-theorists (cf., e.g., Strömberg 1988, 7 ff.) who would say that Hage's rules are no complete legal rules but merely prescriptions. A complete legal rule already includes limits of the application of a rule in time and space and proper exceptions. But this means that the logic of constituting of complete rules from prescription is evaded by such law-theorists as

Strömberg and now taken seriously by Hage. To such theorists as Strömberg, the step (jump) from "prescriptions" to "complete legal rules" is a non-analysed black box, while the corresponding step from rules to applications in Hage's framework is analysed, clearly and by formal means.

The fact that Hage analyses things previously not analysed is, of course, an achievement. It has also far-reaching consequences. For example, Hage (1997, III, 11) criticises the present author for ambivalence as regards the concept of analogy in law. He points out that I one time treat analogy as an application of a rule to case outside, another time as a creation of a more abstract rule. The criticism is well-founded. Let me add the following. If one thinks like Strömberg, it is natural to see analogy as rule creation, if one wants to have a logical analysis of analogy, it is more plausible to see analogy as preceding the creation of a more abstract rule. He is right that I did not see it clearly in 1989 (but a bit more clearly in 1995, 341 ff.).

So far so good. A jurist can certainly profit from tools enabling him to analyse of things previously not analysed. But Hage's analysis (this issue, Section 15.2) is even more profound: "The inclination to treat analogous rule application as the application of a more abstract rule is explainable from the tendency to consider rules from a logical point of view as a kind of statements. Clearly statements cannot be applied analogously; they even cannot be applied at all. The only way to deal with analogy in the case of statements is to assume that the statements were actually more abstract than they originally seemed to be ... (R)ules are not statements, and they can obey a different logic than statements ... Rules should be considered as a kind of tools, applied by humans to structure the (legal) world." In order to understand Hage's views, one must pay attention to the fact that he accepts Searle's distinction between the directions of fit: word-to-world in the case of propositions and world-to-word in the case of rules: "descriptive sentences ... have word to world direction of fit ... On the other hand we have (amongst others) principles, which have the world to word direction of fit". Consequently, the "principle *makes* a fact into a reason, and this reason makes it the case that ... the final conclusion that John ought to be punished" (Hage, this issue, Section 7).

By the way, I made the same observation, independently from Searle, cf. Peczenik 1989, 199–200 with references to some much older articles.

A further consequence (Hage, 1997, III.6.6) is that "the constitution of reasons is based on two kinds of elements. On the one hand there are rules, principles and goals that can generate reasons. On the other hand, there are facts that somehow satisfy the conditions of these rules, principles and goals ... The facts ... may also be the result of a derivation ... form other facts ... or classification". Given this theory, it is plausible to speak about reasons for applying or not applying rules. Moreover, (Hage, this issue, Section 15.2) "reasons to apply a rule even if its conditions are not satisfied will usually be based on principles or goals that led the legislator to make the rule in the first place". And (id.) "e contrario 'application' of a rule can be explained by looking at the goals and principles that underlie the rule".

The possibility to analyse, by techniques developed in AI and logic metaprogramming, what previously has been a black box manifests itself in other ways, too. Cf., e.g. Hage, this issue, Section 21: "Traditionally, individuals are represented in formal logics by means of an unstructured character or a string. The representation of rules as logical individuals in RBL is different, however. The rules of inference of RBL must be able to distinguish between the conditions and the conclusion of an RBL-rule, and as a consequence, the representation of these logical individuals exhibits a structure".

All this is philosophically interesting, though I cannot make up my mind as to how important it is for a reconstruction of legal reasoning.

11. The Limits of Logic

The systems of nonmonotonic logic included in the present volume provide logical tools enabling one to speak precisely about various kinds of "rules about rules", dealing with such things as applicability of rules, what is assumed by rules, priority between rules and the burden of proof. We have thus seen that the domain of logic may be extended. But – and it is important – logic as such cannot provide "material" results. It gives us a framework into which the assessment of weight of various arguments and reasons can be inserted, but the assessment itself is in principle not a matter of logic alone.

> I say "in principle" to omit some special cases. Cf., e.g., Hage, this issue, Section 26.2: "weighing-knowledge is not provided by RBL, but should be incorporated in the theory from which the derivations are made ... There is, however, one important exception. RBL provides the weighing-knowledge that is necessary to weigh a non-empty set of reasons against an empty set".

What Hage writes about his own system is more or less applicable to all the other systems: Nonmonotonic logic is computationally inefficient, but it increases understanding (Hage, this issue, Section 1). Hage's logic, like many others nonmonotonic logics, does not "provide specifications for an inference engine" but "rather provides a list of desiderata, demands that we would like to make on an inference mechanism" (Hage, this issue, Section 1). Roughly speaking, nonmonotonic logic is no calculus but a hint where the calculus must end.

12. An Example of the Limits of Logic. Analogy in the Law – An Inference or an Argument Form?

Nonmonotonic logic thus enables one to construct a much richer logic of law than before. This conclusion can be elucidated by many examples. Let me give only one, concerning the concepts of analogy in the law.

A good starting point is the following observation made by Hage (personal communication) as regards the construction of precedent-based rules: "The rule is reconstructed from the cases to which it can be applied, rather than the other way round. It would be impossible to have a priori knowledge of the rule's conditions".

> A precedent-based rule receives clear content first when a number of precedents occurs. A kind of a zigzag is well-known: a new rule is slowly evolving by trial and error. Both the scope and the clarity of the rule evolve in subsequent cases according to the pattern "two steps forward, one step back" etc, as appears in the following Swedish example.
>
> In the case NJA 1948 p. 584, a general principle for criminal cases was established stating that only the facts explicitly proffered by prosecuting counsel could be used as material for the case and the conviction. This principle was then reasserted in NJA 1976 p. 368. In NJA 1987 p. 194, the same principle was stated and supported with a coherent set of explicit reasons. In NJA 1988 p. 665, the reasons from NJA 1987 p. 194 were stated again verbatim with reference to that case. The same happened once more in NJA 1990 p. 361. (Cf. Bergholtz 1992, 1 ff.).
>
> In the case NJA 1951 p. 1, a customer claimed that a contractor had promised to perform the work in question at a lower price than later demanded. The contractor denied. The Supreme Court (in plenum) decided that the contractor has the burden of proof. Then, in NJA 1975 p. 280, the Court confirmed this rule as regards a case in which a consumer contracted a business establishment. The Court emphasised the consumer-relationship. The case from 1951 was quoted with the comment that there is no need to discuss the burden of proof in general. Finally, in NJA 1989 p. 215, the burden of proof was reversed as regards a bookkeeping contract. The Court mentioned the fact that an established practice was thus changed but the scope of the change remains unclear.

The point is that following precedents is not like following pre-existing rules. It is rather like considering reasons for *making* rules. A reason for deciding the new case like the old one is to be considered. Counter-arguments can prevail in some cases, and it is not known in advance in which ones, albeit the result will almost always be not only to solve the case, but also to confirm of modify the precedent-rule.

Analogy is important not only for constructing the precedent-based rules but also in interpreting statutory provisions. Statutory analogy (*analogia legis*) consists in application of a statutory rule to a case which, viewed from the ordinary linguistic angle, is included in neither the core nor the periphery of the application area of the statute in question, but resembles the cases covered by this statute in essential respects. Statutory analogy is employed in most legal systems, albeit it plays a greater role in the Continental law than in the Common Law countries.

Statutory analogy is justifiable by the principle "like should be treated alike" and thus by considerations of justice, universalisability and coherence. However, the juristic use of statutory analogy is extremely complex.

> The importance of analogy in the law encouraged some jurists (notably *Arthur Kaufmann*) to claim that the legal language in general has an analogical nature. In a loose – perhaps metaphorical – sense, they are right: the lawyers constantly see to it that the like are treated alike. But statutory analogy – implying a radical extension of the scope of application of the statutory prescription – must be distinguished from the so-called *analogia intra legem*. Other jurists (e.g., *Alf Ross*) reject the vague distinction between statutory analogy and extensive interpretation of a statute. But the legal tradition uses this distinction, e.g. statutory analogy in criminal law is to be employed more cautiously than extensive interpretation. By ignoring the distinction, a legal philosopher can thus unconsciously encourage an excessive use of analogy. On the other hand, one must doubt whether this distinction may be made sharp enough to be useful for logicians.

When deciding not to reason by analogy, one can use the so-called *argumentum e contrario*. This is again a hint that statutory analogy and *argumentum e contrario* are no complete arguments but mere argument forms, each supported by a different set of arguments. Only important similarities between cases constitute a sufficient reason for conclusion by analogy. Judgements of importance are justifiable by weighing and balancing of various reasons, often principles. Such a justification is based on the legal culture and tradition of the society. The tradition may change, yet the new elements can constitute a coherent evolution of the old ones (see below on coherence). Important resemblances can concern many different things, such as persons, material objects, documents, rights, duties, circumstances concerning space and time, social effects of the application of the law to different cases, and, finally, the place of the cases in respective "stories" ("narratives"). The judgement of importance is often understood as "finalist", i.e. justifiable by a general principle expressing the *purpose* of the statute.

> The following reasoning norms – widely recognised in a legal tradition – help one to make a choice between the use of analogy and *argumentum e contrario*. One should not construe provisions establishing time limits by analogy. One should not construe provisions constituting exceptions from a general norm by analogy, unless strong reasons for assuming the opposite exist. The so-called principle of legality in penal law demands that no action should be regarded as a crime without statutory support and no penalty may be imposed without a statutory provision (*nullum crimen sine lege, nulla poena sine lege*). In taxation law, the principle *nullum tributum sine lege* justifies the conclusion that one should apply analogy with restraint if it leads to increased taxation. The precise meaning of these restrictions is, however, debatable. Cf., e.g., Frändberg 1973, Kaufmann 1982, Nerhot 1991 and Peczenik 1971.

Returning to Hage's system let me state that Hage seems to consider analogy as an inference. A more orthodox view is to regard it as heuristic for finding new premises. Regarded as a procedure, statutory analogy implies an effort to achieve a "reflective equilibrium" of the generalised rule and particular judgements of analogy. As we have seen above, this is an extremely complex business, full of unanalysed "black boxes". This means that analogy is difficult to conceptualise as an inference. It is only natural that some scholars regard it as a mere hint at what direction an inference shall be directed. In *Robert Alexy's* terminology, analogy is not an argument, but an argument form (cf. Alexy 1985, 343 ff).

It is not easy to take a position on this point. In general, one must be cautious when allowing for non-deductive inferences.

The conclusion of all this is that a logician who allows for analogy as an inference, makes in fact a reference to this complex legal tradition. The tradition may be understanding as contributing to the total coherence of legal reasoning, but only a very small part of it can be presented in the language of logic.

13. Strength of Evidence and Abduction

Some other extensions of logic, presented in this volume, are more daring. For example, Freeman and Farley define the following levels of support for what they call the burden of proof:

scintilla of evidence
find at least one weak, defendable argument

preponderance of evidence
find at least one weak, defendable argument
outweigh the other side's argument

dialectical validity
find at least one credible, defendable argument
defeat all of the other side's arguments

beyond a reasonable doubt
find at least one strong, defendable argument
defeat all of the other side's arguments

beyond a doubt
find at least one valid, defendable argument
defeat all of the other side's arguments

Disregarding technical details, let me say that this kind of differentiation of strength of evidence is well-known to the lawyers, especially in the law of civil procedure. (A Swedish authority in this subject was late Professor *Per Olof Ekelöf*). Another question is, however, whether such things should be incorporated into a *logical* system.

The same question may be asked as regards the model of dialogue, assumed by the authors. Of course, regarding legal argumentation as a dialogue is plausible for a lawyer.

> Notice that also Prakken and Sartor, this issue, Section 5.1, work with proofs that take the form of a dialogue. ("A proof that an argument is justified will take the form of a dialogue tree ... However ..., this does not make our system an example of the 'dialectical' or 'procedural' approach to modelling legal argument, since the dialectical form is only used to state a proof theory for a logic of defeasible argumentation".)

Freeman and Farley's model of dialogue allows for some weak arguments which seem to be dubious. As regards weak arguments, the following controversy is particularly interesting.

> Freeman and Farley, this issue, Section 'Related Research': "The idea of more specific arguments viewed as exceptions, and thus defeaters, was ... adopted by ... Prakken 1991. Since (Freeman and Farley) allow unsound, weak argumentation steps to be applied, (they) introduce other opportunities for defeat between arguments ... A weak argument is fragile, but may prove to be crucial if left unanswered."
>
> Prakken and Sartor, this issue, Section 9.2: In Farley and Freeman's "architecture, the strength of each argument is based on its intrinsic features: the cogency of the used rules (... sufficient, default and evidential) and the performed argumentation steps (which include modus ponens, modus tollens and abduction)... {some} features are left outside of our present work, such as abductive inference; as we said in the introduction, we prefer to conceptualise it as a way of finding and/or backing additional premises, rather than as an additional inference type".

What is at stake here is that Farley and Freeman consider abduction as an inference, warranting at least the "scintilla of evidence". But no lawyer would regard the premise $p \rightarrow q$ together with q as any evidence of p. Of course, the discovery that there is a relationship of the type $p \rightarrow q$ may arouse his curiosity whether the relationship in fact is not stronger, e.g., equivalence $p \equiv q$. In such a case p would follow, but the abduction *per se* is not any reason for it.

> Freeman and Farley have stated the following: "Sartor ... comes closest to capturing our various notions of proof level. He defines plausible argument to be one with no defeating counterargument. This would be an argument sufficient to win a scintilla of evidence ... He then describes a justifying argument as a plausible argument for a claim and no plausible argument for its counterclaim or negation. This is what we require of a dialectically valid argument; Prakken introduces related concepts as well ... Neither explore the application of burden of proof at different levels as an important element of control for generating coherent, dialectical arguments". In my opinion, a formal system grasping the role of the burden of proof in the law is certainly

> an achievement. But such a formalism must not go so far, as allowing for abductive inference.

From this point of view, there is an important difference between abduction and, for example, analogy. Neither is a deductive inference. Yet, the statement "there is analogy between x and y" is a hint that coherent reasons exist to support equal treatment between x and y, albeit such reasons may be complex, and possible to grasp in a "synthetic", holistic way only. In my understanding, abduction is not even such a hint.

14. Enter Coherence

In brief, nonmonotonic logic is an example of an extension of the domain of logic. But the more far-reaching the extension is, the greater problems it meets. It seems impossible to make logical reconstruction of the totality of legal argumentation. Behind the analysed reasons are other ones, not fully analysed, perhaps not analysable at all. Some are grasped by nonmonotonic logic, other are too elusive for that. One can see nonmonotonic logic as an example for an unending search for reasons, even in the domains previously treated as non accessible for rational analysis.

The search for reasons deserves more comments. It has no obvious end point. Obviously, reasoning performed by any person must stop somewhere, because we are neither immortal nor infinitely ingenious. Ideally, the search for reasons may end when one arrives at a coherent totality of knowledge.

In other words, coherence is the termination condition of reasoning. To have a fully justified belief , it is not sufficient to reach a set of justified arguments, on the basis of the premises accepted by the involved subject. This set has also to be coherent with the subject's reflective system of beliefs.

> One way to explicate the latter notion is Keith Lehrer's: "A person, S, is personally justified in accepting that p at t if and only if p coheres with the acceptance system of S at t" (Lehrer 1989, 253). "When one or more errors in the acceptance system of a person are corrected, a new system is formed, what I call a member of the ultrasystem of the person. When what a person accepts fails to cohere with one of these systems, even though it cohered with his acceptance system, I say that her personal justification is defeated. Whatever one accepts with personal justification is converted into knowledge by being undefeated" (id. 254). "S is justified in accepting that p in t in a way that is undefeated if and only if S is justified in accepting that p in t on the basis of every system that is a member of the ultrasystem of S at t" (id. 255). "My claim that justification depends on coherence is not intended as an argument to prove to a sceptic that we are truthworthy. It is the claim that our justification for what we accept depends on a system of acceptance containing general claims about our competence and truthworthiness. When there is an adequate match between acceptance and reality, coherence converts to knowledge" (id. 275).

But what is coherent? "Coherence" is a notoriously contested concept, eluding logical reconstruction. Let me start with the following restatement of Laurence BonJour's explication of it:

> "A system of beliefs is a justification-conferring, coherent system iff:
> (i) It is logically consistent,
> (ii) It has a high degree of probabilistic consistency,
> (iii) It has a significant number of relatively strong inferential connections among component beliefs,
> (iv) It is relatively unified, i.e., does not divide into relatively unconnected subsystems,
> (v) It contains few unexplained anomalies,
> (vi) It provides a relatively stable conception of the word and remains coherent (i.e. satisfies (i)–(v) in the long run) and
> (vii) It satisfies the Observation Requirement, i.e., it must contain laws attributing a high degree of reliability to a reasonable variety of cognitively spontaneous beliefs, including introspective beliefs. (Bender 1989, 5, referring to BonJour 1985, 9, 10, 92, 102–3, 106, 116, 123–4, 141, 151–4, 170, 191).

Alexy and Peczenik (1990) have developed a rather similar theory, containing, among other things, what follows. The more the statements belonging to a given theory approximate a perfect supportive structure, the more coherent the theory. Logical consistency is a necessary condition of perfect coherence at any moment. Logical consistency is, however, no sufficient condition of coherence. There are some additional criteria of coherence. *Ceteris paribus*, the degree of coherence of a theory depends on such circumstances as how great a number of supported statements belong to it; how long chains of reasons belong to it; how great number of connections exists between various supportive chains belonging to the theory, e.g., how many chains of reasons support one and the same conclusion; how many statements belonging to the theory are relevant in the type of argumentation the theory uses; how great number of universal statements belong to the theory; how great number of general concepts belong to it; how high the degree of generality of these concepts is; how great number of cases it cover; and how great number of fields of life it covers. The degree of coherence is determined by weighing and balancing of the criteria.

> By the way, in this approach, justification is a crucial element of coherence, and not an idea to be contrasted with coherence. I thus do not follow the line drafted by Gärdenfors 1990, that is the distinction between a justification theory according to which one has to keep track of justification for beliefs (beliefs that have no justification should not be accepted), and a coherence theory, according to which the focus in not on the pedigree (justification) of beliefs but just on their coherence with other beliefs.

In brief: moral and legal weighings are correct if they are coherent enough. But coherence depends on another kind of weighing.

15. Coherence and Consistency

To be sure, the criteria of coherence require a further analysis. Let me give two examples of the need of such analysis. The first example concerns the chains of reasons (or arguments), see above. The second example of the necessity of an analytical refinement of the coherence theory is more fundamental. One must say something more about the relation between coherence and consistency. Coherence theorists tend to assume that coherence presupposes logical consistency. On the other hand, all nonmonotonic approaches presented in this volume seem to assume that the premises set of legal argumentation may be inconsistent. Does it follow that they are incoherent? To answer this question, one must make two distinctions.

1. The first distinction is between perfect and reasonable coherence. Logical consistency is necessary for perfect coherence. On the other hand it is not necessary for a reasonable coherence. Alexy and Peczenik have missed this point, and this mistake must be corrected here. For example, anyone who believes that at least one of his beliefs is false has an inconsistent belief set. But it certainly is wrong that none of the beliefs in this set can be justified. If many are, the personal system of the subject is reasonably coherent, in spite of this ("unimportant") inconsistency. This is a version of the well-known paradox of the preface (cf. Goldman 1989, 122).
2. The second distinction is between *prima facie* statements and all-things-considered statements.

As regards the *prima facie* statements, let me tell the following. Such premises of legal argumentation as statutory provisions are *prima facie* statements. If such statements are read literally, the requirement of logical consistency seems not to be applicable to them. Indeed, if the statement

(1) A should *prima facie* do H

is interpreted *simpliciter* as

(2) A should do H

(that is, without the clause "prima-facie"), then the statements

A should *prima facie* do H

and

A should *prima facie* not do H

are logically inconsistent, precisely as the statements

A should do H

and

A should not do H

are. The only way to make sense of a set of premises including *prima facie* statements which are inconsistent in this manner is to use a nonmonotonic approach. One of the strong sides of the articles presented in this volume is that they give us precise logical means to supplement the apparently contradictory *prima facie* premises with priority orders which allow for deriving justified conclusions from them.

But it is also possible to read "A should *prima facie* do H" as

(3) there exists a possible situation p, such that p requires that A does H, and there exists a possible situation q, such that q requires that A does not do H.

This interpretation is consistent (cf., e.g., Chisholm 1974, 118 ff. and Åqvist 1992; notice that Åqvist does not use the person variable A).

Moreover, the "situation" can be stated precisely in terms of contextual priority orders of arguments. Then, one obtains the following:

(4) there are reasons for A's doing H, these reasons should be taken into account when one performs moral weighing and balancing and A should do H when these reasons outweigh the counter-arguments.

The complex statement

there are reasons for A's doing H, these reasons should be taken into account when one performs moral weighing and balancing

and

A should do H when these reasons outweigh the counter-arguments

and

there are reasons for A's not doing H, these reasons should be taken into account when one performs moral weighing and balancing

and

A should do H when the former weigh more

and

A should not do H when the latter weigh more

is not logically inconsistent.

Now, reading of

(1) A should *prima facie* do H

as

(4) there are reasons for A's doing H, these reasons should be taken into account when one performs moral weighing and balancing and A should do H when these reasons outweigh the counter-arguments

is by no means a matter of ordinary language. Just the opposite, it involves a complex theoretical reconstruction. This reconstruction is done by philosophical means, not involving any logical formalism. On the other hand, the nonmonotonic approaches presented in this volume give us formal means to replace this reconstruction by a more strict theorising. This is perhaps a significant progress.

As regards all-things-considered statements (justifiable as a result of weighing and balancing of the *prima facie* ones), one may instead require straightforward that they must be consistent. This is not only reasonable but consistency can also be an analytical (logical) implication of the notion itself of all-things-considered statements. For example in the system of Sartor and Prakken, it is a theorem that justified arguments (and justified conclusions, which in their framework express all-things-considered conclusions) are consistent.

> Another thing is that it is not at all sure that all thing considered, one can solve any doubt. Perhaps in certain questions there would be no all-things considered answer, at all or at least in the state of our knowledge. This is what Sartor and Prakken call defensible arguments.

It seems reasonable that in practical reasoning consistency must be only required in regard to individual statements. Only individual statements can be all-things considered, since only individual statements refer to a specific situation, of which all things can be considered. This is not the case for general statements, which consider just partial aspects of the situations in which they may be applied. Cf. Peczenik 1995, 504. General statements, such as statutory provisions and moral principles must be regarded as *prima facie*. On the surface reading, logical consistency is not required for a set of such statements to be coherent (see above!). But what is required for reasonable coherence is that one can construct a nonmonotonic model, such as Sartor and Prakken's, giving us a framework for priority-orders between the *prima facie* statements.

16. Coherence in Time. Tradition

The problem of coherence is even more elusive when one considers the role of time. This can be illustrated by BonJour's requirement that a system of beliefs is coherent enough to justify knowledge only if it is stable, that is "converges on and eventually presents a relatively stable long-run picture of the world" (BonJour 1985, 170). Time is a laboratory in which stability of the system of beliefs is tested.

A legal order, a juristic theory, a moral system etc. can be justified as coherent in the light of a legitimate tradition, understood as a transmission of a pattern of thought or action. A living tradition is, however, not static, but it evolves. Old questions find thus new answers which give raise to new questions. The bearers of the tradition have a latent receptivity for new questions and can develop a new and more profound perspective, regarded as closer to the truth (cf. Rolf 1991, 147 ff. with references to Polanyi 1962; concerning legal tradition, cf., e.g., Krygier 1991, 68).

The continuity of and the changes within legal tradition has already been described above. But I do not know of any general theory which can state precisely what makes the change of tradition coherent.

17. Theory of Science: Trial and Error

One is now tempted to say, that this dependence on tradition explains why the law appears to be non-logical. Yet, not only the law but all knowledge, and also empirical science, depends on trial and error, ultimately based on conventions and consensus. To be sure, the so-called foundationalists claim that all knowledge ultimately rests on evident foundations, such as empirical data (cf., e.g., Chisholm 1966, 30 ff.). However, foundationalism has been confronted by coherentism: the alleged foundations are by no means more certain than some other beliefs (cf., e.g., Dancy 1985, 123 ff.). In the context of theory of science, *Karl Popper* (cf., e.g., 1959, 28 ff.) has developed another important insight. He has thus claimed that the proper method of scientific research consists of creating bold hypotheses. One should try to falsify the hypotheses. One accepts them conditionally, as long as they are not falsified (Popper 1959, 40 ff.). The growth of knowledge is the result of a process closely resembling what Darwin called natural selection, that is, the natural selection of hypotheses (Popper 1959, 108 and 1972, 261). It is important to realise that Popper's falsificationism is ultimately based on conventions. This is so because the data which allegedly falsify a hypothesis are theory-laden. There are no unshakeable foundations of science. Not even empirical reference can be determined without some underpinning theories. Let me merely quote the famous sentence by Quine: "The unit of empirical significance is the whole of science" (1953, 42). Pierre Duhem noticed already before Popper's time that one may criticise and eliminate the observations, apparently falsifying a hypothesis. Suppose the theory T combined with the auxiliary hypothesis A implies e but observation suggests non-e. For instance, physics (T) combined with the hypothesis of expanded universe (A) implies a given position of a start (e), but the star is not exactly where it should be (non-e). What should one do? (1) One may challenge the derivation by showing that e does not follow from T and A. (2) One may show that the observation which purports to show non-e is unreliable ("the telescope is wrong"). (3) One may reject the auxiliary hypothesis A. (4) One may reject the theory T. How should one choose? (cf. Koertge 1978, 255). To solve this problem, Popper (1959, 83) has formulated some methodological rules. The most important is the rule forbidding *ad hoc* auxiliary hypotheses, introduced in order to save the theory while not explaining anything else. The problem is, however, that the methodological rules have no better ground than choice and convention.

According to *Thomas Kuhn* (1970, 23 ff.), one should judge scientific theories as parts of a broader totality called a paradigm. Each paradigm includes, inter alia, (1) some examples of concrete scientific achievements imitated by scientists in subsequent research, e.g. Einstein's research; (2) some value judgements, norms and basic beliefs shared by scientists, e.g. the criteria of correctness of physical experiments; and (3) the so-called symbolic generalisations, concerning the sense of scientific terms, such as "mass", "energy" etc. Paradigms are relatively stable. In the phase of "normal science", all the experts agree to work within the framework of a paradigm. A change of a paradigm is in principle a matter of "scientific revolution". See also Popper 1959, 13: "a structure of scientific doctrines is already in existence; . . . This is why (a scientist) may leave it to others to fit his contribution into the framework of scientific knowledge." No wonder that the role of conventions - and consequently also traditions – in science is a serious and controversial matter.

Conventions, traditions, paradigms and the like are indispensable for all kinds of knowledge. *Hector-Neri Castañeda* stated the following: "Knowledge and justified belief are multifarous in their species and types ... The species or types of knowledge and justified belief are determined by the background takens-for-granted" (1989, 232). In this context, I would rather remain tacit about knowledge and say more cautiously that *justified beliefs* are multifarous in their species and types. The species or types of justified belief are determined by the background takens-for-granted. This background decides about what is relevant within a particular species, e.g., what is relevant natural science, and what is relevant in the law and legal argumentation. And of course, the backgrounds are a kind of social conventions.

As regards legal argumentation and legal "science", the problems are particularly complex, but to an important extent similar. Legal research contains certainly some hypotheses and their testing, even if it is not entirely clear what the term "to falsify a hypothesis" means in the legal context. One can also find analogies between paradigms in natural science and basic assumptions of legal research (cf., e.g., Aarnio 1984, 25 ff.). The big difference is, however, that the paradigm of legal "science" is rather vague, and it is difficult to conceive this "science" as a succession of distinct paradigms, each dominating at a certain period.

> According to Aarnio, the "matrix" of legal dogmatics, in a modified Kuhnian sense, consists of the following four components. (1) A set of philosophical background presuppositions, *inter alia* the assumption that legal argumentation is based on valid law. (2) Presuppositions concerning the sources of the law. One assumes that some of these are either binding or at least constituting authority reasons. (3) Presuppositions concerning legal method. One thus assumes that legal argumentation is and should be governed by some methodological norms. (4) A set of values, first of all concerning legal certainty and justice.
>
> All these components are less precise than the paradigms of natural science. They have also remained unchanged since the Roman times.

This means that growth of legal knowledge resembles the process of achieving reflective equilibrium.

> The so-called reflective equilibrium in morality means that one aims at mutual adaptation of the general principles and individual moral convictions (cf. Rawls 1971, 20). Both the principles and the individual convictions are modified so much that they support each other. Sometimes the principle goes before the individual convictions, sometimes it is the other way around.

Legal knowledge grows by trial and error, but there are no clear rules deciding what an "error" means. "Error" is discovered in a way depending on, among other things, intuition and consensus. What is an error, is not determined by facts and logic alone. Yet one can hardly doubt that this procedure is reasonable and increases coherence of the argumentation.

The outcome of all this is that both scientific knowledge and knowledge of legal and moral norms progresses by trial and error, and that one must resort to a certain convention to define what "error" means. The main difference is, however, that conventions of science are much more precise than those of legal scholarship. Consequently, determination of "error" in legal science is often holistic and circular. The reasons determining that a legal theory is "erroneous" are not more certain than the contested theory itself.

This difference has important consequences: According to the methodology of Popper, when an hypothesis is contradicted by more basic beliefs, it should be thrown away or at least modified. Instead in the legal argumentation – and indeed also in the defeasible reasoning in general! – we often keep in our set of premises both the defeated "hypothesis" and its "exceptions" and continue to use the first for dealing with future cases, even though it was contradicted in specific circumstances. This is a typical feature of principles. And this is also a great advantage of the nonmonotonic approaches presented in this volume. To be sure, this is not always the case. For example, a supreme court of a country may be a precedent-making instance. This means in many cases, that when the situation and valuations change, the court may throw our the old precedent-based rule and make another one. (I omit here the technical details as to how this is done in different legal orders). But in many other cases, the court would rather keep conflicting principles within the system, and balance them in particular cases, thus not creating any fixed precedent-rules. A very important difference between practical (among other things legal) and scientific reasoning is that this method of balancing is much more usual in the former than in the latter one (even though both approaches are applied, though in different degrees, in both domains).

Returning to the articles in this volume, let me state that Hage's theory pays also due attention to the holistic character of the legal argumentation. Hage's logic has extra 'rules of inference' next to those of FOPL . These extra rules are not constructive. In particular, (cf. Hage, 1997, IV.7.1 and V.1.2), R2 indicates that a rule is not applicable to a case if it can be derived that it is excluded., R5 stipulates that if an action or a state contributes to a goal state, and it cannot be derived that the goal is excluded in this case, there is a reason why the action ought to be performed and R6 stipulates that. a conclusion can be derived if the derivable reasons that plead for it outweigh the derivable reasons that plead against it. Hage concludes as follows: "Notice that the rules R1 to R8 above cannot easily be turned into an inductive construction of the set of sentences that can be derived from a theory T, because the Rules R2 and R5 mention a sentence that cannot be derived and therefore indirectly refer to the whole set of sentences that can be derived. R6 makes use of all the reasons for and against". In this manner, Hage's theory may be consider as a good model of legal argumentation. But it must be added that in the real life, legal argumentation continually receives new "input", that is, new goals, principles, rules and standpoints in particular cases. What can be derived now is perhaps no longer derivable tomorrow. And the legal language is too vague to allow the interpreter a certainty as regards what can and what cannot be derived.

18. The Great Circle of Coherence

Now, we approach the most profound problem of a coherentist justification, that is, its circularity. Conventions, paradigms, traditions, frameworks and the like are indispensable for coherence. Then, Is coherence conventional? If this is the case, how can it give us knowledge? Is knowledge conventional? But on the other hand, one can argue in the opposite direction: traditions and the like are relevant for knowledge only if they are, to a relevant extent, coherent. All this appears hopelessly circular. Indeed, coherence . . . circles. For example, the above-mentioned coherence theory by Alexy and Peczenik rests on the following circle: weighing and balancing in law and morality is said to be right, if it follows the balance of coherence criteria. But it is doubtful whether the latter balance is independent from the former. Both kinds of balance may very well affect each other. Balancing is thus circular, in a sense close to reflective equilibrium.

Other coherence theories do not fare better. Let me give a couple of examples. Laurence BonJour assumes that the subject S is empirically justified in his belief B only if "S has at least implicit access to the metajustification for his system of beliefs, viz., that the coherence and stability of the system is best explained by the fact that the epistemic standards embodied in his system are highly likely to yield truth in the long run. Satisfaction of this condition involves a metabelief (or at least an implicit understanding) that B is a belief of a certain type F, as well as an (apriori justified) belief that beliefs of type F are likely to be true." (cf. Bender 1989, 5, referring to BonJour 1985, 9, 10, 92, 102–3, 106, 116, 123–4, 141, 151–4, 170, 191). This is, however, open to the following objection: "What BonJour seems to be saying, then, is that S's belief B is justified only if B not only meets a correct standard of epistemic justification, but also S possesses a metajustification for the correctness of that standard . . . But if this requirement is imposed, nothing can constitute a correct standard of justification understood as (necessary and) sufficient condition for justifiedness, because justifiedness requires, in addition, possession of a metajustification . . . " (Goldman 1989, 106).

Another famous coherentist, *Keith Lehrer*, has also admitted circularity. The problem Lehrer raises for fallible foundations is what follows. The "foundations" are described in particular propositions, e.g., about the colour of a specific object. What is said to make them justified is that the subject is confronted with particular circumstances. When I receive an experience of something red (in a philosophical jargon, when I am "appeared to redly") and have no grounds for doubt that I see a red thing, then I am justified in accepting that I see a red thing. But Lehrer adds that in order to achieve justification, certain general information must be available to me. In particular, I must accept that I have the ability to recognise the kind of thing in question. But this general information is not basic. It could only be justified on the basis of particular instances of success in recognition. We must cycle back and forth between particular and general information. "Thus, just as my justification for accepting particular claims may depend on the inclusion of some general principle of my truthworthiness, so my justification for accepting the general claim may depend on the inclusion of specific claims of obtaining the truth and avoiding error in my acceptance system ... No justified statement is an island. Coherence cycles ... Reasoning for the conclusion that one is generally truthworthy in the quest for truth from particular claims of past successes might result in circularity" (1989, 274–275).

To be sure, "the coherentist response suggested above ... begs the question, since it simply assumes that a person has a reason to think that a belief is true if it coheres with the rest of her beliefs ... This is a depressing but perhaps not surprising conclusion" (Tersman 1993, 102). I do not see any obvious way out of this dilemma. Coherentism seems to be the only reasonable epistemology, yet it is in a particular way – incoherent:

> On the one side, coherentism is based on general, philosophical, and in a sense foundationalist, assumptions. I have argued elsewhere (Peczenik 1989, 177 f.) that at least the following weak assumption is (not proved but) reasonable: If a theory can be made highly coherent, then there exist something in the world, some "truth-makers" which decide about this possibility. A stronger, and thus more controversial assumption may be considered, too: *Ceteris paribus*, the more coherent a theory, the closer it corresponds to what is the case.
>
> On the other hand, such assumptions are (and perhaps even must be) controversial. This means that one must be able to argue the assumptions themselves. This means giving reasons – and these must be a part of a coherent system. However, the coherent system has a power of justifying the reasons and the conclusions only because we rely on the basic coherentist assumptions we have started with. Here we are back at the square one.

19. Some Comparisons

All this does not rule out fully precise, noncircular and perhaps axiomatic theories, in physics, for example. But it shows that these theories have no deeper epistemological base than Popper's evolutionary trial-and-error-conventionalism. Indeed, a phenomenon resembling reflective equilibrium occurs in empirical science and in mathematics (cf. Goodman 1955, 65 ff., quoted by Rawls 1971, 20 n. 7). The outcome of all this is the following.

> Knowledge as a whole is inevitably circular. To cut the circle, one must insert controversial assumptions linking coherence with truth.
>
> Knowledge grows by trial and error.
>
> The concept of "error" is resistant to exact analysis. "Erroneous" means often "not coherent enough", in a sense open for debates.

What – then – is the basic difference between strict science and the study of law? Let me merely make some brief remarks.

> In natural science, a cluster of sophisticated, precise, complex and useful theories has already evolved. It is a good luck of mankind that it has.
>
> In the humanities, we are somewhat less lucky, as for example the history of sociology amply shows. In practical contexts, among other things those concerning the question of what ought to be (as opposed to what actually is), we are even less lucky.

20. The Role of Personal Preferences

Is this just a historical coincidence, or can these differences be explained? In my opinion, the crucial point is that personal systems of moral opinions are necessarily vague and subject to irrational (emotional) change. For that reason, human beings are unable to develop sophisticated and relatively stable moral theories.

In this context, one may return to the distinction between *prima facie* and definitive practical statements. Our cultural heritage decides which norm- and value-statements are relevant for legal and moral argumentation. In other words, the cultural heritage decides what *prima facie* moral and legal reasons are. Some foundationalists may claim that also some definitive (that is, morally compelling, not merely *prima-facie*) practical statements are certain, evident in themselves. However, only few definitive moral statements are thus indubitable. It is doubtful whether they can constitute the foundation of all justifiable acts of moral weighing and balancing. One must thus accept another kind of ultimate grounds for weighing, as well. It consists of statements which constitute a coherent system, in which each component can be put in question, but not all or nearly all components simultaneously. One can thus doubt p_1 if one assumes p_2 and p_3 and doubt p_3 if one assumes p_1 and p_2. But one cannot simultaneously doubt p_1, p_2, and p_3. An attempt to simultaneously doubt all or nearly all moral heritage of our culture would force one to change one's life in a radical, unacceptable and almost. Yet, a moral person can make a choice between different ultimate steps of weighing, allowed for his cultural heritage. It is thus reasonable to state the following. The ultimate step of moral argumentation is determined by an individual's personal preferences and feelings, within the flexible and ever-changing framework of the cultural heritage (cf. Peczenik 1995, 439–520 and 652–676).

> No doubt, this view of values and preferences requires a lot of comments. Indeed, it requires a complex theory. Instead of taking up the impossible task of developing such a theory in this paper, let me simply quote two passages which I find convincing:
>
> > On values: "Values are not part of the mind-independent word but something that we project upon the word, or – more precisely – upon the whole set of possible words" (Rabinowicz and Österberg 1996, 225).

> On preferences: "Comparing preferences that represent different dimensions in one's personality and constructing an all-things-considered preference on the basis of such comparisons is a complicated enterprise, in which there is not much room for easy sacrifices of the weaker to the stronger. Nor is there any guarantee that such an enterprise will always be successful. Amalgamation of heterogeneous preferences may sometimes be impossible" (id. 224).

In a way, this is reflected in all the papers presented in this volume. Of course, all the discussed logical theories assume – and indeed must assume – that the (legal, moral, political or other) domain theory can deliver some material fixed points, like the rules of burden of proof, rules of recognition, collision rules etc. But all those rules are open to revision in a particular, ever-changing and spontaneously – irrationally? – developing context. Hage recognised it clearly (this issue, Section 16): "Rules and principles differ from statements not only in their direction of fit, but also in that they need to be applied. Application of premises does not play a role in traditional logical inferences such as Modus Ponens ... The premise has a certain information content, and given this content it must be the case that ... Rules and principles, on the contrary, need to be applied ... (I)t is always possible to adduce reasons why a principle or rule should not be applied in a particular case ... The fact that rules and principles need to be applied explains two characteristics ... The first ... is that reasoning with rules (and principles) is defeasible; the second one is that rules can be applied analogously". This means that application of rules is a decision, involving not only reason but also the decider's attitude – to use a known philosophical metaphor – his "passion". In particular (cf. Hage, this issue, Section 17): "If we have no reasons why one set of reasons outweighs another set of reasons, we cannot make a rational decision. (But) We can make decisions without having reasons ... This does not mean that the decisions are fully random. On the contrary, very often different persons will weigh the same reasons in the same way ... From a rational point of view, however, such decisions are nothing more than cutting the knot". Yet, from his internal point of view, the decider always or almost always assumes that his decision, his "cutting the knot" is supported by reasons and logic. If no reasons are known to him, he searches for reasons. Indeed, he expects to find them, and other persons, interacting with him in various social roles, expect him to do so. They all seem to have – and in an elusive way must have? – a passion for reason.

The law and morality are subject to reason, but, ultimately, they are governed by passion. We, humans, have a passion for reason, but we also have other kinds of passion.

21. A Conclusion?

A strict and formal logical analysis cannot give us the full grasp of legal rationality. A weaker logical theory, allowing for nonmonotonic steps, comes closer, at the expense of an inevitable loss of computational efficiency. Coherentist epistemology grasps even more of this rationality, at the expense of a loss of preciseness.

If this is the case, one must be satisfied with such a degree of stability, preciseness and (indeed) coherence that the subject permits. It is as wrong to demand of the speaker in a political council strict proof as to accept mere probable grounds from a mathematician (Aristotle, *Nicomachean Ethics* 1094b).

This view can be linked to Aristotle's theory of prudence, understanding and comprehension as "concerned with the final moment in the deliberation process and with that which is considered in detail" (cf. Pattaro 1988, 112, referring to *Nicomachean Ethics* 1142a–1143b and *Rhetoric* 1394a–1395b, 1418a). One can also associate it with Aristotle's view of ethics and good deliberation, based on dialectics, and hence on the commonly held opinion (cf. Pattaro id., referring to *Nicomachean Ethics* 1098b, *Topics* 100a–108b etc.).

But there are some deep problems behind this contrast. Weighings play a role in many contexts, not only in the law and morality. One example has already been mentioned above: the weighing of criteria decides about the optimal coherence of a theory. Hage (1997, VI.5.1) regards weight as a dimension of reason. In his view, it is plausible that probability and weight interfere.

I am using here the word "weight" instead of Hage's word "relevance". This is permissible because Hage assumes that "the dimension of relevance is the same as the dimension of weight that is involved in the weighing of reasons". Since in my vocabulary, relevance cannot be graded (cf. Peczenik 1995), I prefer here the word "weight". The change of terminology has no implication to the content of this paragraph.

Another dimension of reason according to Hage is that of degree (of facts), e.g., "dolphin is to a less degree a fish than a pike". Hage states that "probably degrees interfere with probability and with relevance" (in my terminology: with weight). Then he writes the following (Hage, 1997, VI.5.3): "From the three mentioned dimensions, RBL takes only the dimension of relevance (in my terminology – weight – AP) into account. The probability of reason-giving facts is assumed to be a hundred percent, just as the degree in which they obtain. Probability reasoning such as Bayesian statistics takes only degrees of probability into account, while fuzzy logic takes degrees into account. Ideally a logic would deal with all three dimensions". This is a profound theory of weighing. Notice that "degrees" cannot be reduced to probability. The dolphin-example shows this: one cannot say correctly that dolphin is less probably a fish than a pike is. Can weight be reduced to probability and degrees? I do not know. If it can, the contrast between theoretical knowledge and practical weighing will disappear. But let me have my doubts.

References

Aarnio, Aulis. 1984. Paradigms in Legal Dogmatics. In: A. Peczenik, L. Lindahl and B. van Roermund (edd.), *Theory of Legal Science*. Dordrecht/Boston/Lancaster: Reidel.

Alchourrón, Carlos and Bulygin, Eugenio. 1971. *Normative Systems*. Wien New York: Springer-Verlag.

Alchourrón, Carlos and Makinson, David. 1982. On the Logic of Theory Change: Contraction functions and their associated revision functions. *Theoria* Vol. XLVIII Part 1.

Alchourrón, Carlos; Gärdenfors, Peter and Makinson, David. 1985. On the Logic of Theory Change: Partial Meet Functions for Contractions and Revisions. *Journal of Symbolic Logic* 50: 510–530.

Alexy, Robert. 1985. Theorie der Grundrechte. Baden-Baden: Nomos (Frankfurt/M. 1986: Suhrkamp).

Alexy, Robert. 1985b. Rechtsregeln und Rechtsprinzipien. ARSP Beiheft 25.

Alexy, Robert. 1992. Begriff und Geltung des Rechts. Freiburg/München: Verlag Karl Alber.

Alexy, Robert. 1993. Justification and Application of Norms. *Ratio Juris* Vol. 6 No. 2.

Alexy, Robert and Peczenik, Aleksander. 1990. The Concept of Coherence and its Significance for Discursive Rationality. *Ratio Juris* Vol. 3 No. 1bis.

Åqvist, Lennart. 1992. *Prima facie* Obligations in Deontic Logic: A Chisholmian Analysis Based on Normative Preference Structures. In press in: Proceedings of the Saarbrücken Colloquium PREFERENCES. Saarlouis. June 1992.

Bender, John W. (ed.). 1989. The Current State of the Coherence Theory. Critical Essays on the Epistemic Theories of Keith Lehrer and Laurence BonJour, with Replies. Dordrecht Boston/London: Kluwer Academic Publishers.

Bergholtz, Gunnar. 1992. Åtal och kontradiktion. Marginalanteckningar till några yngre rättsfall. In: *Festskrift till Per Olof Bolding*. Stockholm: Juristförlaget.

BonJour, Laurence. 1985. *The Structure of Empirical Knowledge*. Cambridge, Mass.: Harvard University Press.

Castañeda, Hector-Neri. 1989. The Multiple Faces of Knowing: The Hierarchies of Epistemic Species. In: Bender 1989.

Chisholm, R. M. 1966. *Theory of Knowledge*. Englewood Cliffs: Prentice-Hall.

Chisholm, R. M. 1974. Practical Reason and the Logic of Requirement. In: J. Raz (ed.). *Practical Reasoning*. Oxford 1978: Oxford University Press.

Dancy, Jonathan. 1985. *An Introduction to Contemporary Epistemology*. Oxford & Cambridge, Mass.: Blackwell.

Frändberg, Åke. 1973. *Om analog användning av rättsnormer. With a Summary in English: On Analogical Use of Legal Norms*. Stockholm: Norstedts.

Gärdenfors, Peter. 1990. The Dynamics of Belief Systems: Foundations vs. Coherence Theories. *Revue Internationale de Philosophie* 172 (1): 24–46.

Goldman, Alvin. 1989. BonJour's Structure of Empirical Knowledge. In: Bender 1989.

Goodman, Nelson. 1955. *Fact, Fiction and Forecast*. Cambridge, Mass.: Harvard University Press.

Hage, Jaap C. 1997. *Reasoning with Rules*. An Essay on Legal Reasoning and Its Underlying Logic. Dordrecht: Kluwer Academic Publishers.

Kaufmann, Arthur. 1982. Analogie und *"Natur der Sache"; Zugleich ein Beitrag zur Lehre vom Typus*. 2nd ed. Heidelberg: Decker und Müller. English translation of the first edition by Ilmar Tammelo: "Analogy and the Nature of Things; A Contribution to the Theory of Types". *Journal of the Indian Law Institute* 8 (1966), 358–401.

Koertge, Noretta. 1978: Towards a New Theory of Scientific Inquiry. In: G. Radnitzky and G. Andersson (edd.), *Progress and Rationality in Science*. Dordrecht – London: Reidel.

Krygier, Martin. 1991. Thinking Like a Lawyer. In: Wojciech Sadurski (ed.), *Ethical Dimensions of Legal Theory*. Amsterdam – Atlanta, Ga: Rodopi.

Kuhn, Thomas S. 1970. *The Structure of Scientific Revolutions*. 2nd ed. Chicago: Chicago University Press.

Lehrer, Keith. 1989. Coherence and the Truth Connection: A reply to my critics. In: Bender 1989.

Luhmann, Niklas. 1993. *Das Recht der Gesellschaft*. Frankfurt/M.: Suhrkamp.

Nerhot, Patrick (ed.). 1991. *Legal Knowledge and Analogy. Fragments of Legal Epistemology, Hermeneutics and Linguistics*. Dordrecht/Boston/London: Kluwer Academic Publishers.

Opalek, Kazimierz and Wolenski, Jan. 1975. Das Problem der Axiomatisierung des Rechts. In: *Forschungen aus Staat und Recht, Band 32: Rechtstheorie und Rechtsinformatik*. Wien: Springer-Verlag.

Pattaro, Enrico. 1988. Models of Reason, Types of Principles and Reasoning. *Ratio Iuris*. Vol. 1 No. 2.

Peczenik, Aleksander. 1989. *On Law and Reason*. Dordrecht/Boston/London: Kluwer Academic Publishers.

Peczenik, Aleksander. 1995. *Vad är rätt*? Stockholm: Norstedts juridik.

Peczenik, Aleksander. 1971. "Analogia legis. Analogy from Statutes in Continental Law". *In Le Raisonnement Juridique. Proceedings of the World Congress for Legal and Social Philosophy*. Ed. Hubert Hubien. Brussels: Établissements Émile Bruylant: 329–336.

Polanyi, Michael. 1962. *Personal Knowledge*. Towards a Post-Critical Philosophy. Corrected Edition. Chicago: University Press.

Pollock, John L. 1986. Contemporary *Theories of Knowledge*. Totowa, NJ: Rowman and Littlefield.

Popper, Karl R. 1959. *The Logic of Scientific Discovery*. New York: Basic Books.

Popper, Karl R. 1972. *Objective Knowledge*. Oxford: Clarendon Press.

Prakken, Henry and Sartor, Giovanni. 1995. Argumentation Frameworks: The Missing Link Between Arguments and Procedure. Preliminary Proceedings of the 17th IVR World Congress, Bologna, CLUEB, Vol. 5.

Quine. Willard Van Orman. 1953. *From a Logical Point of View*. Cambridge, Mass.: Harvard University Press.

Rabinowicz, Wlodek and Österberg, Jan. 1996. Value Based on Preferences. On Two Interpretations of Preference Utilitarianism. In: *Preference and Value. Preferentialism in Ethics*. Lund: Studies in Philosophy, Department of Philosophy, Lund University.

Rawls, John. 1971. *A Theory of Justice*. Oxford: University Press.

Rolf, Bertil. 1991. *Profession, tradition och tyst kunskap*. En studie i Michael Polyanyis teori om den professionella kunskapens tysta dimension. Lund: Nya Doxa.

Ross, W. D. 1930. *The Right and the Good*. Oxford: Clarendon Press.

Strömberg, Tore. 1988. *Rättsordningens byggstenar. Om normtyperna i lag och sedvanerätt*. Lund: Studentlitteratur.

Sundberg, Jacob. W.F. 1978. *Fr. Eddan t. Ekelöf. Repetitorium om rättskällor i Norden*. Malmö: Studentlitteratur.

Tersman. Folke. 1993. *Reflective Equilibrium*. An Essay in Moral Epistemology. Stockholm: Almqvist & Wiksell International.

von Wright, G. H. 1957. Logical Studies. London: Routledge & Kegan Paul.

Zahle, Henrik. 1986. Polycentri i retskildelaere. *Festskrift til Torstein Eckhoff*. Oslo: Tano.

Zahle, Henrik. 1992. Findes det kun én bevisret? *Festskrift till Per Olof Bolding*. Stockholm: Juristförlaget.

Artificial Intelligence and Law **4:** 331–368, 1996.

A Dialectical Model of Assessing Conflicting Arguments in Legal Reasoning

H. PRAKKEN*
Computer/Law Institute, Faculty of Law, Free University Amsterdam, De Boelelaan 1105, 1081 HV Amsterdam, The Netherlands
E-mail: henry@rechten.vu.nl

G. SARTOR
Faculty of Law, The Queen's University of Belfast, Belfast BT7 1NN, Northern Ireland
E-mail: sartor@cirfid.unibo.it

Abstract. Inspired by legal reasoning, this paper presents a formal framework for assessing conflicting arguments. Its use is illustrated with applications to realistic legal examples, and the potential for implementation is discussed. The framework has the form of a logical system for defeasible argumentation. Its language, which is of a logic-programming-like nature, has both weak and explicit negation, and conflicts between arguments are decided with the help of priorities on the rules. An important feature of the system is that these priorities are not fixed, but are themselves defeasibly derived as conclusions within the system. Thus debates on the choice between conflicting arguments can also be modelled.

The proof theory of the system is stated in dialectical style, where a proof takes the form of a dialogue between a proponent and an opponent of an argument. An argument is shown to be justified if the proponent can make the opponent run out of moves in whatever way the opponent attacks. Despite this dialectical form, the system reflects a 'declarative', or 'relational' approach to modelling legal argument. A basic assumption of this paper is that this approach complements two other lines of research in AI and Law, investigations of precedent-based reasoning and the development of 'procedural', or 'dialectical' models of legal argument.

Key words: argumentation, defeasibility, dialectics, rule conflicts, logic programming

1. Introduction

In recent years, adversarial legal argumentation has been a major topic of AI-and-Law research, approached from different angles. Some researchers, e.g. (Ashley, 1990; Rissland & Skalak, 1991; Skalak & Rissland, 1992), have developed theories or programs that are mainly descriptive, in that they are meant to model the way lawyers actually argue. Others, including the present authors, have studied the logical notions involved in legal argumentation, and again others, e.g. (Hage et al., 1994; Gordon, 1994) have formalised the role of legal procedures in legal argument.**

* Supported by a research fellowship of the Royal Netherlands Academy of Arts and Sciences, and by Esprit WG 8319 'Modelage'.

** With 'procedure' and 'procedural' we refer to procedural law and not to logical or computational procedures.

In our view, these approaches complement each other: descriptive theories and programs need logical and procedural standards for correct argumentation, and procedural models of dispute are built around a logical theory of notions like 'argument', 'counterargument' and 'defeat'. Finally, logical and procedural theories of argumentation are sterile if they are not susceptible of being embedded in actual reasoning practice.

The present paper extends the logical line of research. Our aim is to develop a formal theory on the assessment of conflicting arguments that takes as many argumentation features of legal language into account as possible. This is based on our view that strategies of attack and defence in dispute are partly based on the logical aspects of the language in which arguments are stated. In particular, lawyers can take advantage of some specific features of legal language, such as 'unless' clauses, applicability statements and statements about preference relations between legal rules.

This paper is also relevant for theories about non-adversarial aspects of legal reasoning. The structures we study are often deliberately used by the legislator as a technique for drafting well-structured legal texts or as a way of anticipating changes in the law. If the aim of a computational representation is to maintain these features, then our work points at ways of doing so.

While introducing complexity in the argumentative features of our language, we reduce complexity in another respect: syntactically, our system will be restricted in logic-programming style. In particular, we will build on (Dung, 1993)'s argumentation-theoretic semantics of extended logic programming. We make this restriction in order to make the discussion of the other types of complexity more transparent, but also to reduce the computational complexity and increase the potential for implementation.

The theory presented in this paper, which was presented in an earlier form in (Prakken & Sartor, 1995) and with more technical details in (Prakken & Sartor, 1996a), extends our own previous work, reported in e.g. (Prakken, 1991; Prakken, 1993; Sartor, 1993; Sartor, 1994). (Prakken & Sartor, 1995; Prakken & Sartor, 1996a) contained two main additions to this work. Firstly, a weak negation operator was used to model the fact that legal reasoning combines the use of priorities to choose between conflicting rules, with the use of 'unless' or similar phrases within a rule to make it inapplicable in exceptional circumstances. Secondly, the means to reason *about* priorities was introduced, i.e. the possibility to derive the ordering on the rules from the rules themselves. This captures the fact that in the legal domain everything is debatable, including the standards for comparing arguments.

This article adds two main features to (Prakken & Sartor, 1995; Prakken & Sartor, 1996a). It adds the category of strict rules to the language, and it replaces the earlier fixpoint definition of a justified argument with a constructive proof theory in dialectical style, which is inspired by work of (Vreeswijk, 1993b; Dung, 1994; Brewka, 1994b; Loui & Norman, 1995). The proof theory is defined as a dialogue game: a proof takes the form of a dialogue between a proponent and an opponent of an argument, where each player attempts to defeat the previous move of the other player; an argument is shown to be justified if the proponent can make the opponent run out of moves in whatever way the opponent attacks. A companion paper of the present article is (Prakken & Sartor, 1996b), which has less emphasis on legal issues and examples but contains more formal details and results.

The structure of this paper is as follows. We will start in the next section by putting our work in the context of related argument-based developments in AI and Law. Then, in Section 3, we will discuss some structural features of legal language that we want our system to be able to deal with. After that, the system is presented and applied to a wide range of examples in Sections 4 to 7. These sections form the heart of the paper. After some remarks on implementation in Section 8, we end with a discussion of related research and some concluding remarks.

2. Argumentation Frameworks: General Ideas and Their Role in Models of Legal Argument

Our system takes the form of a system for defeasible argumentation, or an 'Argumentation Framework' (AF). In this section we discuss the general ideas behind AFs, and we also discuss how research on AFs relates to other argument-oriented developments in AI and Law research.

Most AFs have been developed in general Artificial-Intelligence research on nonmonotonic reasoning, although Pollock's work on defeasible argumentation, e.g. in (Pollock, 1992), was developed to analyze epistemological issues in the philosophy of science. In AI argument-based systems have been developed as a reformulation of, (Bondarenko et al., 1993; Dung, 1995), or an alternative to, (Loui, 1987; Simari & Loui, 1992; Vreeswijk, 1993a), earlier formalisations of nonmonotonic reasoning. The idea here is that nonmonotonic reasoning can be analyzed in terms of the interactions between arguments for alternative conclusions. Nonmonotonicity, or defeasibility, arises from the fact that arguments can be defeated by stronger counterarguments. As is commonly accepted in AI and Law, legal reasoning is also defeasible, and since in our domain notions like argument, counterargument, rebuttal and defeat are very common, it comes as no surprise that several AFs have already been applied to the legal domain (Prakken, 1991; Prakken, 1993; Loui et al., 1993; Sartor, 1993; Gordon, 1994; Gordon, 1995; Prakken & Sartor, 1995).

To describe the general structure of AFs, they contain the following five elements, although sometimes implicitly: an underlying logical language, definitions of an argument, of conflicts between arguments and of defeat among arguments and, finally, an assessment of arguments.

AFs are built around an underlying logical language. Some AFs, like ours, assume a particular logic, while other systems, e.g. (Vreeswijk, 1993a; Bondarenko et al., 1993; Dung, 1995), leave the underlying logic partly or wholly unspecified; thus these systems can be instantiated with various alternative logics, as (Dung,

1993) has done for extended logic programming. Then AFs have the notion of an argument, which corresponds to a proof in the underlying logic. This is a narrow use of the term 'argument', which should not be confused with the broader meaning it often has in AI and law, when it also includes inductive, abductive and especially analogical arguments.

The notions of an underlying logic and an argument still fit with the standard picture of what a logical system is. The remaining three elements are what makes an AF a framework for adversarial argumentation. The first is the notion of a conflict between arguments. The typical case is when arguments have contradictory conclusions. An AF also has ways of comparing arguments, on the basis of certain standards, to see whether an argument defeats a counterargument. In AI the specificity principle is regarded as very important, but one of the main themes of this paper is that any standard might be used: their content is part of the domain theory, and is debatable, just as the rest of the domain theory is.

Since attacking arguments can themselves be attacked by other arguments, comparing pairs of arguments is not sufficient; what is also needed is a definition of the status of arguments on the basis of all ways in which they interact. It is this definition that produces the output of an AF: it divides arguments in, typically, three classes: arguments with which a dispute can be 'won', respectively, 'lost' and arguments which leave the dispute undecided. In this paper we will denote these classes with the terms 'justified', 'overruled' and 'defensible' arguments.

Systems which fit this description have been called 'declarative' (Loui & Norman, 1995) and 'relational' (Gordon, 1994; Gordon, 1995). The reason is that AFs are not intended to model the *process* of argumentation; i.e. they are not meant to define standards for fair and effective dispute, or to define strategies for adding new information into the debate. Instead AFs define the nature of the relation between the premises put forward at a certain stage of a dispute, and the possible conclusions at that stage; i.e. they declare an argument to be in one of the three classes on the basis of the premises and the standards (for comparing arguments) that are given at a certain stage of a dispute.

Two other developments in AI and Law have focused more on the process of argumentation, in the setting of a two-party adversarial dialogue. The first development is research in precedent-based reasoning of e.g. (McCarty & Sridharan, 1982; Ashley, 1990; Rissland & Skalak, 1991; Skalak & Rissland, 1992), where the dialogue moves are possible dialectical uses of precedents, such as analogizing, distinguishing and rule discrediting. Whereas this line of research mainly focuses on the specific moves that can be made with precedents, and on the ways in which the precedents can best be represented to support these moves, another development, e.g. (Gordon, 1994; Gordon, 1995; Lodder & Herczog, 1995), focuses more on the general procedural properties of disputes. The leading idea here is that justice and rationality have a procedural side: a legal argument is acceptable if it has been defended against criticism in a properly conducted dispute. The main aims of this line of research are to define the general form of dialectical protocols, and to study what makes such a protocol proper, i.e. what makes it fair and effective.

As already mentioned in the introduction, and as earlier defended in (Prakken, 1995b), we think that these three developments complement each other. A dialectical model of fair and effective legal argument needs an argumentation framework to determine at each stage of a dispute which party is winning, and logical and procedural models are sterile if not complemented with theories on generating particular disputes in a realistic way. On the other hand, the logical and procedural models formulate standards with which actual disputes should comply.

An interesting attempt to synthesize these approaches is (Loui & Norman, 1995), which defines the allowed types of moves in a dispute, uses the AF of (Simari & Loui, 1992) to assess arguments at each stage of the debate, and presents ways of exploiting rationales of precedents to introduce new or remove old pieces of input information.

Finally, note that from this description two notions of an argument have emerged: the logical notion of an argument as a necessary relation between premises and a conclusion, and the dynamic notion of an argument as a move in a disputational setting. We think that these notions complement each other; in particular, we think that analogical arguments, as studied in e.g. (Ashley, 1990), can best be conceived as types of such argument moves, i.e. as heuristics for adding premises (for more detail see (Prakken, 1995b)).

3. Attacking Points in Legal Language

We now illustrate with some examples the features of legal language that we aim to formalise. Legal language offers a wide inventory of argumentative structures, such as contradictory rules, rules with assumptions, inapplicability statements, and priority rules. These structures can be found in legal discussions and documents recording them, but also in non argumentative legal documents, such as statutory texts or contracts.

Sometimes different arguments use rules with contradictory consequents. In statutory texts such 'head-to-head' conflicts can be found for a variety of reasons, extensively discussed in our earlier work. In legal debates they typically arise when parties appeal to competing principles, as in the following example from Italian law. According to the principle of the protection of privacy, it is forbidden to propagate private information, while according to the principle of the freedom of communication, it is allowed to propagate every piece of information, at least when it has a public significance. A piece of information about the private life of a person having a public role both concerns the privacy of an individual and has public relevance, so that its propagation puts the two just mentioned principles into conflict.

Another example of this type concerns a conflict between European and Italian law. According to a general principle of the European community law, if a product is lawfully put into commerce in an E.C. country, it can be freely sold in any other E.C. country, unless special reasons occur, such as the preservation of public health or consumer protection. In Italy it had been forbidden to sell products called 'pasta' not being made of hard corn. According to a decision of the European court of justice European law prevails, and 'pasta' products not made of hard corn, merchandized in other European countries, can also be sold in Italy.

The next feature we want to formalise is reasoning about priorities. To decide a head-to-head conflict between arguments with incompatible rules often priority rules are used, establishing which one of the competing rules is to prevail. The law offers well-known general priority rules such as the principles of specificity (Lex Specialis), temporality (Lex Posterior) and hierarchy (Lex Superior). Other domain-dependent general priority rules are explicitly stated by the legislator. For instance, in Italy, in town planning regulations we can find a priority rule stating that rules intended to protect artistic buildings prevail over rules concerning town planning; and in The Netherlands section 1637c of the Civil Code gives priority to statutory rules concerning labour contracts over statutory rules concerning any other type of contract.

Besides general priority rules, there are implicit specific priority assertions, which the interpreter may detect, just by a combined interpretation of the involved rules. For example, the Italian Criminal Code includes a prescription establishing that he who acted in self defence is not responsible. This prescription is obviously (although implicitly) intended to prevail over each particular criminal provision establishing responsibility for a specific crime.

Finally, substantive priority rules may be used, adducing special domain dependent grounds for preferring certain rules. For instance, in the privacy example the conflict could be solved by a rule stating that if the involved person is a politician, and the private information concerns aspects which may affect his/her political functioning, then the communication rule should be preferred.

It is important to note that priority rules behave exactly like any other legal rule: also these rules make their consequent (a priority assertion) dependent on the satisfaction of certain conditions, and also between these rules the conflicts can be solved appealing to priority rules. For instance, the town planning priority rule may be in conflict with Lex Posterior and to this conflict Lex Superior, Lex Specialis and, as we will see in Section 6.2, even Lex Posterior itself may apply. Our formalisation will respect this, i.e. it will treat priority rules like any other premise.

We will also include assumptions in our formalisation. Often, the satisfaction of the antecedent provided by a legal rule is able to produce the effect of the rule only if certain conditions are not proved to hold: the complements of these conditions will here be called the assumptions of the rule. For instance, in the above pasta example the EC rule contains a clause 'unless special reasons occur'. Another example is Section 3:32-(1) of the Dutch Civil Code, which declares every person to have the capacity to perform juridical acts, "to the extent that the law does not provide otherwise". Often the methods of representing exceptions explicitly, with assumptions, and implicitly, with priorities, are presented as alternatives. However, in legal texts also rules with explicit exceptions are subject to defeat by rules with higher priority, for instance, on the basis of Lex Superior or Lex Posterior; therefore a full theory of legal argument should be able to deal with the combination of assumptions and priorities.

In some cases assumptions may be 'discovered' by the legal interpreter; then they are considered implicit presuppositions of the involved rules. Other assumptions are explicitly established by the involved rule, by including an unless clause or a similar expression, as, as in the two above-given examples.

Finally, we want to formalise applicability rules. In legal texts and judicial debates rules frequently occur which deny the applicability of certain other rules, under certain conditions. Those rules do not exclude a determinate legal conclusion, but intend just to exclude the possibility of using a specific rule or set of rules. For instance, Section 2 of the Dutch rent act states that the act is not applicable to lease contracts which by their nature concern a short termed usage. Note that rules denying applicability may themselves be contradicted by rules affirming it.

4. The Formal System I: Fixed Priorities

We now present our own argumentation framework, along the lines of the informal description in Section 2. We will present the system in two stages: in this and the following section we will assume that the priorities are fixed and undisputable, while in Section 6 we will make them defeasible, by allowing also arguments about the priorities.

4.1. The Language

The object language of our system is of familiar logic-programming style: it contains a twoplace one-direction connective that forms rules out of literals, which can contain two kinds of negation, weak and strong negation. A *strong* literal is an atomic first-order formula, or such a formula preceded by strong negation $\neg$. For any atom A we say that A and $\neg A$ are the complement of each other; in the metalanguage we will denote the complement of a literal L with $\overline{L}$. A *weak* literal is a literal of the form $\sim L$, where L is a strong literal. Informally, $\sim L$ reads as 'there is no evidence that L is the case', while $\neg L$ says 'L is definitely not the case'.

DEFINITION 4.1. A *rule* is an expression of the form

$$r : L_0 \wedge \ldots \wedge L_j \wedge \sim L_k \wedge \ldots \wedge \sim L_m \Rightarrow L_n$$

where r, a first-order term, is the name of the rule and each L_i ($0 \leq i \leq n$) is a strong literal. The conjunction at the left of the arrow is the *antecedent* and the literal at the right of the arrow is the *consequent* of the rule. As usual, a rule with variables is a scheme standing for all its ground instances.

Note that a rule may have zero literals in its antecedent. Such a rule can be used to express an unconditional statement. Although informal discourse might prefer to call unconditional rules 'facts' (when they are strict) or 'assumptions' (when they are defeasible), we will also call such rules 'rules', to stress that in our system they are treated in exactly the same way as proper conditional rules.

Variables will in this paper be denoted with the letters x, y and z, and constants with any other letter, or with words.

Next we define the input information of our system, which will be called an *ordered theory*. Obviously, the input contains rules. However, we will assume that the input rules are divided into two categories, the set D of *defeasible* rules and the set S of *strict* rules; we assume that no member of S contains a weak literal. Informally, the defeasible rules express information that is intended by the user of the system to be subject to debate, while the strict rules represent the information that is intended to be beyond debate. Thus the strict rules can be used to express meaning postulates, like 'Bachelors are not married', and properties of relations, like transitivity of the 'older than' relation or asymmetry of the 'father of' relation. Note that a defeasible rule can be defeasible in two ways: it can be overridden by stronger rules with a contradicting consequent, and it can contain assumptions that are not warranted.

Syntactically, strict and defeasible rules differ in only one respect: only defeasible rules can contain assumptions. For the rest we have chosen to make the distinction between strict and defeasible rules not at the syntactic but at the pragmatic level. That is, the logic governing the conditional operator is the same for both types of rules; they differ only in their epistemological status. Yet, for notational convenience we will, when writing down rules, use $\rightarrow$ when a rule is strict and $\Rightarrow$ when a rule is defeasible. However, formally the symbol $\rightarrow$ is not part of our object language; it is just a shorthand for saying that a rule is in the set of strict rules.

As discussed in the introduction, in legal reasoning conflicts between defeasible rules are often resolved with the help of statements on which rule takes precedence. Accordingly, our input information will also contain an ordering $<$ on the set D, which we will assume to be a strict partial order, i.e. transitive (if $x < y$ and $y < z$ then $x < z$) and asymmetric (if $x < y$ then $y \not< x$). $x < y$ means that y has priority over x. Because strict rules are beyond debate, no ordering needs to be defined on S.

In sum, our system assumes input information in the form of an *ordered theory* $(S, D, <)$, where S and D are sets of, respectively, strict and defeasible rules and $<$ is a strict partial order on D.

4.2. ARGUMENTS

The basic notion of a system for defeasible argumentation is that of an argument. In general, the idea is that an argument for a certain proposition is a proof of that proposition in the logic of the underlying language. In our system, the simple language gives rise to a simple notion of an argument, viz. as a sequence of rules that can be chained together, and that is 'grounded' in the facts. This is captured by a slight variant of (Dung, 1993)'s notion of a 'defeasible proof'.

DEFINITION 4.2. An *argument* is a finite sequence $A = [r_0, \ldots, r_n]$ of ground instances of rules such that

1. for every i $(0 \leq i \leq n)$, for every strong literal L_j in the antecedent of r_i there is a $k < i$ such that L_j is the consequent of r_k.
2. No two distinct rules in the sequence have the same consequent.

An argument A is *based on* the ordered theory $(S, D, <)$ iff all rules of A are in $S \cup D$.*

Condition (1) says that arguments are formed by chaining rules together. A subtlety is that in doing so, weak literals may be ignored. Condition (2) prevents arguments from containing circular chains of rules.

For any ordered theory Γ we will denote the set of all arguments on the basis of Γ with $Args_\Gamma$. Likewise, for any set R of rules, $Args_R$ stands for the set of all arguments that consist of only rules in R.

We will also use the following notions.

DEFINITION 4.3. For any argument A:

1. A is *strict* iff it does not contain any defeasible rule; it is *defeasible* otherwise.
2. An argument A' is a *(proper) subargument* of A iff A' is a (proper) subsequence of A.
3. a literal L is a *conclusion* of A iff L is the consequent of some rule in A;
4. A literal L is an *assumption* of A iff $\sim \overline{L}$ occurs in some rule in A.

Note that Condition (3) makes the consequent of any rule in the chain a conclusion of the argument. The alternative, to regard only the consequent of the last rule as a conclusion, is perhaps philosophically more usual, but our choice makes some other definitions simpler.

To illustrate these notions, for the (defeasible) argument

$$A = [r_1 :\rightarrow a, r_2 : a \wedge \sim \neg b \Rightarrow c, r_3 : c \wedge \sim d \Rightarrow e]$$

we have that A's conclusions are $\{a, c, e\}$, its subarguments are $\{[\,], [r_1], [r_1, r_2], [r_1, r_2, r_3]\}$, of which only $[\,]$ and $[r_1]$ are strict, and A's assumptions are $\{b, \neg d\}$.

* Where there is no danger of confusion, we will leave 'based on $(S, D, <)$' implicit.

EXAMPLE 4.4. The next example illustrates the distinction between weak and strong negation. Rule r_1 states that a person who cannot be shown to be a minor has the capacity to perform legal acts, and rule r_2 requires that a person is positively shown not to be a minor, in order that s/he can exercise the right to vote. The point is that these rules give rise to an argument for 'x has legal capacity' but not for 'x has the right to vote', since there is no rule providing the antecedent of r_2.

$$r_1: \quad \sim x \text{ is a minor } \Rightarrow x \text{ has legal capacity}$$

$$r_2: \quad \neg x \text{ is a minor } \Rightarrow x \text{ has the right to vote}$$

4.3. Conflicts between Arguments

So far the notions have been fairly standard; now we will present the adversarial aspects of our system. We first define in which ways an argument can attack, i.e. be a counterargument of another argument. This definition does not yet include any way of checking which argument is better; it only tells us which arguments are in conflict. As already indicated in Section 3, the two different kinds of negation give rise to two ways of attacking an argument. Let us first explain them informally. Assume an argument A has a conclusion L. Then the first way of attack consists in contradicting a conclusion: i.e. A attacks any argument B which has a conclusion $\overline{L}$. Clearly, such a head-to-head conflict is symmetric: if A head-to-head attacks B, then B head-to-head attacks A. The second way of attack, with weak negation, consists in contradicting an assumption: i.e. A attacks any argument B which has an assumption $\overline{L}$. Obviously, this way of attack is not symmetric.

However, strict rules complicate the matter. To see this, consider the following example.

EXAMPLE 4.5. Assume we have two defeasible rules

$$r_1: \quad A \Rightarrow x \text{ is a lease}$$

$$r_2: \quad B \Rightarrow \neg\, x \text{ is a contract}$$

and a strict rule

$$s_1: \quad x \text{ is a lease } \rightarrow x \text{ is a contract}$$

and assume we have the strict facts f_1: $\rightarrow A$, f_2: $\rightarrow B$. Now the rules with complementary consequents are* r_2 and s_1. However, intuitively it seems that r_2 does not compete with the strict rule s_1 but with the defeasible rule r_1; s_1 just expresses a linguistic convention.

Here is a variant of this example.

* Sometimes we will leave implicit that we refer to ground instances of rules.

EXAMPLE 4.6. Assume we have

r_1 : $A \Rightarrow x$ is married

r_2 : $B \Rightarrow x$ is a bachelor

s_1 : x is married $\rightarrow \neg x$ is a bachelor

s_2 : x is a bachelor $\rightarrow \neg x$ is married

and the strict facts f_1: $\rightarrow A$, f_2: $\rightarrow B$. Again, the rules that intuitively are in conflict with each other are not the rules with complementary consequents (r_1 vs. s_2 and r_2 vs. s_1), but the two defeasible rules r_1 and r_2. The strict rules just declare the predicates 'married' and 'bachelor' to be incompatible.

These examples suggest the following way of defining a conflict between arguments: if an argument A has a conclusion or assumption L, we should consider A as being attacked by all those arguments which can *with only strict rules* be extended to an argument with conclusion $\overline{L}$.

To illustrate this, in Example 4.5 the argument $[f_1, r_1]$ attacks the argument $[f_2, r_2]$, since $[f_1, r_1]$ can with the strict rule s_2 be extended to an argument for 'x is a contract'. More generally, in the first way of attack we have to extend *both* arguments with only strict rules, to see if eventually they will have complementary conclusions. This is captured by the following definitions, which, like all other definitions, are implicitly assumed to be relative to an ordered theory $(S, D, <)$. First we have to define the notion of extending an argument.

DEFINITION 4.7. Let A be an argument and T a sequence of rules. Then $A + T$ is the concatenation of A and T.*

Now the notion of attacking/conflicting/counterarguments is defined as follows.**

DEFINITION 4.8. Let A_1 and A_2 be two arguments. Then A_1 *attacks* A_2 iff there are sequences S_1, S_2 of strict rules such that $A_1 + S_1$ is an argument with conclusion L and

1. $A_2 + S_2$ is an argument with a conclusion $\overline{L}$; or
2. A_2 is an argument with an assumption $\overline{L}$.

We have already discussed some peculiarities of this definition when strict rules are involved. We can add that if two arguments contain defeasible rules with complementary consequents, the definition is satisfied if S_1 and S_2 are empty. We now give some examples of this type, illustrating some more features of Definition 4.8.

* Since the order of rules does not matter except that the antecedents of a rule should come from a previous rule, we ignore the fact that $A + T$ is not uniquely defined.

** To prevent terminological confusion, it should be noted that (Dung, 1993) and (Bondarenko et al., 1993) use the term 'attack' in a different way, coming closer to our notion of 'defeat', to be defined below. They do not have an explicit notion of what we call 'attack'.

EXAMPLE 4.9. The first example shows that in order to attack an argument, a counterargument can point its attack at that argument itself, but also at one of its proper subarguments, thereby indirectly attacking the entire argument. So if we have

$r_1: \quad \Rightarrow f$ forged evidence e

$r_2: \quad f$ forged evidence $e \Rightarrow \neg e$ is admissible evidence

$r_3: \quad \Rightarrow \neg f$ forged evidence e

we have that $[r_3]$ does not only attack $[r_1]$, but also $[r_1, r_2]$.

EXAMPLE 4.10. And if we vary this example into

$r_1: \quad \Rightarrow f$ forged evidence e

$r_2: \quad f$ forged evidence $e \Rightarrow \neg f$ is honest

$r_3: \quad f$ is police officer $\Rightarrow f$ is honest

$r_4: \quad f$ is honest $\Rightarrow \neg f$ forged evidence

together with the fact

$s_1: \rightarrow f$ is police officer

then we have that $[r_1, r_2]$ does not only attack $[s_1, r_3]$ but also $[s_1, r_3, r_4]$. And $[s_1, r_3, r_4]$ does not only attack $[r_1]$, but also $[r_1, r_2]$.

The concept of 'attack/counterargument' is very important, since clearly a minimum requirement on any system for defeasible argumentation is that if two arguments are in conflict with each other, they cannot both be accepted as justified: at best, they can be accepted alternatively. We want our system to agree with this, in the sense that the set of 'justified arguments', to be defined later, is unique and conflict-free. To this end, we now define the following notions.

DEFINITION 4.11. An argument is *coherent* iff it does not attack itself.

Two examples of incoherent arguments are $[r_1 : \Rightarrow a, \ r_2 : \ a \Rightarrow \neg a]$ and $[r_1 : \ \sim a \Rightarrow b, r_2 : \ b \Rightarrow a]$.

DEFINITION 4.12. A set *Args* of arguments is *conflict-free* iff no argument in *Args* attacks an argument in *Args*.

COROLLARY 4.13. *If* $Args_S$ *is not conflict-free, then every argument is incoherent.*

4.4. DEFEAT AMONG ARGUMENTS

Now that we know which arguments are in conflict with each other, the next step is to compare conflicting arguments. To this end we define, in two steps, a binary relation of defeat among arguments.* It is important to realise that this comparison does not yet determine with which arguments a dispute can be won; it only tells us something about the relation between two individual arguments (and their subarguments).

To capture the different 'force' of the two ways of attack, we define 'defeat' in terms of two other notions, rebutting and undercutting** an argument. Their difference depends on whether the attacking argument contradicts a conclusion or an assumption of the attacked argument. Only in the first case will the priorities be used. This is based on our view that in legal reasoning the priorities are only used to resolve head-to-head conflicts between rules, not to resolve head-to-body conflicts. The definition of defeat will state how to use the notions of rebutting and undercutting an argument in combination.

Let us first concentrate on head-to-head conflicts and see how the priorities can be used to compare the conflicting arguments. In its simplest form, with a head-to-head conflict between two defeasible rules, we will compare the arguments with respect to the priority relation between these two rules (for a defence of this approach over comparing the arguments with respect to their 'weakest links', the reader is referred to (Prakken, 1991; Prakken, 1993)). However, if the conflict involves strict rules, then each argument may contain more than one rule of which the priority is relevant. To see this, suppose that $A = [r_1\colon \Rightarrow Rab, r_2\colon \Rightarrow Rbc]$, $B = [r_3\colon \Rightarrow Rca]$, and that S contains transitivity and asymmetry axioms for R. Then A can with these axioms be extended to an argument for $\neg Rca$, which means that A attacks B and vice versa. Now if we examine A, it seems natural to regard the priority of both r_1 and r_2 as relevant to deciding the conflict. So we want to compare r_3 with the set of rules $\{r_1, r_2\}$. In general, both arguments involved in a conflict can have more than one rule directly relevant to the conflict, and therefore in general we have to compare two *sets* of defeasible rules.

So what are the rules that are relevant for the comparison? In the simple case, when the conflict is between two defeasible rules with complementary consequents, they are exactly those defeasible rules. In the more complex case, when the conflict is determined by strict rules, they are, for each argument, all defeasible rules that are used to satisfy the antecedents of the strict rules with which the argument is (hypothetically) extended to establish a conflict. In the special case when the conflict is entirely caused by strict rules, the sets of relevant defeasible rules will be empty. Formally:

---

* Note that the argument relations and properties defined below are relative to an implicitly assumed ordered theory.

** As further discussed in (Prakken & Sartor, 1996b), our notion of undercutting is a special case of Pollock's (1992) 'undercutting defeaters'

DEFINITION 4.14. For any argument A and set S of strict rules such that $A + S$ is an argument with conclusion L we define the set $R_L(A + S)$ of the defeasible rules relevant to L in the argument $A + S$ as follows. $R_L(A + S) =$

1. $\{r_d\}$ iff A includes a defeasible rule r_d with consequent L;
2. $R_{L_1}(A+S) \cup \ldots \cup R_{L_n}(A+S)$ iff A is defeasible and S includes a strict rule r_s: $L_1 \wedge \ldots \wedge L_n \rightarrow L$.

Observe that since by definition no argument contains two rules with the same consequent, the set $R_L(A + S)$ is always unique.

To illustrate this definition, in Examples 4.6 and 4.10 the rules to be compared are r_1 and r_2. Consider next $A = [r_1\colon \Rightarrow Rab,\ r_2\colon \Rightarrow Rbc,\ s_1\colon Rab \wedge Rbc \rightarrow Rac]$. Then $R_{Rac}(A) = \{r_1, r_2\}$. However, if we make s_1 a defeasible rule, then $R_{Rac}(A) = \{s_1\}$.

Next we define how sets of rules are ordered on the basis of an ordering on their members.

DEFINITION 4.15. For any two sets R and R' of defeasible rules, $R < R'$ iff for some $r \in R$ and all $r' \in R'$ it holds that $r < r'$.

The intuitive idea behind this definition is that if $R < R'$, R can be made better by replacing some rule in R with any rule in R', while the reverse is impossible.

Now we have enough tools to give the definition of rebutting and undercutting arguments. In fact, it will be almost the same as the one of attack; the only difference is that in the first case of attack, when arguments have complementary conclusions, we will use the priorities to assess them. Since we will not use the priorities in the second case, this means that an attack on an assumption always succeeds.

DEFINITION 4.16. Let A_1 and A_2 be two arguments. Then

- A_1 *rebuts* A_2 iff condition (1) of Definition 4.8 holds, provided that $R_L(A_1 + S_1) \not< R_{\overline{L}}(A_2 + S_2)$.
- A_1 *undercuts* A_2 iff condition (2) of Definition 4.8 holds.

To inspect some properties of the definition, note first that from the definition of attack these definitions inherit that also rebutting and undercutting an argument can be 'direct', or 'indirect'. Let us now investigate some other properties. Observe first that if A rebuts or undercuts B, then A attacks B. Obviously, it does not hold that if A undercuts B, then B undercuts A. However, neither does it hold that if A undercuts B, then B does not undercut A. A counterexample is $A = [r_1\colon \sim b \Rightarrow a]$, $B = [r_2\colon \sim a \Rightarrow b]$. It is also not the case that if A rebuts B, then B rebuts A. Just assume we have $A = [r_1\colon \Rightarrow a]$, $B = [r_2\colon \Rightarrow \neg a]$, and $r_2 < r_1$. However, rebutting involving a $<$ relation between conflicting rules is not always one-directional. To see this, assume in Example 4.10 that $r_1 < r_4$ and $r_3 < r_2$; then $[r_1, r_2]$ and $[s_1, r_3, r_4]$ rebut each other.

Finally we can give our definition of defeat. It states how in evaluating arguments the notions of undercutting and rebutting attack are combined. As a border case it regards any incoherent argument as defeated by the empty argument. Apart from this, the definition is based on two ideas, of which the first is implicit, and inherited from the definitions of attack, rebutting and undercutting: defeat of an argument can be direct, or indirect, by defeating one of its strict subarguments. The other idea is that our reading of $\sim A$ not only makes attacks on assumptions always succeed, but also makes an attack on an assumption stronger than an attack on a conclusion: if one argument undercuts the other, and the other does not undercut but only rebuts the first, the first defeats the second but the second does not defeat the first. Below we will explain the reason for our choice with an example.

DEFINITION 4.17. Let A_1 and A_2 be two arguments. Then A_1 *defeats* A_2 iff A_1 is empty and A_2 is incoherent, or else if
- A_1 undercuts A_2; or
- A_1 rebuts A_2 and A_2 does not undercut A_1.

We say that A_1 *strictly defeats* A_2 iff A_1 defeats A_2 and A_2 does not defeat A_1.

To check some boundary cases, from Definition 4.15 we have that for any nonempty set of rules R, $R < \emptyset$; this makes strict arguments strictly defeat conflicting defeasible arguments. Moreover, we have that $\emptyset \not< \emptyset$, so that no strict argument strictly defeats any conflicting strict argument (recall that strict rules contain no weak literals).

The following example illustrates that undercutting an argument is stronger than rebutting it.

EXAMPLE 4.18. Consider

$$r_1: \quad \sim \neg OJ \text{ is innocent } \Rightarrow OJ \text{ is innocent}$$

$$r_2: \quad \Rightarrow \neg OJ \text{ is innocent}$$

And assume that $< = \emptyset$. Then, although $[r_1]$ rebuts $[r_2]$, $[r_1]$ does not defeat $[r_2]$, since $[r_2]$ undercuts $[r_1]$. So $[r_2]$ strictly defeats $[r_1]$.

With this example we can explain why we regard undercutting attack as stronger than rebutting attack. This is since the only way to accept both rules is to believe that OJ is not innocent: in that case the condition of r_1 is not satisfied. By contrast, if it is believed that OJ is innocent, then r_2 has to be rejected, in the sense that its antecedent is believed but its consequent is not. In fact, we here employ the logical counterpart of the legal principle that the law should be interpreted as coherently as possible.

If we examine the nature of our notion of defeat, we see that it is a weak one, since for rebutting an argument no $>$ relation is needed between the sets of relevant rules, but only a $\not<$ relation. So, rather than having to be 'really better' than the argument that is to be defeated, a defeating argument only has to be not inferior. The reason we have this weak notion of defeat is that we want that our notion of 'justified arguments', to be defined next, really regards only those arguments as justified that, given the premises, are beyond any reasonable doubt or challenge. And reasonable doubt can be cast on an argument just by providing a counterargument that is not inferior to it.

For the same reason we also need the notion of strict defeat, which, being asymmetric, captures the idea of 'really being better than'. In the following section this notion will be used to ensure that a counterargument fails to cast doubt if it is inferior to at least one counterargument that is itself protected from defeat.

5. The Status of Arguments

5.1. The General Idea

Since defeating arguments can in turn be defeated by other arguments, comparing pairs of arguments is not sufficient; what is also needed is a definition that determines the status of arguments on the basis of all ways in which they interact. In particular, the definition should allow for reinstatement of defeated arguments, if their defeater is itself (strictly) defeated by another argument. Also, the definition should respect the 'weakest link' principle that an argument cannot be justified unless all of its subarguments are justified.

Defining this notion, then, is the central part of our system. This part takes as input the set of all possible arguments and their mutual relations of defeat, and produces as output a division of arguments into three classes: arguments with which a dispute can be 'won', respectively, 'lost' and arguments which leave the dispute undecided. As remarked above, the winning arguments should be only those arguments that, given the premises, are beyond reasonable doubt: the only way to cast doubt on these arguments is by providing new premises, giving rise to new, defeating counterarguments. Accordingly, we want our set of justified arguments to be unique, and to be conflict-free.

Inspired by earlier work of (Vreeswijk, 1993b; Dung, 1994; Brewka, 1994b; Loui & Norman, 1995) we develop this part of our framework as a proof theory in dialectical style, as a dialogue game. A proof that an argument is justified will take the form of a dialogue tree, where each branch of the tree is a dialogue, and the root of the tree is that argument. The idea is that every move in a dialogue consists of an argument based on the input theory, where each stated argument attacks the last move of the opponent in a way that meets the player's burden of proof. That a move consists of a complete argument, means that the search for an individual argument is conducted in a 'monological' fashion, determined by the nature of the underlying logic; only the process of considering counterarguments is modelled dialectically. The required force of a move depends on who states it. Since the proponent wants a conclusion to be justified, a proponent's argument has to be strictly defeating, while since the opponent only wants to prevent the conclusion from being justified, an opponent's move may be just defeating.

Before we illustrate and define these ideas, a remark is in order on the origin of the input theory. Logically, the dialogue game that we will define assumes a given 'pool' of rules from which the arguments are to be constructed. At first sight, this would seem to run counter to the way actual legal disputes proceed, where the parties can freely introduce new premises with every argument move. However, our assumption of a prior pool of premises is just a theoretical abstraction; nothing prevents applications to situations where the pool of premises consists of everything put forward by any of the parties in a dialogue.

Let us illustrate our ideas with a dialogue based on the following example.

EXAMPLE 5.1. Assume we have the following input theory.

r_1 : $\sim \neg e$ is admissible evidence $\Rightarrow e$ proves guilt

r_2 : $\Rightarrow f$ forged evidence e

r_3 : x forged evidence $y \Rightarrow \neg y$ is admissible evidence

r_4 : x is police officer $\wedge \sim x$ is dishonest $\Rightarrow \neg x$ forged evidence y

f_5 : $\rightarrow f$ is police officer in LA

f_6 : x is police officer in LA $\rightarrow x$ is police officer

r_7 : x is police officer in LA $\Rightarrow x$ is dishonest

r_8 : $\Rightarrow f$ has received a medal of honour

r_9 : x is police officer $\wedge\, x$ has received a medal of honour $\Rightarrow$
$\neg f$ is dishonest

and assume that, for whatever reason, $r_2 < r_4$, $r_7 < r_9$ and that all other rules are incomparable. Let us denote the arguments stated by the proponent by P_i and those of the opponent by O_i. The proponent starts the dispute by asserting that $[r_1]$ is a justified argument for 'e proves guilt'.

P_1 : $[r_1 : \sim \neg e$ is admissible evidence $\Rightarrow e$ proves guilt$]$

Now the opponent has to defeat this argument. It can do so in only one way, by undercutting it with

O_1 : $[r_2 : \Rightarrow f$ forged evidence e,
$r_3 : f$ forged evidence $e \Rightarrow \neg e$ is admissible evidence$]$

The proponent now has to counterattack with an argument that strictly defeats O_1. It finds the following rebuttal, using the fact that $r_2 < r_4$.

P_2 : $[f_5 : \rightarrow f$ is police officer in LA,

$$f_6 : f \text{ is police officer in LA } \rightarrow f \text{ is police officer,}$$
$$r_4 : f \text{ is police officer} \wedge \sim f \text{ is dishonest}$$
$$\Rightarrow \neg f \text{ forged evidence } e]$$

Again the opponent has only one way to respond, with the undercutting attack:

$$O_2 : \quad [f_5 :\rightarrow f \text{ is police officer in LA,}$$
$$r_7 : f \text{ is police officer in LA } \Rightarrow f \text{ is dishonest}]$$

This time the proponent responds with a strictly defeating rebuttal, using that $r_7 < r_9$.

$$P_3 : \quad [r_8 :\Rightarrow f \text{ has received a medal of honour,}$$
$$f_5 :\rightarrow f \text{ is police officer in LA,}$$
$$f_6 : f \text{ is police officer in LA } \rightarrow f \text{ is police officer,}$$
$$r_9 : x \text{ is police officer } \wedge x \text{ has received a medal of honour}$$
$$\Rightarrow \neg f \text{ is dishonest}]$$

Now the opponent has run out of moves: no argument on the basis of our ordered theory defeats P's last argument. And since at no point could O create alternative branches, P can successfully defend its argument against every possible way of attack: r_1 is a provably justified argument.

In dialectical proof systems a 'loop checker' can be implemented in a very natural way, by stating that no two moves of the proponent in the same branch of the dialogue may have the same content.

EXAMPLE 5.2. Assume for illustration that our ordered theory Γ is the following familiar logic-programming example.

$$r_1 : \quad \sim a \Rightarrow b$$

$$r_2 : \quad \sim b \Rightarrow a$$

This is how the attempt to prove b fails.

$$P_1 : \quad [r_1 :\sim a \Rightarrow b]$$

$$O_1 : \quad [r_2 :\sim b \Rightarrow a]$$

Now P has run out of moves, since any defeating attack on O_1 would have the same content as P_1.

It is easy to see that a non-repetition rule will not harm P; if O had a move the first time P stated the argument, it will also have a move the second time, so no repetition by P can make P win a dialogue.

5.2. THE DIALOGUE GAME

We now formally define the dialogue game. Our aim is to make it agree with the fixpoint definition of (Prakken & Sartor, 1995; Prakken & Sartor, 1996a), which is a variant of (Dung, 1993)'s grounded (skeptical) semantics of extended logic programming. More precisely, we want our dialogue game, when interpreted as a proof theory for this semantics, to be sound in the general case, and for justified arguments also complete for finitary ordered theories, i.e. for theories in which each argument has at most a finite number of attackers. For the proofs that this is the case we refer to (Prakken & Sartor, 1996b).

Justified arguments

We start with the notion of justified arguments.

DEFINITION 5.3. A *dialogue* based on an ordered theory Γ is a finite nonempty sequence of moves $move_i = (Player_i, Arg_i)$ $(i > 0)$, such that

1. $Arg_i \in Args_\Gamma$;
2. $Player_i = P$ iff i is odd; and $Player_i = O$ iff i is even;
3. If $Player_i = Player_j = P$ and $i \neq j$, then $Arg_i \neq Arg_j$;
4. If $Player_i = P$, then Arg_i is a minimal (w.r.t. set inclusion) argument strictly defeating Arg_{i-1} on the basis of Γ;
5. If $Player_i = O$, then Arg_i defeats Arg_{i-1} on the basis of Γ.

The first condition makes a dialogue relative to a given ordered theory, while the second condition says that the proponent begins and then the players take turns, and condition (3) prevents the proponent from repeating its attacks. The last two conditions form the heart of the definition: they state the burdens of proof for P and O. The minimality condition on P's moves makes it impossible to make arguments trivially different by combining them with some other, irrelevant argument.

In the remaining definitions we leave Γ implicit.

DEFINITION 5.4. A *dialogue tree* is a finite tree of moves such that

1. Each branch is a dialogue;
2. If $Player_i = P$ then the children of $move_i$ are all defeaters of Arg_i.

The second condition of this definition makes dialogue trees candidates for being proofs: it says that the tree should consider all possible ways in which O can attack an argument of P.

DEFINITION 5.5. A player *wins a dialogue* if the other player cannot move. And a player *wins a dialogue tree* iff it wins all branches of the tree.

The idea of this definition is that if P's last argument is undefeated, it reinstates all previous arguments of P that occur in the same branch of a tree, in particular the root of the tree.

DEFINITION 5.6. An argument A is *justified* iff there is a dialogue tree with A as its root, and won by the proponent.

Formal properties

In (Prakken & Sartor, 1996b) we have proven the desired results on soundness and completeness with respect to (Prakken & Sartor, 1996a). This means that every argument that is justified according to the dialogue game, is also justified according to the fixpoint semantics, while for finitary ordered theories every semantically justified argument is also dialectically justified. We have also shown that the set of justified arguments is unique and conflict-free, as desired. Finally, we have shown that our system respects the 'weakest link' principle that an argument cannot be justified if not all its subarguments are justified. Some systems incorporate this principle in the definition of a justified argument, e.g. (Vreeswijk, 1993a; Prakken, 1993; Sartor, 1993; Nute, 1994). In the present system this is not the case; instead it makes the principle follow from the other definitions, as also in e.g. (Pollock, 1992; Simari & Loui, 1992; Geffner & Pearl, 1992).

Overruled and defensible arguments

In (Prakken & Sartor, 1995; Prakken & Sartor, 1996a) the categories of overruled and defensible arguments are defined in a purely declarative way: an argument is *overruled* iff it is attacked by a justified argument, and it is *defensible* iff it is neither justified nor overruled. This definition is still possible in our present system, but then the question arises what are the corresponding dialogue rules. We will only discuss this for defensible arguments, since we do not expect that many parties in a dispute will want to defend their own argument as overruled.

So when is an argument dialectically shown to be defensible? The key idea is to reverse the burden of proof for O and P: the opponent now has to find an argument that *strictly* defeats the proponent's previous move, while the proponent only needs to find an argument that *defeats* the opponents last move. Moreover, the non-repetition condition now holds for the opponent instead of the proponent. For the rest the definitions remain unchanged: in particular, if the proponent can make the opponent run out of moves against every attacking strategy of the opponent, the argument is shown to be at least defensible.

Soundness of this definition with respect to (Prakken & Sartor, 1996a) is straightforward. Issues of completeness and the relation with other credulous semantics defined by (Dung, 1995), such as stable semantics, are left for future research. Here we confine ourselves to an example. Consider again the ordered theory of Example 5.2. Above we saw that P's attempt to prove P_1 to be justified failed. However, P can prove it to be defensible.

$$P_1 : \ [r_1 : \sim a \Rightarrow b]$$

And already O has run out of moves, since O_1, although defeating P_1, does not strictly defeat it, as is now required.

The status of conclusions

Since ultimately we are not interested in arguments but in the conclusions they support, we also have to define the status of strong literals. This can be done straightforwardly, by saying that L is a *justified conclusion* iff it is a conclusion of a justified argument; L is a *defensible conclusion* iff it is not justified and it is a conclusion of some defensible argument; and L is an *overruled conclusion* iff it is not justified or defensible, and a conclusion of an overruled argument.

5.3. ILLUSTRATIONS

EXAMPLE 5.7. The following example illustrates that our definitions respect the 'step-by-step' nature of argumentation: conflicts about conclusions or assumptions earlier in the chains are dealt with before 'later' conflicts.

$$r_1: \Rightarrow a \quad r_2: \ a \Rightarrow b \quad r_3: \ b \Rightarrow c$$
$$r_4: \Rightarrow \neg a \ r_5: \ \neg a \Rightarrow d \ r_6: \ d \Rightarrow \neg c$$

Assume that $< = \{r_4 < r_1, r_3 < r_6\}$. Then the arguments $[r_1 - r_3]$ and $[r_4 - r_6]$ defeat each other. However, the first argument can still be proven to be justified, because its subargument $[r_1]$ wins a conflict with a subargument of the second, viz. $[r_4]$. Here is the proof.

$$P_1: \ [r_1: \Rightarrow a, \quad r_2: \ a \Rightarrow b, \quad r_3: \ b \Rightarrow c]$$
$$O_1: \ [r_4: \Rightarrow \neg a, \ r_5: \ \neg a \Rightarrow d, \ r_6: \ d \Rightarrow \neg c]$$
$$P_2: \ [r_1: \Rightarrow a]$$

O cannot counter with $[r_4\!: \Rightarrow \neg a]$: that argument does not defeat P_2, since $r_4 < r_1$.

EXAMPLE 5.8. Finally, we show that our system does not exhibit a form of 'extreme skepticism', to be found, for instance, in (Horty et al., 1990; Nute, 1994). Informally speaking, a system is extremely skeptical if arguments have to be 'cut off' not only when they are overruled, but also when they are merely defensible. In our system this is not the case, as is illustrated by the following example.

r_1: $\Rightarrow f$ forged evidence e

r_2: f forged evidence $e \Rightarrow \neg e$ is admissible evidence

r_3: $\Rightarrow \neg f$ forged evidence e

r_4: $\sim \neg e$ is admissible evidence $\Rightarrow e$ proves guilt

Assume that $< = \emptyset$. Here is how the proof for 'e proves guilt' fails.

$$P_1: \quad [r_4: \sim \neg e \text{ is admissible evidence } \Rightarrow e \text{ proves guilt}]$$

$$O_1: \quad [r_1: \Rightarrow f \text{ forged evidence } e,$$
$$r_2: f \text{ forged evidence } e \Rightarrow \neg e \text{ is admissible evidence}]$$

Now P has run out of moves, since $[r_3]$ defeats O_1 only nonstrictly. By contrast, in extremely skeptical systems $[r_1, r_2]$ is, in our terms, not allowed to prevent $[r_4]$ from becoming justified, since it has a subargument that is only defensible. As a result, in such systems $[r_4]$ is justified, even though it is attacked by an argument that is not worse than any counterargument.

Although this difference reflects a 'clash of intuitions', we think that our intuitions are justified by our general approach. Recall that we regard an argument as justified only if, given the premises, no doubt at all can be cast on the argument. Now here doubt can be cast on the argument $[r_4]$, since it has a counterargument that is not weaker than any argument attacking it. We think that in a dispute a judge would feel compelled to determine whether $r_1 < r_3$ before deciding in favour of P.

5.4. The Dialogue Game: Declarative or Procedural?

In Section 2 we remarked that argumentation frameworks are not procedural but declarative, or relational theories, since their only job is to define a relation between premises and conclusions: given a body of input information they declare arguments to have a certain status. Now the dialogue game defined in the present section clearly has a procedural flavour; does this mean that we have shifted from a declarative to a procedural perspective?

We think that this is partly the case. Although the definitions of Section 4, together with the fixpoint characterisation of the justified arguments of (Prakken & Sartor, 1996a) clearly form an AF, the present dialogue game may be regarded as the logical core of a dialectical protocol, i.e. as that part of a protocol that applies the AF. Thus our dialogue game links the AF with a dialectical protocol. We can even state this more generally: our dialogue game links any theory that produces a binary relation of defeat among arguments with any dialectical protocol that incorporates our dialogue rules.

6. The Formal System II: Defeasible Priorities

6.1. The New Definitions

So far we have simply assumed that there is a fixed and undisputable ordering on the rules. However, as we already said in the introduction, this assumption is unrealistic: in legal reasoning, and also in several other domains of practical reasoning, the standards for conflict resolution are themselves subject to debate and disagreement. A full theory of defeasible argumentation in law should therefore also be able to formalise arguments about priorities.

Obviously, we cannot simply do this by only adding a priority predicate symbol to our object language; in addition the priorities derived at the object level somehow need to be lifted to the metatheory of the system, in particular to Definition 4.15. So we have to define a formal connection between object and metalevel.

We start by assuming that our language contains a distinguished twoplace predicate symbol $\prec$, with which information on the priorities can be expressed in the object language. This makes the third component of an ordered theory redundant, so an *ordered theory* is from now on just a pair (S, D). Next we have to make sure that the ordering thus derived is of the desired type, i.e. that it is a strict partial order. This can be done by adding the axioms of a partial order to the strict rules. A slight complication is that, since strict rules do not allow for contraposition, we also have to add the contrapositive rules for transitivity (for asymmetry the contrapositive is redundant). Thus, in the rest of this paper we assume that of every input theory the set S of strict rules contains all and only the following rules containing the $\prec$ predicate.

$$t_1: \quad x \prec y \land y \prec z \rightarrow x \prec z$$

$$t_2: \quad x \prec y \land \neg x \prec z \rightarrow \neg y \prec z$$

$$t_3: \quad y \prec z \land \neg x \prec z \rightarrow \neg x \prec y$$

$$a: \quad x \prec y \rightarrow \neg y \prec x$$

We now need to link the priority conclusions that can be drawn at the object level to the metalevel of our system: i.e. we want to make sure that $(r, r') \in <$ if and only if there is a justified argument for $r \prec r'$. We retain the idea of (Prakken & Sartor, 1995) and (Prakken & Sartor, 1996a) that the ordering component of an ordered theory Γ is now determined by the set of all priority arguments that are justified on the basis of Γ. Therefore, we have to define the following notation, capturing what a certain set of arguments says about the priorities.

DEFINITION 6.1. For any set *Args* of arguments

$$<_{Args} = \{r < r' \mid r \prec r' \text{ is a conclusion of some } A \in Args\}$$

And we say for any set of arguments *Args* that A (strictly) *Args*-defeats B on the basis of Γ iff according to Definition 4.17 A (strictly) defeats B on the basis of $(\Gamma, <_{Args})$. Occasionally, we will also use the analogous notion *Args*-rebuts. And for any argument A we write $\{A\}$-defeats as A-defeats.

Now we have to change our rules of the dialogue game. The main problem here is on the basis of which priorities the defeating force of the moves should be determined.

What we want to avoid is that we have to generate all priority arguments before we can determine the defeating force of a move. The pleasant surprise is that, to achieve this, a few very simple conditions suffice. For O it is sufficient that its move $\emptyset$-defeats P's previous move. This is so since, as shown in (Prakken & Sartor, 1996b), Definition 4.17 implies that if A is for some S an S-defeater of P's previous move, it is also an $\emptyset$-defeater of that move. So O does not have to take priorities into account, as is illustrated by

$$P_1: \quad [r_1 :\Rightarrow a]$$

Now a possible move of O is

$$O_1: \quad [r_2 :\Rightarrow b, r_3 : b \Rightarrow \neg a]$$

P, on the other hand, should take some priorities into account. However, it suffices to apply only those priorities that are stated by P's move; more priorities are not needed, since Definition 4.17 also implies that if P's argument Arg_i strictly $Args_i$-defeats O's previous move, it will also do so whatever more priorities will be derived. So P can reply to O_1 with

$$P_2: \quad [r_4 :\Rightarrow \neg b, r_5 :\Rightarrow r_2 \prec r_4]$$

However, this is not the only type move that the proponent can make. If O responds with

$$O_2: [r_2 :\Rightarrow b]$$

which $\emptyset$-defeats P_2, then P must have the possibility to 'undo' the defeating force of O_2 with the priority argument

$$P_3: \quad [r_5 :\Rightarrow r_2 \prec r_4]$$

We now incorporate these ideas in the definition of a dialogue. All conditions are the same as above, except for the references to 'defeat'.

DEFINITION 6.2. A *priority dialogue* based on Γ is a finite sequence of moves $move_i = (Player_i, Arg_i)$ $(i > 0)$, where

1. $Arg_i \in Args_\Gamma$;
2. $Player_i = P$ iff i is odd, and $Player_i = O$ iff i is even;
3. If $Player_i = Player_j = P$ and $i \neq j$, then $Arg_i \neq Arg_j$;
4. If $Player_i = P$ then Arg_i is a minimal (w.r.t. set inclusion) argument such that
   - Arg_i strictly Arg_i-defeats Arg_{i-1} on the basis of Γ; or
   - Arg_{i-1} does not Arg_i-defeat A_{i-2} on the basis of Γ;
5. If $Player_i = O$ then Arg_i $\emptyset$-defeats Arg_{i-1} on the basis of Γ.

The only change in the definition of a dialogue tree is that the defeat condition on O's moves is made relative to the empty set.

DEFINITION 6.3. A *priority dialogue tree* is a finite tree of moves such that

1. Each branch is a dialogue;
2. If $Player_i = P$ then the children of $move_i$ are all $\emptyset$-defeaters of Arg_i.

The other definitions stay the same.

In (Prakken & Sartor, 1996b) we prove that the abovementioned formal properties of the system with strict priorities also hold for the defeasible case.

6.2. Applications

In the remaining examples we will use the following method for naming rules. Every rule with terms $t_1, \ldots, t_n$ is named with a function expression $r(t_1, \ldots, t_n)$, where r is the informal name of the rule.

First we propose a systematic way of formalising reasoning about multiple legal orderings. The idea is to just write 'if' definitions, so that the ordering is possibly partially unspecified. The three general principles Lex Superior, Lex Specialis and Lex Posterior thus become:

$$H(x,y): \quad x \text{ is inferior to } y \Rightarrow x \prec y$$

$$T(x,y): \quad x \text{ is earlier than } y \Rightarrow x \prec y$$

$$S(x,y): \quad y \text{ is more specific than } x \Rightarrow x \prec y$$

Other rules can then specify when the antecedents of these rules hold. For example,

$$r_1(r_3(x), r_4(x)): \quad \Rightarrow r_4(x) \text{ is more specific than } r_3(x)$$

$$r_2(x,y): \quad x \text{ is in a statute } \wedge y \text{ is in the constitution} \Rightarrow x \text{ is inferior to } y$$

$r_1(r_3(x), r_4(x))$ says of two particular rules $r_3(x)$ and $r_4(x)$ that one is more specific than the other. This premise could be specified 'by hand' by the user but it could also be the outcome of a logical specificity checker, as e.g. used by (Simari & Loui, 1992).

Finally, the relation between the three principles can be specified by

$$O_1(T(x,y), H(x,y)): \quad \Rightarrow T(x,y) \prec H(x,y)$$

$$O_2(S(x,y), T(x,y)): \quad \Rightarrow S(x,y) \prec T(x,y)$$

EXAMPLE 6.4. We now formalise an example in which the Italian priority rule on building regulations, mentioned in Section 3, conflicts with the temporality principle that the later rule has priority over the earlier one. They state contradicting priorities between a town planning rule saying that if a building needs restructuring, its exterior may be modified, and an earlier, and conflicting, artistic-buildings rule saying that if a building is on the list of protected buildings, its exterior may not be modified.

Note that rule r_9 states that rule r_3 is later than the Lex Posterior principle T, which implies that r_3 prevails over T, according to T itself. The application of a priority rule to itself (or better, to one of its instances), is an interesting peculiarity of this example.

$r_1(x)$:	x is a protected building $\Rightarrow \neg$ x's exterior may be modified
$r_2(x)$:	x needs restructuring $\Rightarrow$ x's exterior may be modified
$r_3(x,y)$:	x is about the protection of artistic buildings $\wedge$ y is a town planning rule $\Rightarrow y \prec x$
$T(x,y)$:	x is earlier than $y \Rightarrow x \prec y$
$r_4(r_1(x))$:	$\Rightarrow r_1(x)$ is about the protection of artistic buildings
$r_5(r_2(x))$:	$\Rightarrow r_2(x)$ is a town planning rule
$r_6(r_1(x), r_2(y))$:	$\Rightarrow r_1(x)$ is earlier than $r_2(y)$
$r_7(\mathit{Villa}_0)$:	$\Rightarrow$ *Villa*$_0$ is a protected building
$r_8(\mathit{Villa}_0)$:	$\Rightarrow$ *Villa*$_0$ needs restructuring
$r_9(T(x,y), r_3(x,y))$:	$\Rightarrow T(x,y)$ is earlier than $r_3(x,y)$

To maintain readability, we will below only give the function-symbol part of the rule names. Here is a proof that the exterior of *Villa*$_0$ may not be modified.

P_1 : [r_7 : $\Rightarrow$ *Villa*$_0$ is a protected building,
r_1 : *Villa*$_0$ is a protected building $\Rightarrow \neg$*Villa*$_0$'s exterior may be modified]

O can respond in only one way.

O_1 : [r_8 : $\Rightarrow$ *Villa*$_0$ needs restructuring,
r_2 : *Villa*$_0$ needs restructuring $\Rightarrow$ *Villa*$_0$'s exterior may be modified]

P can now neutralize O's defeater with the following priority argument, saying that the protection rule prevails over the town planning rule.

P_2 : [r_4 : $\Rightarrow r_1$ is about the protection of artistic buildings,
r_5 : $\Rightarrow r_2$ is a town planning rule,

r_3 : r_1 is about the protection of artistic buildings $\wedge$

r_2 is a town planning rule $\Rightarrow r_2 \prec r_1]$

But O can $\emptyset$-defeat this priority argument with a conflicting priority argument based on the Lex Posterior principle.

O_2 : $[r_6 : \Rightarrow r_1$ is earlier than r_2,

T : r_1 is earlier than $r_2 \Rightarrow r_1 \prec r_2]$

Now P takes the debate to the meta-meta-level, by asserting a priority argument that neutralizes O's defeater at the meta-level. P's argument says that, since the Lex Posterior principle is earlier than the building regulations principle, the former is inferior to the latter on the basis of the former. Although this seems to be self-referential, formally it is not, since it is one instance of Lex Posterior that speaks about another instance of itself.

P_3 : $[r_9 : \Rightarrow T$ is earlier than r_3,

T' : T is earlier than $r_3 \Rightarrow T \prec r_3]$

Now O has run out of moves, and we know that the villa's exterior may not be modified. Note that in this dialogue the function arguments of T and r_3 are instances of r_1 and r_2, while of T' they are the full versions of T and r_3. We leave it to the computer to write the full name of T'.

EXAMPLE 6.5. Consider next the pasta example from the introduction, which combines priorities and assumptions.

$r_1(x, y, z)$: x can be sold in $y \wedge$
y is an E.C. country $\wedge$
z is an E.C. country $\wedge$
$\sim$ the selling of x in z endangers public health $\wedge$
$\sim$ the selling of x in z prejudices the consumer $\Rightarrow$
x can be sold in z

$r_2(x, Italy)$: x is called "pasta" $\wedge$
$\neg x$ is made of hard corn $\Rightarrow$
$\neg x$ can be sold in $Italy$

Let us assume the following facts

$f_3(BRD)$: $\rightarrow$ *BRD* is an EC-country
f_4(Italy): $\rightarrow$ *Italy* is an EC-country
$f_5(P_0, BRD)$: $\rightarrow P_0$ can be sold in *BRD*
$f_6(P_0)$: $\rightarrow P_0$ is called "pasta"
$f_7(P_0)$: $\rightarrow \neg P_0$ is made of hard corn

We can then derive, as the European Court of Justice did, that P_0 can be sold in *Italy*, by means of the justified argument $A_1 = [f_3, f_4, f_5, r_1]$, which strictly defeats the rebutting argument $A_2 = [f_6, f_7, r_2]$. However, if we also ascertain that:

$$r_8(P_0, \mathit{Italy}) : \Rightarrow \text{ the selling of } P_0 \text{ in Italy prejudices the consumer}$$

then argument A_1 is undercut by argument $A_3 = [r_8]$, so that the before overruled argument B_2 for "$\neg P_0$ can be sold in *Italy*" becomes justified.

7. Applicability

Finally, we discuss the formalisation of statements about applicability. In legal language weak exceptions to rules are often made with a phrase like 'in these circumstances rule r is inapplicable'. Instead of attacking a particular assumption of a rule, such a phrase says that in these circumstances the whole rule may not be used for constructing arguments, in other words, that the rule is not a premise.

Basically, there are two methods for formalising applicability arguments. The first does not require a change of the definitions but complicates the representations of defeasible rules, while the second involves a change of the notions of attack and defeat, but leads to simpler representations.

The first method essentially boils down to the use of standard AI techniques for reasoning with 'abnormality' or 'applicability' predicates. For instance, if one has the view that any rule can make any other rule applicable, regardless of their preference relation, then it suffices to give each rule r an extra condition $\sim \neg appl(r)$. Then any argument with a conclusion $\neg appl(r)$ undercuts an argument using r.

Alternatively, if one thinks that a rule can only make another rule inapplicable if the first is not of lower priority, then to every defeasible rule r a condition $appl(r)$ can be added, and to D a new rule r_0 should be added of the form

$$r_0(r) : \Rightarrow appl(r)$$

Note that r here is a variable. Then arguments with defeasible rules can only be constructed by including instantiations of $r_0(r)$ for these rules. If now an argument has a conclusion $\neg appl(r_i)$, it does not attack an assumption but a conclusion of an argument using r_i and so needs priorities to succeed.

Here is how section 2 HPW, discussed in the introduction, can be formalised in this method. Recall that this section declares all other sections in the Dutch rent act inapplicable in case a lease is short-termed.

$$\begin{aligned} \mathit{2HPW}(x,y):\quad & appl(\mathit{2HPW}(x,y)) \wedge \\ & x \text{ is a short-termed lease} \wedge \\ & y \text{ is a section of the rent act} \wedge \\ & y \neq \mathit{2HPW}(x,y) \Rightarrow \\ & \neg appl(y) \end{aligned}$$

Moreover, *2HPW* should be given priority over the instances of r_0 for every other rule in the HPW. For more illustrations of this method, see (Prakken, 1993).

The second method, which was initially developed by (Sartor, 1994), involves a change of our formal system. The idea is to define inapplicability arguments as an additional way of attacking an argument: A attacks B also if B contains a defeasible rule r such that A has a conclusion $\neg appl(r)$. Note that thus rules are assumed to be applicable. Also (Hage, 1995) makes applicability a condition of the metatheory (of a system which is not argument- but extension-based), but he does not assume rules to be applicable; instead in his system a rule can only be applied if a conclusion that it is applicable is derivable.

Here is how the definitions of attack and defeat should be changed. First we add to Definition 4.8 a third condition to the disjunction:

(3) $A_2 + S_2$ is an argument with for some $r \in A_1$ a conclusion $\neg appl(r)$.

Then we add to Definition 4.16 a third possibility, *excluding* an argument by attacking the applicability of a rule in that argument. Again there is a choice whether the priorities should be relevant. If not, the following condition suffices.

(3) A_1 *excludes* A_2 iff condition (3) of Definition 4.8 holds.

Otherwise, we should add that the relevant rules for $\neg appl(r_1)$ are not all inferior to r_1.

(3) A_1 *excludes* A_2 iff condition (3) of Definition 4.8 holds, provided that $R_{\neg appl(r_1)}(A_1) \not< \{r_1\}$.

Finally, we redefine defeat as

DEFINITION 7.1. Let A_1 and A_2 be two arguments. Then A_1 *defeats* A_2 iff A_1 is empty and A_2 is incoherent, or else if

- A_1 undercuts A_2; or
- A_1 rebuts or excludes A_2 and A_2 does not undercut A_1.

With this definition it is not necessary to include applicability conditions in defeasible rules.

8. Some Remarks on Implementation

Our dialogue game already has the form of the top level of an implementation. Moreover, we have stated some results on completeness: if the input theory is finitary, i.e. it is such that each argument has at most a finite number of attackers, each argument that is semantically justified according to (Prakken & Sartor, 1996a) has a dialectical proof that it is justified. However, it should be noted that this is a kind of completeness that does not imply semi-decidability: if the language contains function symbols, the logic for the construction of arguments will not be decidable, and then the search for counterarguments is not even semi-decidable. So in the finitary case there is no algorithm that is guaranteed to find all proofs that exist.

In the case that an ordered theory has only a finite number of rules, decidability follows from the fact that, since arguments may not contain more than one rule with the same conclusion, a finite ordered theory has only a finite number of arguments. Note that since rules are schemes for all its instances, this condition implies that the language has no function symbols. At first sight, the exclusion of function symbols would seem problematic, since our just-explained naming convention makes heavily use of them. Yet we expect that in many practical applications also a simpler naming convention, with terms instead of function symbols, will do.

9. Comparison with Related Work

9.1. Logic and General AI

With respect to related research, we first indicate what we add to the earlier developments in defeasible argumentation, mentioned in Section 2, in particular to (Loui, 1987) and (Simari & Loui, 1992). What we retain is the use of one-direction rules for representing conditionals, but we add assumptions, we replace specificity with any possible source of priorities and, finally, we make the priorities defeasible.

Next we focus on some logic-programming-like systems for defeasible reasoning. (Dung, 1993) has developed various argumentation based semantics of extended logic programming, based on more abstract work of (Dung, 1995) and (Bondarenko et al., 1993). As already indicated above, in (Prakken & Sartor, 1995) and (Prakken & Sartor, 1996a) we build on one of (Dung, 1993)'s definitions, in particular on his formulation of well-founded semantics of extended logic programs. However, there are some differences. Firstly, Dung does not consider reasoning with or about priorities. Moreover, since Dung only reformulates the various semantics of logic programs, in the case of well-founded semantics he inherits some of its features that we find less attractive. In particular, Dung defines, like (Bondarenko et al., 1993), arguments as being the set of assumptions of what we define as an argument. Thus the program $r_1\colon \Rightarrow a$, $r_2\colon \Rightarrow \neg a$, $r_3\colon \Rightarrow b$ has only one argument, viz. $\emptyset$, which defeats itself, so that the set of justified arguments is empty. By contrast, in our system we have a justified argument $[r_3]$ and two defensible arguments $[r_1]$ and $[r_2]$. This problem occurs in any program with head-to-head conflicts between rules.

Dung's assumption-based approach can be defended by saying that it determines sets of assumptions (i.e. weak literals) with which a program or theory can be given a noncontradictory interpretation. If no such set exists, the program is in some sense incoherent and the system draws no justified conclusions. Our system, however, is also meant to be used in adversarial contexts, where coherency is rare.

An early application of extended logic programming in which head-to-head conflicts between rules do not trivialise a program is (Kowalski & Sadri, 1990). In their method, rules with negative consequents are interpreted as exceptions to rules with the corresponding positive consequent. This reading is preserved by a translation of the extended program into a general logic program, i.e. a program with only weak negation. This method still has some limitations, such as the inability to express exceptions to exceptions.

In the case of fixed priorities our system is a variant of (Dung, 1994)'s dialogue game formulation of the well-founded semantics of (Dung, 1993). Our main contribution to Dung's version is that we extend it to the case of defeasible priorities. Already (Rescher, 1977) suggested the dialectical form to analyze defeasible reasoning. (Brewka, 1994b) gives a logical reconstruction of Rescher's suggestion with the help of default logic. (Vreeswijk, 1993b) has developed a dialectical proof theory for his own system for defeasible argumentation developed in (Vreeswijk, 1993a). Finally, Loui has in various publications defended a dialectical approach to the formalisation of defeasible reasoning, e.g. in (Loui, 1993).

(Brewka, 1996) has developed a version of well-founded semantics with defeasible priorities which is not argument-based. His version partly avoids the just-discussed problems, viz. in cases where the rules that are in a head-to-head conflict assume their head in their body. An important difference with our system is that Brewka reduces rebutting to undercutting defeat, by assuming of every rule that is intended to be defeasible its consequent in its antecedent. Although this makes the definitions simpler, it also gives up some expressive power. In particular, the difference between defeasible rules like 'If A then B' and 'If A then B, unless the contrary can be shown' cannot be expressed. On the other hand, it makes the priorities also applicable to mutually undercutting arguments, which Brewka finds desirable.

Also two other logic-programming-like systems are relevant, 'ordered logic' (Laenens & Vermeir, 1990)) and (Nute, 1994)'s 'defeasible logic'. Both systems have prioritized rules but not assumptions, while the priorities are fixed. They also both reflect the kind of skepticism discussed above with Example 5.8. Nute's language also has a 'might conditional', which roughly is the conditional denial of a rule. To obtain decidability, Nute assumes the input theory to be finite, and the language to have no function symbols.

Also, Nute's system has, like ours, the category of strict rules. However, Nute's treatment of such rules is different, since he regards only rules with complementary consequents as conflicting. Thus in the Examples 4.5 and 4.6 he regards the arguments $[s_1, r_1]$ and $[s_2, r_2]$ as not conflicting, for which reason he does not take the priority relation between r_1 and r_2 into account when deciding the conflicts between the strict and defeasible arguments.

Finally, an alternative approach to reasoning about priorities, especially suitable for extension- or model-based nonmonotonic logics, was developed by (Brewka, 1994a) for prioritised default logic, and generalised and slightly revised by

(Prakken, 1995a) for any extension- or model-based system. Roughly, the method checks whether what an extension says about the priorities corresponds to the ordering on which the extension is based.

9.2. AI AND LAW

We now discuss some projects in AI and Law. Here we only focus on relational, or declarative approaches. Most systems below are not formal systems but implemented architectures. As far as they share features with our framework, our work can be regarded as formulating standards for their behaviour.

First we discuss some systems using techniques of logic metaprogramming. (Yoshino & Kithahara, 1988) propose a rule-based system in which priorities between rules are defined on the basis of the principles Lex Superior, Lex Posterior and Lex Specialis, in that order of precedence. These rules are not represented in the knowledge representation language but encoded in the inference engine. Thus the relation between these three priority rules is fixed, other sources of priorities cannot be accounted for, and reasoning about priorities cannot be modelled. In (Yoshino, 1995) a more flexible rule-based inference engine is proposed, which accepts priorities as part of the input information. More exactly, each single priority criterion (such as Lex Posterior, Lex Superior, or Lex Specialis) contributes to the definition of the derogation relation. For example, later rules derogate older ones, and higher rules derogate lower ones. The inference engine checks the validity of every rule it uses, by checking that the rule is not derogated. The output of the system is a single category of conclusions, viz. those that can be drawn from valid rules. The system also checks the validity (i.e., non-derogation) of derogation rules, and this implies, in a way, reasoning about priorities. However, Yoshino does not address the problem of circular derogation statements, and he also leaves it unclear whether derogation statements only apply to rules that are conflicting or to all rules in the knowledge base.

(Hamfelt & Barklund, 1989) address, among other things, reasoning with prioritized legal rules. For this purpose they use the DEMO predicate of logic metaprogramming instead of explicit priorities, which makes their style of representation very different from ours: each preference rule is represented as a metaprogram, which outputs the conclusion of the weaker rules only if the conclusion of the conflicting stronger rules is not derivable. Moreover, in this approach, each set of rules having the same priority, under a determinate ordering criterion, is a separate program, which implies that a hierarchy of separated levels of legal knowledge is assumed. We have chosen not to make this assumption, because, as Example 6.4 shows, a conflict resolution rule may apply not only to object level rules, but also to conflict resolution rules, including itself.

Also (Routen, 1989) has suggested the use of logic metaprogramming, in particular, for dealing with rules and exceptions. However, Routen does not directly address the problem of reasoning with or about priorities.

The Helic system of (Nitta et al., 1995) is a software tool for legal reasoning, including an 'argumentation function', which builds arguments, and a 'debating function', which compares and evaluates them, implementing the model proposed in (Prakken, 1991; Prakken, 1993) and (Sartor, 1993; Sartor, 1994). The input of the system includes legal rules and priorities, which are called viewpoints. An example of a viewpoint is that flexibility in law is more important than strict interpretation of penal rules. A restriction is that viewpoints can only be stated as unconditional facts, while in our system they can be conditional upon other facts, just as any other rule.

Finally, (St-Vincent et al., 1995) use logic metaprogramming to define a filtering mechanism for building arguments, which selects the applicable rules by taking into consideration the contexts associated to them. A context is a set of clauses, representing, for instance, a set of facts, a legal text (such as a statute) or a category of legal texts (such as statutes or municipal regulations). Also in this framework a formalisation of priority rules is presented but the priority conclusions derived from them are not used to solve conflicts and evaluate arguments: the exclusive object of this work is argument construction.

Let us now pass to some other relational models of legal argumentation. Some of them are purely formal, while others implement a formal or informal theory of adversarial argument.

(Farley & Freeman, 1995) describe a dialectical model of legal reasoning with a heuristic flavour. They maintain that different legal problem solving contexts require different levels of proof. For instance, for the question whether a case can be brought before court, only a 'scintilla of evidence' is required, while for a decision in a case 'dialectical validity' is needed. They correspondingly describe a dialogue game in which parties dialectically construct arguments in order to satisfy (or to make unsatisfied) the required level of proof. The basic idea of their model is the same as of our dialogue game: only those moves are allowed that meet a certain level of burden of proof. However, there are also differences.

Firstly, Farley & Freeman divide the rules not in two but three epistemic categories: 'sufficient', 'evidential' and 'default', in decreasing order of priority. All three types of rules are in our sense defeasible, since they can all make arguments subject to defeat.

Farley & Freeman extend our model in that they also allow arguments based on modus tollens, and even nondeductive arguments, viz. simple forms of abductive and a contrario reasoning, with corresponding ways to attack such arguments. A subtlety is that nondeductive arguments can be disallowed by defining a certain level of burden of proof. Because of the presence of nondeductive arguments, arguments are not only compared on the strength of their rules, but also on the intrinsic strength of their reasoning steps.

Some aspects of Farley & Freeman's approach can be directly captured in our framework: for instance, their 'scintilla of evidence' corresponds to a defensible argument, while a dialectically valid proof corresponds to a justified argument.

In general, their various levels of burden of proof can be captured by varying the required force of arguments in our dialogue game. On some other aspects our model generalises Farley & Freeman's approach, for instance, by including strict rules and weak negation. Also, rather than having to classify defeasible rules according to their epistemic nature, we can base the rule priorities on any possible ground, and we model reasoning about these priorities. Again other features are left outside our present framework, such as non-deductive arguments; since we want a completely formalised model, we prefer to study such arguments better, before including them in our system. Finally, as far as the inference rule of modus tollens for defeasible rules is concerned, we prefer not to introduce it into our system, for reasons extensively discussed in (Prakken, 1991; Prakken, 1993).

In various publications Hage has stressed the need for combining reasoning with and about priorities and about applicability; in fact, he reduces priority statements to applicability statements (cf. Yoshino's reduction to validity statements). A difference on details is that Hage does not study reasoning with assumptions. Also his general approach is different: technically since, like default logic, it is an extension-based system instead of an argument-based system; and philosophically, since it is inspired by (Raz, 1975)'s theory of reasons in practical reasoning. The latest version is described in (Hage, 1995).

One important issue raised by Hage is that of weighing reasons. He objects to systems like ours, where the defeat relation is defined between individual arguments. Instead, Hage wants to compare *sets* of arguments, to model the fact that in practical reasoning often reasons that individually have not enough weight to support a certain conclusion, do have that weight in combination. For instance, it might be that the individual reasons that it is hot, and that it is raining, are insufficient for not going jogging, but that they are sufficient in combination.

We agree that weighing reasons is an important feature of practical reasoning, but we prefer not to model it as an aspect of the assessment of arguments. Instead, we propose to express the weight of reasons in terms of priority relations between rules. For instance, the individual rules 'If it is hot, I don't go jogging' and 'if it is raining, I don't go jogging' can be given lower priority than 'If I haven't been jogging for two days, I go jogging'. And if the combination of the first two reasons outweighs the latter reason, this can be expressed by adding a new rule 'If it is hot and raining, I don't go jogging' and giving this rule higher priority than the jogging rule (note that also in Hage's system the information that a set of reasons outweighs another set has to be explicitly added).

The main reason why we prefer this approach is that reasons for a certain proposition cannot always be combined. For instance, for a certain person it can be that the individual circumstances that it rains and that it is hot are reasons for not going jogging, but that the combination is so pleasant that it is instead a reason for going jogging. Therefore, we don't want to be forced to regard the combination of two reasons for a certain conclusion also a reason for that conclusion, as is the case in Hage's approach. And precisely because this freedom to combine or not exists, we think that a decision to combine them in a particular case has the character of stating a new premise.

Next we discuss Gordon's work in (Gordon, 1994; Gordon, 1995). Part of his dialectical protocol for civil pleading is what can be called a declarative argumentation framework, based on (Geffner & Pearl, 1992)'s logic for conditional entailment. Within full first-order logic, Geffner and Pearl define a preferred-model semantics for any ordered set of defeasible conditionals, and then they define a sound and complete proof theory for this semantics. An important requirement on the ordering on defaults is 'admissibility', which in essence is that more specific defaults should have priority over more general ones. Gordon adds to Geffner & Pearl's theory of admissible orderings a method for expressing any given ordering (an issue not discussed by Geffner and Pearl), and also describes a method for representing explicit ordering information. In fact, his system has all the elements of the present framework: assumptions, applicability, strict and defeasible rules, and reasoning with and about priorities.

Still, there are some differences. In our system, the derived priorities are directly 'transported' to the metatheory. Since the predicate symbol $\prec$ in our object language denotes the relation $<$ in our metatheory. In Gordon's method, instead, priority statements are linked to priorities of conditional entailment's metatheory in a less transparent way. This is so since in conditional entailment specificity is hardwired in the logic (via the requirement that orderings are admissible), so that more specific rules always prevail. Therefore Gordon needs to transform winning rules (according to any priority criterion) into more specific ones. Obviously, since such a transformation does not succeed when the losing rule is more specific than the winning one, specificity becomes the overriding kind of defeat. As stated above, and as Gordon acknowledges in (Gordon, 1995), this is in legal applications undesirable: in the law, any priority relation is subject to debate.

10. Conclusion

To summarise the main results of the present paper, inspired by the rich structure of legal language and legal argument we have provided a formal argument-based system for the combination of several features of legal language: reasoning with priorities, reasoning about priorities and reasoning with assumptions and applicability statements. We have stated the system in a dialectical form, which easily suggests possible implementations. We have also shown that the system can be used to formalise a wide range of realistic examples from legal reasoning.

Several issues for future research remain. Firstly, on some points alternative definitions may be possible. For instance, examples might be found which motivate a different relation between rebutting and undercutting arguments, or different dialogue moves. However, we think that our system is robust enough to allow for such adjustments without having to change its overall structure.

We also want to investigate the use of our framework, in particular its dialectical features, for representing precedents in HYPO-style case-based reasoners. Here we want to explore an idea of (Loui & Norman, 1995) to represent precedents as argument structures, i.e. as a set of possibly conflicting arguments, including arguments on the resolution of such conflicts. We think that this is a promising application of argumentation frameworks, which can shed further light on the relation between rule-based and case-based theories of legal argument.

Acknowledgements

The authors thank Mark Ryan for his comments on an earlier version of this paper, the SG1 Working Group of ModelAge, led by Pierre-Yves Schobbens, for useful discussions, and the referees for their interesting comments.

References

Ashley, K.D. 1990. *Modeling legal argument: reasoning with cases and hypotheticals.* Cambridge, MA: MIT Press, 1990.

Bondarenko, A., Toni, F. & Kowalski, R.A. 1993. An assumption-based framework for non-monotonic reasoning. *Proceedings of the Second International Workshop on Logic Programming and Non-monotonic Reasoning*, 1993, 171–189. Lisbon: MIT Press.

Brewka, G. 1994a. Reasoning about priorities in default logic. *Proceedings AAAI-94*, 247–260. Seattle.

Brewka, G. 1994b. A logical reconstruction of Rescher's theory of formal disputation based on default logic. *Proceedings of the 11th European Conference on Artificial Intelligence*, 366–370. Amsterdam: Wiley.

Brewka, G. 1996. Well-founded semantics for extended logic programs with dynamic preferences. *Journal of Artificial Intelligence Research* 4, 19–36.

Dung, P.M. 1993. An argumentation semantics for logic programming with explicit negation. *Proceedings of the Tenth Logic Programming Conference*, 1993, 616–630. MIT Press.

Dung, P.M. 1994. Logic programming as dialogue games. Unpublished paper.

Dung, P.M. 1995. On the acceptability of arguments and its fundamental role in nonmonotonic reasoning, logic programming, and *n*-person games. *Artificial Intelligence* 77, 321–357.

Farley, A.M. and Freeman, K. 1995. Burden of Proof in Legal Argumentation. *Proceedings of the Fifth International Conference on Artificial Intelligence and Law*, 156–164. College Park, MD: ACM Press.

Geffner, H. and Pearl, J. 1992. Conditional entailment: bridging two approaches to default reasoning. *Artificial Intelligence* 53, 209–244.

Gordon, T.F. 1994. The Pleadings Game: An Exercise in Computational Dialectics. *Artificial Intelligence and Law* 2: 239–292.

Gordon, T.F. 1995. *The Pleadings Game. An Artificial Intelligence Model of Procedural Justice.* Kluwer, 1995.

Hage, J.C. Teleological reasoning in reason-based logic. *Proceedings of the Fifth International Conference on Artificial Intelligence and Law*, 11–20. College Park, MD: ACM Press.

Hage, J.C., Leenes, R. & Lodder, A.R. 1994. Hard cases: a procedural approach. *Artificial Intelligence and Law* 2: 113–167.

Hamfelt, A. & Barklund, J. 1989. Metalevels in legal knowledge and their runnable representation in logic. *Preproceedings of the III International Conference on "Logica, Informatica, Diritto"*, Vol. II, 557–576. Florence.

Horty, J.F., Thomasson, R.H. & Touretzky, D.S. 1990. A skeptical theory of inheritance in non-monotonic semantic networks. *Artificial Intelligence* 42, 311–348.

Kowalski, R.A. & Sadri, F. 1990. Logic programs with exceptions. *Proceedings of the Seventh International Logic Programming Conference*, 598–613. MIT Press.

Laenens. E. & Vermeir, D. 1990. A fixed points semantics for ordered logic. *Journal of Logic and Computation* Vol. 1 No. 2, 159–185.

Lodder, A.R. & Herczog, A. 1995. DiaLaw: A dialogical framework for modelling legal reasoning. *Proceedings of the Fifth International Conference on Artificial Intelligence and Law*, 146–155. College Park, MD: ACM Press.

Loui, R.P. 1987. Defeat among arguments: a system of defeasible inference. *Computational Intelligence* 2, 100–106.

Loui, R.P. 1993. Process and policy: resource-bounded non-demonstrative reasoning. Report WUCS-92-43, Washington-University-in-St-Louis, 1993. To appear in *Computational Intelligence.*

Loui, R.P. & Norman, J. 1995. Rationales and argument moves. *Artificial Intelligence and Law* 3: 159–189.

Loui, R.P., Norman, J., Olson, J. & Merrill, A. 1993. A design for reasoning with policies, precedent, and rationales. *Proceedings of Fourth International Conference on Artificial Intelligence and Law*, 202–211. Amsterdam: ACM Press.

McCarty, L.T. & Sridharan, N.N. 1982. A computational theory of legal argument. Technical Report LRP-TR-13, Laboratory for Computer Science Research, Rutgers University, 1982.

Nitta, K. et al. 1995. New HELIC-II: a software tool for legal reasoning. *Proceedings of the Fifth International Conference on Artificial Intelligence and Law*, 287–296. College Park, MD: ACM Press.

Nute, D.N. 1994. A decidable quantified defeasible logic. In D. Prawitz, B. Skyrms and D. Westerståhl (eds.): *Logic, Methodology and Philosophy of Science IX*. Elsevier Science B.V., 1994, 263–284.

Pollock, J.L. 1992. How to reason defeasibly. *Artificial Intelligence* 57, 1–42.

Prakken, H. 1991. A tool in modelling disagreement in law: preferring the most specific argument. *Proceedings of the Third International Conference on Artificial Intelligence and Law*, 165–174. Oxford: ACM Press.

Prakken, H. 1993. *Logical tools for modelling legal argument*. Doctoral Dissertation Free University Amsterdam, 1993.

Prakken, H. 1995a. A semantic view on reasoning about priorities (extended abstract). *Proceedings of the Second Dutch/German Workshop on Nonmonotonic Reasoning*, 152–159. Utrecht.

Prakken, H. 1995b. From logic to dialectics in legal argument. *Proceedings of the Fifth International Conference on Artificial Intelligence and Law*, 165–174. College Park, MD: ACM Press.

Prakken, H. & Sartor, G. 1995. On the relation between legal language and legal argument: assumptions, applicability and dynamic priorities. *Proceedings of the Fifth International Conference on Artificial Intelligence and Law*, 1–9. College Park, MD: ACM Press.

Prakken & Sartor, G. 1996a. A system for defeasible argumentation, with defeasible priorities. *Proceedings of the International Conference on Formal Aspects of Practical Reasoning*, Springer Lecture Notes in AI 1085, 510–524. Bonn: Springer Verlag.

Prakken & Sartor, G. 1996b. Argument-based extended logic programming with defeasible priorities. To appear in *Journal of Applied Non-classical Logics*.

Raz, J. 1975. *Practical reason and norms*. Princeton University Press, 1975.

Rescher, N. 1977. *Dialectics: a controversy-oriented approach to the theory of knowledge*. State University of New York Press, Albany, 1977.

Rissland, E.L. & Skalak, D.B. 1991. CABARET: statutory interpretation in a hybrid architecture. *International Journal of Man-Machine Studies* 34, 839–887.

Routen, T. 1989. Hierarchically organised formalisations. *Proceedings of the Second International Conference on Artificial Intelligence and Law*, 242–250. Vancouver: ACM Press.

Sartor, G. 1993. A simple computational model for nonmonotonic and adversarial legal reasoning. *Proceedings of the Fourth International Conference on Artificial Intelligence and Law*, 192–201. Amsterdam: ACM Press.

Sartor, G. A formal model of legal argumentation. *Ratio Juris* 7, 212–226.

Simari, G.R. & R.P. Loui, R.P. 1992. A mathematical treatment of defeasible argumentation and its implementation. *Artificial Intelligence* 53, 125–157.

Skalak, D.B. & Rissland, E.L. 1992. Arguments and Cases. An Inevitable Intertwining. *Artificial Intelligence and Law*, 3–44.

St-Vincent, P., Poulin, D. & Bratley, P. 1995. A Computational Framework for Dialectical Reasoning. *Proceedings of the Fifth International Conference on Artificial Intelligence and Law*, 137–145. College Park, MD: ACM Press.

Vreeswijk, G. 1993a. *Studies in defeasible argumentation.* Doctoral dissertation Free University Amsterdam, 1993.

Vreeswijk, G. Defeasible dialectics: a controversy-oriented approach towards defeasible argumentation. *Journal of Logic and Computation*, Vol. 3, No. 3, 317–334.

Yoshino, H. 1995. The systematization of legal meta-inference. *Proceedings of the Fifth International Conference on Artificial Intelligence and Law*, 266–275. College Park, MD: ACM Press.

Yoshino, H. and Kithahara, M. 1988. Les-Project. In H. Fiedler, F. Haft, R. Traunmüller (eds.): *Expert systems in law. Impacts on legal theory and computer law*. Attempto Verlag, Tübingen, 1988, 47–65.

Artificial Intelligence and Law **4:** 369, 1996.

Index of Key Words

Artificial Intelligence and Law **4:** 371–372, 1996.

CONTENTS OF VOLUME 4

Volume 4 No. 1 1996

Volume 4 No. 2 1996

Volume 4 Nos. 3–4 1996

SPECIAL DOUBLE ISSUE:
LOGICAL MODELS OF LEGAL ARGUMENTATION

Editors:
Henry Prakken and Giovanni Sartor